The Retirement Sourcebook

Mary Helen Smith
Shuford Smith

ROXBURY PARK

LOWELL HOUSE

LOS ANGELES

NTC/Contemporary Publishing Group

Library of Congress Cataloging-in-Publication Data

Smith, Mary Helen.
    The retirement sourcebook / Mary Helen & Shuford Smith.
    p. cm.
    "A Roxbury Park book."
    Includes bibliographical references and index.
    ISBN 0-7373-0039-6 (alk. paper)
    1. Retirement—United States—Planning—Handbooks, manuals.
    I. Smith, Shuford. II. Title.
    HQ1063.2.U6S65 1999
    646.7'9—dc1

                          98-27741
                              CIP

Published by Lowell House
A division of NTC/Contemporary Publishing Group, Inc.
4255 West Touhy Avenue,
Lincolnwood (Chicago), Illinois 60646-1975 U.S.A.

Lowell House books can be purchased at special discounts when
ordered in bulk for premiums and special sales. Contact Department
CS at the following address:

    NTC/Contemporary Publishing Group
    4255 West. Touhy Avenue
    Lincolnwood, IL 60646-1975
    1-800-323-4900

Roxbury Park is a division of
NTC/Contemporary Publishing Group, Inc.

Managing Director and Publisher: Jack Artenstein
Editor in Chief, Roxbury Park Books: Michael Artenstein
Director of Publishing Services: Rena Copperman
Editorial Assistant: Nicole Monastirsky
Interior Design and Production: Robert S. Tinnon

Printed and bound in the United States of America
10 9 8 7 6 5

Contents

Preface

Congratulations! If you are fifty or older, you have lived longer than 99 percent of all humans who have ever lived on the face of this earth. And, if you are sixty-five or older, you and your contemporaries are members of a select group that represents more than half of all humans who have lived to this age! In the twentieth century, the average life expectancy of Americans has increased by six and one-half hours every day—almost two days every week and more than twenty-five years in this century. In these times of ever-lengthening life spans, at age fifty-plus, either you are planning for or you are living in your "golden years"—your retirement years.

More and more Americans are living longer and enjoying retirement. As reported by the Bureau of Labor Statistics, more than 30 percent of American men and 48 percent of American women over the age of fifty-five have retired from the work-force. Only a generation or two ago, our parents and grandparents labored through a lifetime of work to reach an exhausted middle or old age. Nowadays, you can look forward to a full "second" life in your retirement years. It is possible to start an entirely different career, to weave together exciting vocations and avocations, to travel, and to volunteer your efforts to improve your community. The possibilities are almost endless.

You have been anticipating this time since you began working. It is the time when you no longer have to work, when you can draw upon your savings, take more complete control of your time, and enjoy new experiences. It has been an elusive state in your mind for years—you've wanted to quit working since you were twenty-five, thirty-five, or forty-five. . . . Now's

the time to do what you want—without career demands or societal pressures.

You are preparing to chart your course. This passage of life
calls for considering the various challenges ahead, analyzing
personal needs, and setting up plans. Then, as changes occur—
whether they are in your body, impact a family member or
friend, concern a health-care plan, or are caused by government regulations—you will need to modify aspects of your
plans. You may make changes to your diet or exercise program,
you may join a support group, you may move, or you may
set up a living trust. The goal of this book is to help you understand the concept of retirement, its challenges, and its manageable aspects regarding your health and well-being, social
and emotional changes, work and play opportunities, financial
and legal issues, "here or there" decisions, and safety and security concerns.

The first challenge is to understand the terms and the process
of retirement. A question many of us have is: Why is this exciting life passage called retirement? How did the word *retirement* come into being? According to the *Oxford English
Dictionary*, the word *retire* appears to have originated in France.
The first English usages were recorded in the 1500s. The preferred word usage meant to withdraw into seclusion, as a monk
would do. In 1648, Cromwell makes a reference concerning a
"desired retirement from the army." And, in 1667, diarist Samuel
Pepys made allusions to "how to retire and live a country life."
Consider these references. "The monk moved himself to a different physical space to enhance his mental space." "The army
officer sought to escape the rules, regimens, and the violence
inherent in his career. The lady and gentleman changed locales
to live an idyllic life." Three to four hundred years later, we are
doing the same things: escaping careers and/or changing locations to enhance our physical and mental performance.

Another frequently asked question is: Why is the age of sixty-
five so strongly associated with retirement? It was the methodical Germans who identified age sixty-five as the retirement
age. In 1889, Chancellor Otto von Bismarck added twenty-five
years to the average life span of forty-five to obtain a retirement age of seventy. He figured that few citizens would live

that long, so demand for government pensions would be minimal. The German government, however, pushed the age back to sixty-five. In America, our legislature also chose the age sixty-five when it established the 1935 Social Security Act. At that time, the average American's life expectancy was almost sixty-two years.

Now, with more than five thousand Americans reaching sixty-five each day, it is important for each of us to understand retirement—what it is and what it can be. Let's accept what we cannot change: aging. All of us are aging; we're doing it every day! But let's not accept the misconception that retirement means old age or that retirement is a negative. And more importantly, let's correct harmful approaches to retirement planning, such as procrastinating about planning and saving or considering retirement planning a single event. You've heard, "We do have a plan—we'll take a trip." "There are too many things we need now—we'll start saving for retirement later." "I've got a good pension and there's always Social Security." "We own our home—we can always get a loan." "We won't need much money during retirement." "We'll decide what to do after retirement." Whoa! You're never too young or too old to start preparing to enjoy the rest of your life. The planning involves more than money (and more than one trip). You must be flexible—changing your plans as situations change.

It is most important to be in touch with *your* perceptions of retirement. Do you look forward to it or do you dread it? Interestingly, the attitude you adopt will be an accurate predictor of what you will or will not achieve and enjoy. It is vital to approach this time in life with a positive attitude.

Realize that anxiety about retirement peaks *before* the actual event. Naturally, you fear changes such as loss of income, loss of occupation (and, sometimes, the self-esteem tied to that endeavor), and the loss of relationships with your coworkers.

Realize, too, that though retirement is a new experience for each person, the process has almost the same phases for everyone. You'll feel exhilaration, followed by a brief dissatisfaction, then a realignment phase in which you begin to relax and enjoy yourself. To achieve this final adjustment, you have to be honest as you answer questions, such as: What do you want to

Retirement at sixty-five is ridiculous. When I was sixty-five I still had pimples.

GEORGE BURNS
Comedian

do with the rest of your life? How do you want to maintain your health? How would you finance a long-term-care situation? How do you want to die? Once all this questioning is resolved, a deep contentment sets in—if you have adopted a positive attitude and have planned or are planning to make the most of your retirement. If you refuse to face these questions and take charge of your life, you may end up living in fear of the future or in mourning the past instead of with excitement for the present and the future.

Amory Bradford, a friend who has had many rich experiences in his life, shares this with us: "I like to emphasize that retirees get the last chance in this life to accept that the choice they make is their own, not one imposed on them by others—something that they have been trying to learn since it was time to wean from their mothers. They can choose to be a park ranger or to be depressed, to write their memoirs or to be an alcoholic. There is no one around to choose for them, unless their spouse, children, or doddering parents want to take on the job."

Definitely, retirement is not a single event but a continuing adaptation from an imposed societal structure (outside yourself) called *work*. In reality, you've been making these adaptations all your life—graduating from schools, leaving home, and so on. Now, with retirement, society is saying it's okay to stop working full time and to develop another reality that is self-directed (inside yourself). You draw upon your lifetime of experience to grow into whatever you decide. You must develop a clear perspective on what you want from this stage of your life. Only you can take control of your retirement and, consequently, your life.

Fly trial balloons, test the waters, or take baby steps—whatever you want to call your personal evaluations of the changes you want to make. If you want to travel full time, take a month-long trip and find out if you enjoy being homeless—before you sell your home. Perhaps you have dreamed of going back to school and earning your doctorate. Take a course or two to determine if you still like all the classwork. If you think you want to move to a different region, rent an apartment for a year and experience the locale's seasons. Take a small step and evaluate before you make a giant leap.

You should also have a yardstick to measure your success. Will it be similar to that of the rat-race existence you're leaving behind in the workplace (money, recognition, or responsibility), or will it be one of contentment (self-acceptance, congeniality, cooperation, or love)? If you are going to feel successful, your endeavors must be measurable by your own criteria.

As you age, it is inspirational to note other people who have aged well and are continuing to be creative and constructive. Most of these people have been successful in their professional and personal lives. Here is a short list of accomplished, older people:

- A self-taught artist, GRANDMA MOSES exhibited her paintings at the Museum of Modern Art in New York City when she was seventy-eight. She proceeded to paint until her death, at one hundred years of age.
- FRANK LLOYD WRIGHT worked as one of America's outstanding architects until his death at age ninety-one. Throughout his life, Wright created new architectural concepts. He designed more than one thousand modern structures, including the Guggenheim Museum in New York City.
- ELLA FITZGERALD made her first big appearance as a jazz singer in 1934, then continued to perform into the 1990s—sixty years later!
- A virtuoso pianist of international reputation, ARTHUR RUBINSTEIN was eighty-nine when he performed his last concert at Carnegie Hall.
- *Out of Africa* author ISAK DINESEN (also known as Baroness Karen Blixen-Finecke) penned Danish and English versions of her works from age forty-nine to age seventy-six.
- English playwright and social critic GEORGE BERNARD SHAW wrote from his thirties into his eighties, creating such plays as *Man and Superman* and *Pygmalion.* Shaw continued to write until his death at ninety-four.
- MAHATMA GANDHI led India from age sixty to age

seventy-eight, establishing his country's freedom from Great Britain through nonviolent revolution.

- GOLDA MEIR helped found the state of Israel, then served her country in many positions. Meir was in her seventies when she became prime minister, holding that post for five years.
- MARGARET MEAD, an anthropologist known for her work in child care, adolescence, sexual behavior, and American culture, continued to make contributions to her field into her seventies. Her landmark work, *Coming of Age in Samoa*, and her memoirs, *Blackberry Winter*, remain highly readable.
- Renaissance man ALBERT SCHWEITZER is known for his contributions to music, medicine, theology, and philosophy. Schweitzer started working for world peace at age seventy and lectured until age eighty-four. He continued to care for patients until age ninety. He was awarded the 1952 Nobel Peace Prize.
- MOTHER TERESA, a Roman Catholic nun, founded the Missionaries of Charity, a ministry among the sick of Calcutta. She and her associates took four vows: poverty, chastity, obedience to Christ, and service to the poor. She extended her work to five continents. In recognition of her efforts, she was awarded the 1979 Nobel Peace Prize. She continued her work until her death, in 1997, at age eighty-seven.
- Forced to retire as a secretary for the Presbyterian Church at age sixty-five, MAGGIE KUHN found herself so incensed at how older people were being treated that she formed the Gray Panthers. Concerned with many social issues, she helped end forced retirement, combatted fraud against the elderly in the health-care system, and reformed nursing homes.

These people, from many walks of life and backgrounds, have achieved great things in their later years as artists, musicians, writers, statesmen, scientists, doctors, nurses, and humanitarians. All around us, millions of ordinary aging people have begun to break free of traditional expectations of age to shape new and rewarding lives for themselves.

Interestingly, all of us—all six billion humans on earth—have the same amount of time—twenty-four hours each day. But each of us makes different decisions about what we will do with it. As we age, time seems to rush past us, gaining speed with each year. Before his retirement, *Charlotte Observer* publisher Rolfe Neill wrote

> The clock ticks, impartially rationing to us all. When younger, we have more time than money and regard time as valueless. When we achieve more money than time, we try to substitute. Watch fathers buy expensive presents for children, or husbands for spouses, when what the recipient craves is time with the giver, not money. Nothing has as much value as time well used. . . . Our choices define us.

As a retiree or future retiree, it is a bit daunting to realize that without working, you will be in charge of an additional 8 hours per day, 40 hours per week, more than 170 hours per month, and over 2,000 hours per year. To prevent the days, weeks, months, and years from racing off with your life, savor moments and events. Become caught up in the wonder of the natural world around you. Freely credit those who help you achieve your successes. (On the other hand, stop blaming others for your inability to accomplish what you want.) Celebrate the successes of others, too.

Take up the challenge of independence that is inherent in this gift of time called retirement. Start now. Time is all there is. How you spend your time is your choice.

Acknowledgments

We'd like to thank the following acquaintances and family members who have provided insights into various aspects of retirement:

Porter Anderson
Steve Barsby
Ron Beall
Dorothy Biocini
Chita Birkins
Amory and Laurene Bradford
Evelyn and Howard Bradley
Marge and Lenny Bruss
Peggy Carter
Alice and Charlie Cecil
Elizabeth Cottle
Ernestine Crowell
Jan Daugherty
Fred Fenton
El and Bill Fiero
Pat Foreman
Philip Franklin
Jim Freeman
Danni Geisler
Claudia George
Diana and Bill Gleasner
Joyce and Nelson Graves
Irv Green
Andrea Gross

Toby Heaton
David Hirsch
Nancy Holmes
Charlotte and Robert Hope
Jim Johnston
Barbara Jones
Cassandra and Patrick
    Kennedy
Judi and Bob Koenig
Andy Lee
Judy LeRoux
Liz Malloy
Pat Martin
Wanda May
Ben Mayberry
Emily and Al Michaud
Joyce Murlless
Dot Nann
Marjorie and Charlie Neff
Rolfe Neill
Mila Newcombe
Mel O'Hara
Polly and Howard Olson
Jean Pettigrew

David Pope
Jean Prevost
Jack Pyle
Taylor Reese
Bea and George Scofield
Wyatt E. Smith

Pat Soares
Katharine Spivey
Mary and Bill Staton
Helen Tack
Clarke Taube
Pat and Ike Wilson

And, of course, we'd like to recognize the assistance of our editors, Lindsey Hay and Nicole Monastirsky.

CHAPTER ONE

Challenges of Retirement

There are many challenges to address as you navigate through this passage in life called retirement. The greatest is accepting the responsibility for your life and happiness. To be truly happy, you must recognize the powers within yourself by using your abilities and maintaining a positive attitude. If you have worked for a business or organization rather than for yourself, you may have a greater challenge as you learn to be self-directed in your retirement. And, if you are part of a couple, understanding the changes and wishes of your partner may present another challenge.

Another profound demand is accepting the natural process of aging. An additional task is unmasking the stereotypes connected with the aged. Why read about aging and common misconceptions about old age? The simple answer is that to take charge of your retirement situation, you must understand the aging process—its problems and benefits. Alex Comfort, the editor of *Joy of Sex* and *More Joy of Sex* and author of *A Good Age* and numerous other scientific and literary works, summed up the need to understand the aging process when he said, "All people, of all ages, need the basic facts. Those now old need positive strategies. Those not yet called old need to realize what is in store for them if they let things ride."

Besides meeting challenges dictated by your body as you age, you will face issues imposed by the outside world. And, for the first time in human history, monumental societal changes are accommodating the aging—primarily because the enormous population segment known as the "baby boomer" generation is approaching retirement. Due to these advancements, there are exciting opportunities for people with the right ideas and the right products at the right time.

Power of Self

On the personal level, retirement presents many challenges. You must take charge of your new freedoms: leaving the workplace; switching jobs; volunteering; relishing leisure pursuits; maintaining your physical and mental abilities; enjoying changing relationships (grandparenting and taking care of your parents); savoring more opportunities for sexuality; and coping with the concept of mortality (accepting the death of friends or a spouse and preparing for your own). If you achieve personal independence, you leave behind much struggling and striving. Instead, you set your own goals, see opportunities, devote major chunks of time to others, and speak your mind. A satisfying feeling comes from taking charge of your affairs—whether it is eating a healthy diet, exercising, creating a safe and pleasant environment, maintaining an alert mind, putting your financial and legal matters in order, or planning for the future. You know you are performing at your personal best. You know you are in charge.

Approach Retirement Positively

Retirement also offers choices. You can choose to approach retirement positively, seeking renewal, growth, and relaxation, or you can choose to view it negatively, with resignation and resistance—even anger. A positive perspective comes from being around other happy people; from saying "yes" more often than "no" to new activities; from planning things you want to do; and from improving your daily routines. Make up your mind that you will take care of yourself and enjoy opportunities.

You (and your partner, if you have one) hold the keys to a successful, happy retirement. To increase the probability of turning retirement into a rewarding time in your life, read the next few pages slowly.

The most successful retirees approach the future with a sense of adventure. If you fear the future, stop and ask yourself: What can I gain or lose by changing? What can I gain or lose by not changing? Be honest with yourself. Write down and evaluate your answers. By facing your fears instead of running from them, you will discover you can gain more control over your future and, consequently, your life. As America's great storyteller Garrison Keillor shares, "You're supposed to get reckless as you grow older. That way, you keep saying yes to life. And, perhaps, saying yes, not being safe, is the real point of life."

Attitude Is Everything

What one thing most improves your chances for a happy, successful retirement? *It is your attitude.* Research confirms this belief. Dr. Stephen P. Jewett conducted a study in New York of seventy-nine healthy people who were eighty-seven years and older, reports Dr. Deepak Chopra in *Ageless Body, Timeless Mind.*

> The common thread was a sense of self-sufficiency that runs much deeper than personality. They almost never went to doctors, were never found in nursing homes, and were rarely in homes for the aged. . . . Granted, the seventy-ninety people he studied had escaped catastrophic illness, such as heart attack and cancer, in the critical midlife period, from forty-five to sixty-five (this is when bad genes, hypertension, elevated cholesterol, smoking, alcoholism, and other negative factors tend to take their highest toll). Jewett made clear that his subjects were more than chance survivors or lucky beneficiaries of good genes. . . . The majority of factors Jewett came up with were subjective, having to do with how these people felt about themselves. In comparison, the purely objective factors linked to long life were few and very general.

Retirement was the chance to do the things I had always wanted to do, the things I had postponed because of a multitude of real or imagined reasons why doing them was impossible. With retirement, those excuses no longer existed—I had to face the fact that I was left naked. Those 'dream' cards were in my hand right then, and I knew it was time to hold 'em or fold 'em.

JACK PYLE
Author

The not-so surprising objective factors were that these seniors had reasonable muscle tone, were near their optimal weight, and were physically active. The subjective characteristics are definitely worth considering: superior intelligence (keen interest in current events and good memory), little anxiety, a love of independence, joy in life, adaptability (good recovery from catastrophic events), no obsession about death, a spiritual life, moderate eating and drinking, few medications, nonsmoking, and rising early.

It is as if these people had decided to take care of their minds and bodies, to maintain their independence, and to enjoy life. Psychiatrist Eric Pfeiffer conducted a Duke University Longevity Study of thirty-four men and women in their late sixties who were considered successful agers. Pfeiffer compared the successful agers with thirty-four men and women who were considered worse agers. He discovered that the individuals' perception about themselves, their financial status, and their physical functioning was different between the two groups. Successful agers are positive and engaged with life. The manner in which you perceive your situation has a strong bearing on its outcome!

How to Enjoy Your Retirement

Other doctors and writers have offered additional prescriptions for enjoying your retirement years. Following is a compilation of suggestions that can play a part when you create your own life's goals:

- develop a variety of interests
- keep your health in good repair
- try to find romance and a good sex life
- maintain family ties
- make friends of all ages
- build strong relationships with friends
- live within your means
- become engaged in giving (volunteer or other work)
- use leisure time well

- stay happy and optimistic
- express your feelings
- laugh a lot
- allow for your eccentricities
- create routines, as needed
- develop and respect resiliency
- welcome animals into your life and home

More than anything else, it is our own view of ourselves that determines the richness of our later years.

Study after study indicates it is important to be comfortable with yourself and your situation. Know who you are! Self-understanding and self-acceptance must precede planning for retirement. What roles do you play and why?

Consider the statements in Table 1.1, page 6, and circle the number that typically describes you.

Now that you have finished the first marking, go back through the statements again. This time, look hard in that self-mirror and see if you circled the wished-for response or the real response. No one is looking over your shoulder. You are after insights that help you build a strong retirement direction—a plan for your future which makes the most of your time.

All the statements will be tested during most retirements. The more 5s you can honestly count, the greater the likelihood of a successful future. For statements that don't describe you, try to incorporate them into your daily life by taking action. If you have no passions, begin exploring possibilities; if you avoid exercise, start today by taking a walk; if you avoid talking about your emotions, share your next feeling of contentment with someone close. One West Virginia couple would have circled a 1 on statement number 15 (at least he would have). By his own admission, the husband had talked to almost no one but family members during his life as a coal miner. He realized this shortcoming and decided to change it. Upon retirement, he and his wife decided to become volunteer camp hosts at a National Forest campground so he would be forced to interact with strangers. He loved the experience. They were so proud of his efforts that the pride carried over into other aspects of their seasonal job—the campground was immaculate.

TABLE 1.1 Your Personal Characteristics

		NO	SOMETIMES		DEFINITELY
Personal					
1. I consider myself an optimist.	1	2	3	4	5
2. I feel good about myself.	1	2	3	4	5
3. I sense that in most instances, the right answer will emerge.	1	2	3	4	5
4. I actively consider ideals greater than myself.	1	2	3	4	5
5. I am usually happy and contented.	1	2	3	4	5
Health					
6. When I look in the mirror, I'm satisfied with how I look.	1	2	3	4	5
7. I exercise regularly.	1	2	3	4	5
8. I am conscious of what I eat and strive for healthy meals.	1	2	3	4	5
9. I seldom worry.	1	2	3	4	5
10. My overall stress level is low.	1	2	3	4	5
Social					
11. I listen well and easily sense what others are feeling.	1	2	3	4	5
12. I can talk about how I feel with someone close.	1	2	3	4	5
13. I can communicate about politics and money with my family.	1	2	3	4	5
14. I trust others.	1	2	3	4	5
15. I find it easy to talk with strangers.	1	2	3	4	5
Money					
16. I track my expenses, know my budget, and my net worth.	1	2	3	4	5
17. I don't spend impulsively.	1	2	3	4	5
18. I understand my pension, IRA, and Social Security benefits.	1	2	3	4	5
19. I have figured out what makes for a high quality of life.	1	2	3	4	5
20. I have a sound financial safety net for my dependents.	1	2	3	4	5
Direction					
21. I have several passions I want to pursue.	1	2	3	4	5
22. I have tested each of my future plans.	1	2	3	4	5
23. I know what I need to feel productive.	1	2	3	4	5
24. I don't have to win in every situation.	1	2	3	4	5
25. I know where and how I want to live.	1	2	3	4	5

Another exercise, devised by Dr. Sidney Simon of University of Massachusetts (reported in Grace Weinstein's *Life Plans*), helps you identify what you want to do. Write down twenty things you really enjoy—no matter how small. Now that you have your list, review it. First, mark the items that cost money every time you do them. Next, mark the items you prefer to do alone and those you prefer do with others. For the next mark, identify the items that involve physical, emotional, and financial risk. Next, mark items that would not have been on your list ten years ago; then mark those that may not be there in the future. Finally, mark the last time you actually did each item. If you have a partner, ask him or her do the same thing. Now share. This little exercise might open up a whole world of possibilities, as well as add a large dose of reality to your plans.

In *A Time to Enjoy: The Pleasures of Aging*, Dr. Lillian Dangott encourages us to set aside time for the simple pleasures of everyday life. She advocates that pleasing yourself improves your health, emotionally and physically. Go barefoot, sunbathe, take a hot bath, daydream, nap, sleep late for a change, get a massage, hum and sing. Dangott also recommends activities for self-expression, service to others, social involvement, physical fitness, learning, and contemplation. Notice that there is no stress on figuring if you can afford it. There is an emphasis on your knowing what pleases you and then becoming engaged in activities that satisfy you. Approaching life in this way, you will continue to grow every day. If you have had trouble adjusting to change in the past, it does not mean you will always have that problem. You can learn to adapt now and in the future. Forget the old adage, "You can't teach an old dog new tricks."

Now, close your eyes and picture your ideal day in retirement. Imagine all the details. If you were writing about this day-in-the-life, what kind of book would it be? Would the reader be thrilled, happy, serene, or bored? Do you like the story? Are there any adjustments you find you want to make?

How to Be Ageless

In 1957, Flanders Dunbar, Columbia University professor of medicine, studied centenarians to discover what made them ageless. Psychological adaptability was the strongest common trait among these people. This trait helped them bounce back from disappointment, shock, and grief. Other traits included creative responses to change; capacity to integrate new things into one's existence; continuing ability to invent anew; high energy levels; freedom from anxiety; and the desire to stay alive.

To help yourself become more adaptable, develop resources that matter for your income and your health (physical and mental). Also, develop alliances that count: your mate, your children and grandchildren, brothers and sisters, friends, and groups. (Ask yourself how can a particular someone help you? And, more importantly, how can you help him or her?) Barbara Gallatin Anderson in *The Aging Game* offers additional suggestions: Replace any lost satisfactions and develop different options for measuring success, such as change, novelty, independence, productivity, recognition, conservation, self-acceptance, congeniality, cooperation, love, or concern.

Chart Your Retirement with Simple Steps

Once you know who you are and what you want, you can chart your retirement course. Here's a simplification of the five steps.

Step One: Know Yourself What are your best talents? Take an honest inventory. Concentrate and be objective. Compare those talents with the results of the survey done previously in this chapter. Examine the areas circled as 5s versus the areas with 1s. If you are part of a couple, know your partner's talents. Identify your pattern as a couple—togetherness, parallel tracks, or separate tracks. Are you talking about aging? Remember that one of you may be a surviving partner.

Step Two: Focus on the Life You Desire Set goals for the rest of your life. Keep your goals visible and measurable. Have separate goals for your physical, mental, and spiritual development. Make specific plans to achieve your goals. Basically, know where you are going and how you will get there.

Step Three: Transition into Retirement Activities Income does not need to be the top priority. Develop fresh interests. Performing volunteer work or learning something new could become the source of something meaningful. Successful people give of themselves, as well as invest in themselves.

Step Four: Enjoy the Adventure Choose to find personal satisfaction on the way to achieving your goals. Take better care of your health, create opportunities to stay mentally fresh, spend more time with your family, and share all you have learned. If you want to make a positive change, learn to relish your life.

Step Five: Realize You Have Limits Try to discover a high level of persistence toward your goal (whether it's a sport or a hobby).

As Marian Marzynski, filmmaker for the PBS *Frontline* series production of *A Look at the Land of Our Second Chance*, says, "It's all in your mind. We create who we are by intellectualizing it, imagining it, then doing it."

Time to Transition

By the time retirement rolls around, so many of us have dedicated everything to the job that the career has become synonymous with life itself. "It is sport, pastime, hobby, lover. It provides our friends and our social life. It sets our goals, defines our ambitions, gives us our report cards. Slowly, seductively, it comes to define the very word *important*," according to author Howard Shank in *Managing Retirement*.

If you have been taking rather than giving orders, you may have a more difficult time with retirement. This may be the first time that you must create your own plan to structure your life. Perhaps it would be helpful to think of you giving yourself orders!

Be Prepared for a Change in How You Feel

Be prepared for feelings of purposelessness. You have lost comrades from your workplace. Your self-esteem may disappear with your job title. Simultaneously, you have many choices, yet you have lost your mission. Understand that the basic instinct of survival can be undermined by retirement. Remember the vision of the drowning person desperately grasping at anything that floats? The survivor learns to relax. You will get a grip on your emotions and slowly begin to take action.

You should also be prepared for feelings of boredom. To predict boredom, look at your favorite pastimes. If you take pleasure in them only because they are changes from your usual routine, these activities will probably lead to boredom. You love fishing? Is it because fishing is an escape from a hectic schedule, or is it because you seek the solitary moment? If joy comes because it's an escape, think of fishing as a nice occasional pastime, not as a frequent retirement activity.

Be as prepared as you can for a successful retirement. Make it your latest mission or newest adventure. Start planning now.

Planning

To make your plan tangible, gather all of your work into one place. For example, much of your research and information could be placed in a loose-leaf notebook with the following sections:

- *Financial and Legal*—annual net worth statement with income and expense summaries, investments (and investment strategies), Social Security informa-

tion and periodic updates, and list of important
papers (and their locations)
- *Health*—health-care records and reminders
- *Social*—family and community responsibilities
- *Dreams*—ideas and plans

Remember that a well-planned and executed retirement
can still be dramatically changed by a catastrophic event, such
as the incapacity or death of a spouse. The people who cope
best are those who have exerted control over their lives and
who have worked at adapting to change. Prepare yourself
psychologically, as well as with knowledge in finance, legal,
and medical areas.

It is also a time to prepare for our inevitable deaths. If you
face your fears about death, you can plan better. Do you want
to die with dignity, or do you want your life prolonged at all
costs? Do you want to be cremated or buried? Do you want a
memorial service? If so, what do you want said and what
music do you want played? Have you created a living trust to
distribute your belongings easily to your heirs? Making these
decisions and keeping them up-to-date gives you more confidence because you are in control.

Your Partner's Wishes

If you are part of a couple, it will be an even greater challenge
to reach mutual agreements on what to do as an individual
and what to do as a couple. Many couples have only one plan
upon retiring—to take a major trip. Then what?

If you have not shared your dreams and fears with your
partner, it is time to learn how. With communication, you can
agree on the best courses of action for the two of you. To start
communicating, brainstorm a list of topics. Each of you
responds to each topic with what you seek and, then, what
you can do without or want to avoid. Subjects might include:

house and neighborhood	income and investments
friends and acquaintances	spending preferences

The best way for
couples to adjust to their
retirement is to talk
about it—before,
during, and after!
RETIRED SHOP OWNER
New Jersey

family members	health
weather	physical activity
social preferences	role of television
cultural activities	gardening and yard work
leisure activities	housework
travel	learning
job(s)	luxuries
volunteer work	fears and concerns

Here are some additional questions that require each partner to do some soul-searching:

- What are our dreams? What would we like to achieve? How much change are we going to attempt?
- Will we have more leisure time? What will we do together? How much do we accept, compromise, or combine?
- Is our time together enjoyable? Is our sex life fulfilling? How can we improve our relationship?
- Can we calculate our retirement income? How will we manage financially? How much cushion do we have for emergencies?
- Are we considering jobs or volunteer activities?
- What do we want from our family? Do our children need our help? Do we need their help? What about grandchildren?
- Suppose one of us becomes ill or seriously impaired. Are we ready to take care of the other? What if we are both incapacitated? Who would we turn to? Do we need to consider possible problems in the future?

Dreams to Reality

Look at your plan and the dreams you and your partner have outlined. Take a few moments to place these fantasies into reality. With new ventures, such as travel, education, relocation, or writing the great American novel, realize that your experiences may not measure up to your dreams. You might endure a frustrating trip, encounter a poor teacher, find your new location full of unfriendly people, or run headlong into writer's block. The idea is to have balanced expectations and be prepared to adjust and adapt.

When you plan on a life with your favorite sport, anticipate how you will adjust to injury (either you or a partner), boredom, or tension from over-competitiveness.

When you hope to give back through volunteering, understand that many volunteer operations may be disorganized or staffed with less-than-dependable volunteers. Society may view your efforts as somewhat unimportant since the work is unpaid.

When you envision yourself happily encased in a new career, recognize that you may be seen as an older worker to be patronized and underpaid. If you decide to be the next great entrepreneur and open a small business, understand that many are unprofitable and that there is often no backup for the key player(s).

When you elect to stay with your career because of happiness or money, foresee the inevitable time when you can no longer continue (sudden incapacitation does occur). There will be many other rewarding opportunities if you can open yourself to them.

In short, plan big and envision yourself in perfect scenarios, but also take off any blinders so you can glance at possible pitfalls. Preparation includes a balanced view.

When we work to develop our dreams, we write the scripts for our own movies-of-the-mind. Now in order to bring these movies to life, we must become first-class directors and producers.

ANDREA GROSS
Author

A New Vision

What is your vision? Do you seek opportunities to do things you have never done, to change the world (or at least a small part of it), to continue your lifelong work, to be released from work and family cares, or to sit by a fire surrounded by adoring grandchildren who listen to your every word? All of that and more is possible except, maybe, the last image. More than likely, your children and grandchildren have scattered and have their own lives to lead. After all, you have raised them to be responsible and independent.

And, relax—not everything has to be decided at once or before you retire. It does help, however, to know your partner's thoughts as you face not only the momentous decisions but the day-to-day choices, as well.

Here seems an appropriate place to share what we try to do each morning over the breakfast table. It has become a race to be the first to ask, "What do you want to accomplish today?" We share opportunities, such as a picnic in the park or the movie; we share deadlines, such as the press release that is due at the local newspaper for the volunteer project; we prioritize our time. Then, as phone calls come in, we know each other's preferences well enough to handle any last-minute situations.

Hopefully, improved communication occurs during this process of learning one another's wishes. Some of you may discover, however, that you do not care enough about each other to make planning worth the effort. This may be hard to accept, to express, and even harder to accomplish with fairness and grace, but it may be time to end your relationship. Then each of you can make a fresh start on this next phase of life. (See Chapter 3, "Social and Emotional Changes," for other ideas.)

Acceptance of Aging

The Challenges of Aging

People don't grow old. When they stop growing, they become old.

ANONYMOUS

With aging come challenges. Physician and author Alex Comfort simplifies the aging process by looking at it in two ways: One kind is biological and expresses itself in such changes as the graying of hair, the decline in eye-focusing power, and the loss of top-register hearing. The most serious of these changes is the increased liability to, and lack of recuperative power from, illnesses of various kinds. These changes can be accelerated by diet, abuse, stress, exhaustion, trauma, and disease. These rising "forces of mortality" can make a seventy-five-year-old man about forty-one times more likely to die during that year of his life than a twenty-year-old man. How you fare individually with this sort of aging depends upon luck, genetic inheritance, money, and lifestyle choices.

Comfort writes,

> But the things which make oldness insupportable in human societies don't all commonly arise from consequences of this biological aging process. They arise from 'sociogenic aging.' This means, quite simply, the role which society imposes on people as they reach a certain chronologic age. At this age, they 'retire' or, in plain words, are rendered unemployed, useless and, in some cases, impoverished. After that transition, and in proportion to their chronological age, they are prescribed to be unintelligent, unemployable, crazy and asexual.

Faced with this specter of aging, you can choose to rise to the occasion. The landmark MacArthur Foundation study, which took ten years and $10 million has been published in *Successful Aging* by John Wallis Rowe, M.D., and Robert L. Kahn, Ph.D. The study reveals how the lifestyle choices you make—more than the genes you carry—determine your health and vitality. Your attitude, diet, exercise program, and engagement with the world around you are the main contributors to the quality of your life.

In *Age Wave: The Challenges and Opportunities of an Aging America*, one of America's experts on gerontology, Ken Dychtwald, reported,

> I observed that a lifetime of disregard for personal health usually led not to a death sentence, but to chronic disease, a kind of extended-life imprisonment. It was obvious that many of the painful, punishing illnesses of old age could have been prevented.

Seeing Life Divided into Four Episodes

Think of a full human life in at least four twenty-five-year episodes. The first twenty-five represent the time of learning to perform in our culture and society. The next twenty-five years implement what was learned in the first twenty-five, including starting a career and raising a family. The next twenty-five are the opportunity years, as the children leave home, earnings and savings peak, and a longer perspective aids in individuals making better choices. The fourth set of twenty-five requires a closer monitoring of health and an adjustment of activities. These years can constitute the most meaningful periods in your life.

Illusions of Old Age

It is ironic that humanity has spent much of its history trying to live longer, and that now, when civilization is experiencing some success with medical breakthroughs, it does not know what to make of it. That may be because western society is fixated on looking young and acting youthful. There are all kinds of polarized messages about youth and old age. Passionate youth—young models, young athletes, young stars, and young computer geniuses—fill the media space with their presence. We are left wondering, if youth is so idyllic, then what is it to be old? Older people must be behind the times, slow, feeble, decrepit. . . . In countless ways, our society has learned to like what is young and dislike what is old. The term *geezer* is instructive. Originating from the Germanic *guiser*, meaning to disguise, the word was used to describe women who wore too much makeup. Now, the young use the term in derision to describe everyone who is old. Meanwhile, study after study has reported that while younger people see problems in the elderly, older folks do not have the same view. Approximately one in eight older people (12 percent) has social problems, while only one in six (approximately 16 percent) has financial problems and only one in five (approximately 20 percent) has serious health problems. If the same yardstick were applied to twenty-year-olds, would the numbers and percentages be significantly different? Let's examine some of the individual illusions of old age:

Old Age Happens at Sixty-Five

The already-mentioned economic decisions made in 1889 Germany and 1935 America proclaimed sixty-five as the year of retirement. This arbitrary age was selected so that little pension money would be distributed. Times have changed dramatically. Medical advancements have increased longevity and decreased illnesses. Recent studies show highly active and capable people living beyond the age of sixty-five.

Most Old People Are Decrepit

While, as they age, people may develop chronic health problems, such as arthritis, most are not excessively bothered or limited by them. They learn to adapt through diet and activity including taking medications. Approximately 85 percent of all people older than sixty-five live independently. Of those independent seniors, three-fourths consider their health to be good to excellent. Though there are exceptions, as a general rule, it is not until the last six months of life, as the body shuts down, that one experiences ailing health.

As our society adapts to its aging norm, our notions about health and old age will change, too. Definitions and measurements of abilities will be a result of an individual's level of performance and sense of well-being. Knowledge of the crucial importance of exercise and the wide availability of a quality diet will play substantial roles in allowing people to maintain high levels of functioning as they age. Active seniors will have more opportunities and experience better health than in years past. You probably can expect more (and obtain more) from yourself than you thought possible.

Most Old People Are Sexless

As Ken Dychtwald and Joe Fowler report in *Age Wave*, Doctors Bernard D. Starr and Marcella Bakur Weiner discovered

Dr. William Castelli, head of the Framingham Heart Study, writes of one participant who had a heart attack at age ninety. She made changes. She sent him a jar of fat representing the fat she took out of her diet. She enrolled in college. She became the school's oldest graduate, then wrote a book in her late nineties. Finally, she "retired" at age 100 to New Hampshire. Who is defining the word *old*?

(after interviewing eight hundred people between sixty and ninety-two from all parts of the United States):

- 97 percent like sex
- 91 percent approve of unmarried or widowed people having sexual relations
- 80 percent think sex is good for health
- 75 percent think sex feels as good—or better—than it did when they were young
- 72 percent are sexually satisfied
- approximately 39 percent would like to have new sexual experiences
- almost 10 percent felt women should deal with the shortage of men with arrangements that include several women sharing a man

Do these answers reflect a sexless population?

Most Old People Become Senile

There is no "illness" or even common occurrence called *senility*. The worst part of this illusion is that it can become a self-fulfilling prophecy. There are diseases that can create various forms of dementia, but those affect only a small percentage of the older population. About 95 percent of retirees remain independent and are capable of functioning without assistance. Recent reports show that even seniors with cognitive decline can greatly benefit through mental training. For example, the MacArthur Foundation studies reveal that the higher level mental functions of inductive reasoning and spatial orientation can show substantial improvement after just five training sessions. With memory training, subjects can triple their recall power, scoring even higher than typical young people.

The use-it-or-lose-it concept popularized by sex researchers holds true in other physical activities, as well as mental capacities, such as learning ability. The more you work your brain, the more it will continue to work for you. Author Gail Sheehy shares in *Passages*:

> Highly educated people show little or no decline with age in test performance—indeed, accuracy generally improves over the years—up to the age of fifty. After that, it is lack of speed, not accuracy, that accounts for decline, if there is any. Adult learning ability does not slack off in a generalized way; it is in the ability to absorb unfamiliar or inapplicable material that a loss is noticed later in life.

Psychologists are verifying that human development extends into old age through higher states of awareness—such as wisdom. Wisdom can be defined as:

- understanding the facts related to a situation
- having strategies for getting more information
- applying sensitivity to issues
- recognizing the long-term consequences of any action
- appreciating that all choices have advantages and disadvantages

When you consider the aging process, it is not a bad trade-off—you lose a little mental speed and short-term memory but you gain a broader, deeper perspective on life. When combined with your varied experiences, your perspective can allow you better insight, with wiser solutions.

Most Old People Are Boring and Monotonous

This stereotype arises from ignorance and isolation. No one who has been around a number of older people would even consider it to be true. As Dychtwald and Fowler write, "There is no age group more varied in physical abilities, personal styles, tastes and desires, or financial capabilities than the older population. . . . People in their later years become more, not less, diverse. And tomorrow's elders will be different not only from one another but from today's elders as well."

You do not have to accept or live the role of any stereotype. We met one couple in a Georgia state park. They were traveling in a beat-up Volkswagen camper, with bicycles strapped to the front and other paraphernalia to the top and rear. They were returning to New England after a week-long scuba diving research expedition in the Caribbean. (They had been volunteers.) They had learned scuba so they could be part of this adventure. Over the next few hours, they shared many other tips they had learned since retirement. Finally, the gentleman prodded us to guess their ages. We tried to be as honest as possible—using our observations of their skin, posture, hair, etc. We guessed seventy-two. They were eighty-eight! They taught us lessons that are still vivid in our memories.

Most Old People Are Unproductive

People who retire could think of themselves as self-employed and go from there.

AUTHOR
North Carolina

Productivity in this country is an economic statistic, not a concept. It is defined as performing tasks for money. Are you being productive when you build a house for Habitat for Humanity, when you raise two kids, when you help someone feed themselves, or when you coach a ball team? You are not being productive, based on our current economic definition. Work done by volunteers and help provided someone is productive work, however. Retirees accomplish much of it. According to standards, older workers produce as much (and often more reliably) than their younger counterparts. The U.S. Department of Labor and many senior citizen organizations have performed studies and published information to counter the misbelief that older people are unreliable, inflexible, and unproductive. (See Chapter 4, "Work and Play Opportunities.") In the future, the word *productive* will be redefined.

It is disheartening to watch our society trying to disengage people older than sixty-five from the mainstream. Remain engaged!

Looking at the latest figures from the Census Bureau, the age group of fifty-five and older has, by far, the largest median personal net worth. This pattern is true from the lowest to highest (poorest to richest) classifications. Net worth finally begins to show a small decline after the age of seventy-five, though that group still has a net worth 20 percent higher than the forty-five- to fifty-four-year-olds. The numbers do not suggest an impoverished group. In 1996, less than 11 percent of seniors lived at the poverty level, a slightly lower rate than the rest of the population. It is appropriate to recognize and assist the small percentage of older Americans whose only income is a meager Social Security check and who have few other assets. These are primarily widows whose spouses had no pensions and who, as a couple, had no savings.

You can choose not to live in poverty through the way you spend and the way you save. (See Chapter 5, "Financial and Legal Issues," for ideas.)

Societal Accommodations

Early in human history, few people could expect to live to the age of sixty-five. In 1983, the number of Americans older than sixty-five surpassed the number of teenagers. We are no longer a nation of youths. The Census Bureau forecasts that the over-sixty-five population in 2000 is likely to be close to 35 million, representing approximately one-eighth of the total population.

The Economic Power of Seniors

As politicians, marketing managers, and other executives become aware that the sixty-five-plus age group is the fastest growing segment in the country, that it has money (and is willing to spend it), and that it is willing to make its viewpoints known (read: vote), the power of seniors will spread exponentially.

To give you an idea of the power within this age group, consider these points (several from Cheryl Russell's "The Ungraying of America" in the July 1997 issue of *American Demographics*) about older citizens.

They typically:

- spend more than twenty-five to thirty-four year olds on the major categories of goods and services, from food to housing, transportation, and health care
- spend far more on women's clothes than the younger group
- spend more on pets, toys, and playground equipment for their grandchildren than the children's parents
- eat out 9 percent more than the younger age group
- spend more than any other group (except for the boomers) on transportation and entertainment
- control most of the personal cash in banks, credit unions, and savings and loans
- gamble more than any other age group
- watch television more than any other age group
- buy and read books, magazines, and newspapers more than any other age group

The economic implications are staggering. Retirees possess most of the personal assets in this country and their discretionary spending is far higher than younger consumers. Individuals joining the older-than-sixty-five club in the next couple of decades promise to be healthier, more active, and more prepared to spend. And, the predominant sex of this burgeoning group will be female. When the corporate world understands the implications of these numbers, the marketing blitz will follow. Your challenge is to grasp your needs so you are not swept away in the flood of advertising.

Add to this momentum, the fact that the baby boomers will soon qualify for many services—fasten your seat belts for the changes. As this group has grown up in America, its needs and desires have become prominent considerations for businesses and governments alike. The first of the boomers will turn sixty-five in 2011. Hopefully, the inevitable changes will be those that benefit everyone in America—not just the baby boomers—when there are so many people of all ages who are desperately needy.

Looking at the seniors as consumers, when the Daniel Yankelovich Group performed a study in 1987 for AARP's *Modern Maturity* magazine, fifty-plus consumers showed a higher concern for quality over cost. Following are some of the findings:

- mature consumers do not like to be thought of as old
- mature consumers prefer to be reflected in an attractive, positive fashion
- mature consumers are more interested in purchasing experiences than things
- for an older consumer, convenience and access may be as important as the product
- being comfortable is a key psychological need of the older consumer
- security and safety are important factors in the older consumer's decision to buy

Seniors, more than other age groups, like products and services they can trust (with guarantees, trial periods, service after the sale) and that are marketed with knowledge rather than hype.

There will probably be thousands of new offerings so challenge yourself to develop your own strict standards of what any offering must possess before you buy. You will see new devices and new twists on old ones. A recent poll highlighting the fifty-five-plus population indicates these older individuals could foresee the need for help with common chores (vacuuming, washing and waxing, and using tools), and personal tasks (reading labels, reaching high things, fastening, carrying objects, and using the shower). Brainstorm the kinds of products and services that might be introduced to meet those needs. Write down your ideas—you will probably see them as reality within the next ten years. Better yet, why not register these ideas and invent them?

Beware of Economic Ploys Directed at Seniors

You will be the selected target of many a marketing ploy—good and bad. It will seem as if almost every person and business is attempting to redistribute whatever wealth you have collected in your lifetime into their bank accounts. In the health-care industry, we are already seeing this trend with frequently unnecessary tests, surgeries, and prescriptions. Insurance salesmen sell products you may not need. (Seniors spend far more on insurance than any other age group.) You will be the target of bulk-mail contests offering the chance to win millions—if you make a purchase. Unless you are vigilant, you could be the victim of flimflam operators knocking at your door or calling you, asking for your money. (For avoidance techniques, see Chapter 7, "Safety and Security Concerns.") Unless you have created a living trust that directs the disbursement of your assets after your death, documented reports indicate the probate system can pick over your estate. (See Chapter 5, "Financial and Legal Issues.")

More Good Times Opening Up for Seniors

On the positive side, seniors will enjoy new recreational outlets—more educational and travel opportunities, more magazines and books, more radio and television shows—perhaps, seniors' broadcast channels.

Many matters seem certain. Thanks to medical advances, you will live longer than you expect. Consequently, many physical, social, and emotional aspects of your life will change—your physical environment, family relationships, and love life (who you love, how long you love them, and how you love them). You may never retire or you may retire several times. And, unless our government devises a fair system to distribute Social Security benefits, you will become part of an intergenerational struggle due to an unfair tax burden placed on those who are working for a living. (How can the U.S. government spend eight times more per capita on a senior then it does on a young person, especially when the senior possesses far more wealth?)

Summary

As you determine what you really want for the remainder of your life, it is helpful to write down your wishes. It is valuable to compare your wish list with that of others. Respected doctor, author, and speaker Deepak Chopra shares this list:

- I want to survive even longer, if possible.
- I want to remain healthy.
- I want a clear, alert mind.
- I want to be active.
- I want to have achieved wisdom.

As you transition from your old life to your new one, it is helpful to read about the inspirational experiences of others who also faced that challenge. One of America's first couples, Rosalynn and Jimmy Carter, wrote in *Everything to Gain* that when they retired from the White House, they had to work through self-pity, anger, discouragement, and anxiety. They understood that their lives did not have to be limited by their past experiences. "What we had come to realize as 'retired' people is that we have a lot more leeway than ever before to choose our own path, to establish our own priorities. We had a lifetime of training and experience on which to base these decisions, and our financial resources would be adequate to meet our needs. We had nothing to lose in whatever we did and everything to gain."

Jimmy Carter further describes his retirement as "a less pres-sured, more reflective time with further development of the interior life of the intellect, memory, imagination, of emotional maturity, and of one's own personal sense of spiritual identity. It's a period for giving back to society the lessons, resources, and experiences accumulated and articulated over a lifetime."

Indeed, after his involuntary retirement from the American presidency, Carter has made the world a better place for all of us: constructing a peace center, mediating Mideast talks, over-seeing Nicaraguan elections, helping the World Health Orga-nization incubate premature babies, and much more.

The happiest retirees are the "doers"—those who are involved with life and who give back. They are the people whom others find the most engaging in their lives.

Again, the options exist; the choices are yours.

CHAPTER TWO

Health and Well-Being Matters

One of the most active members in a hiking club, an older retiree, has shared his plans for his 120th birthday party. It includes a five-mile walk along a beautiful section of the Appalachian Trail. He finds it important to give his body the messages that, first, he intends to be around for quite a while and, second, that he expects his body to serve him well during those years. There appear to be positive behavioral benefits to this type of thinking.

The Process of Aging

Until this century, the average life span did not exceed forty years. Now, with possibilities of more than twice that limit, we must face the realization that these extra years exact a price. Our body efficiency decreases with time. We must work harder to maintain a high level of functioning. Our health, in larger measure, depends on how we treat our bodies. Research studies indicate there is plenty of room for us to minimize aging's negative impact.

Aging is not a disease but a natural slowing-down process. We can understand that process and personally take charge so as to minimize its harmful effects. We cannot stop aging, but we can age with more grace and, consequently, experience less

The people around me who are flunking retirement are those who think old. They give up doing things they've done their whole lives because they think it's time to quit. They haven't cultivated interests to carry them through what should be a very exciting time of life. I intend to play handball, water-ski, and keep physically active as long as I'm upright.

SIXTY FIVE-YEAR-OLD
PHOTOGRAPHER

misery. We can remain more independent. Visualize yourself being healthy and mentally alert long into the future. The body does respond to expectations.

It may help to think of your age in three parts. The number of years you have lived would be your chronological age. Your body parts have aged, reflecting how well they have held up to the demands of your chronological age—that is, your biological age. Finally, your attitude has psychological age. The old cliché, "You're as young as you feel" has validity. Scientists are increasingly finding that such an attitude is crucial to predicting success and happiness while aging.

There has been, and will continue to be, much discussion about the influences of heredity (good genes) and environment (lifestyle). The most recent research, however, indicates that if you want to age well, then you must give up a sedentary lifestyle and incorporate a positive attitude. The genes play a smaller and smaller role once you pass retirement age. You are in control.

Keep in mind that flagrant disregard for your health and fitness not only shortens your life, but greatly heightens your chance of suffering from a chronic, debilitating disease.

Exercise

Do you want more energy, less stress (or greater ability to cope with stress), improved quality of sleep, and increased mental acuity? Get moving! Regular exercise is crucial to good health. Many of the problems associated with aging can be lessened with appropriate exercise. This conclusion is one of the most universally accepted findings in the study of gerontology. Everyone, no matter the age or physical condition, benefits from embarking on an exercise program. The latest research demonstrates that exercise improves physical well-being and enhances mental functioning. The second great news is that these benefits are available for free.

We face only two hurdles: motivating ourselves into action and choosing the exercises. That first hurdle can be significant. After all, almost 40 percent of all people older than fifty-five report no leisure-time physical activity. Yet, the older one becomes, the more regular physical activity is necessary.

Use Daily Activities for More Physical Movement

Retirement offers time for you to set your own schedule and priorities. Moderate physical activity should be at the top of your list. Ideally, the activity will be something you enjoy. If it is, that will heighten the motivational component. It is even better if you incorporate exercise as an integral part of your daily activities. For example, we currently live in a small town where many services (post office, grocery, library) are within six blocks, so we walk to each one. We timed driving, finding a parking space, and returning. We discovered walking is almost as fast as the "modern" alternative. Our conclusion? By using a vehicle, we neglected a chance to exercise our bodies, wasted money, and saved little time. Now is the time to examine your old habits and start new ones.

There are so many casual opportunities for enjoyable exercise. If you golf, walk rather than take a cart. If you work in the garden or on your landscaping, use as few power tools as possible—power your efforts with your body. If you like photography, hike to those photo opportunities and carry your camera and tripod. When you watch television, incorporate flexibility and stretching movements while you sit. Take a brisk walk when the urge to snack hits.

With every daily routine, raise your activity level a notch. When talking on the phone, stand rather than sit. When talking to someone, walk around a little. When walking, move a little faster. Take a hilly route on your next stroll. When using the car for shopping, park far away from the store entrance to force yourself to walk more. Use stairs instead of elevators (at least part of the way). Mow your own lawn and rake your own leaves. Dance!

With the soaring cost of health care, why not benefit from one of Dr. Thomas Curtis Namey's free "pills" (reported by

Those who think they have not time for bodily exercise will sooner or later have to find time for illness.

EDWARD STANLEY
Earl of Derby

I ride almost every day.
Every day, I muck the
stalls and feed the
horses. That means I'm
hauling and lifting bales
of hay and fifty-pound
bags of feed.

SEVENTY-NINE-

YEAR-OLD

WIDOW/EQUESTRIAN

Leonard Hansen in *Life Begins at 50*). Take a walk—a brisk one for more than forty minutes at least four to seven times each week. You will feel better and look better, as well as cut your risk of many "old-age" maladies. As a supplemental benefit, your appetite will synchronize with your body's needs. For those who are overweight, exercise appears to cut cravings; for those who are underweight, exercise stimulates the desire for food. In addition, regular exercise provides more energy, makes us feel better, and allows us to engage in more pleasurable activities.

All of us, however, face the problem of motivation. Are you a self-starter? Be honest with yourself and reflect on your past patterns. Did you play team sports or individual sports, or no sports at all? What kept your interest in any physically demanding activity? The answers provide you with insights for implementing a successful retirement exercise program. You may need to join a club or participate in more formal, organized events. You may be able to develop your own individual program and keep it going. Each person has his own pattern of persistence—you must draw upon yours. For classes and groups, check with your community recreation department, local YMCAs and YWCAs, health clubs, and gyms.

To keep your body functioning at a high level, you must incorporate a variety of exercises that aid flexibility, balance, strength, and endurance. Each of these categories ranks important for a physically fit, healthy body. You must ensure that you have some activity available year-round. Come up with many choices. If it is raining or hot or cold, you need an appropriate alternative ready.

Appropriate Activities For improving flexibility and balance, muscles must work through a range of motion. Think of walking, dancing, yoga, martial arts (especially tai chi), swimming, water aerobics, cycling, and rowing. Try simple activities to rotate your hands and feet, stretch your fingers, or curl into a ball to stretch your back. There are many books on stretching, such as the classic *Stretching* by Bob and Jean Anderson, which demonstrates hundreds of beneficial exercises. Yoga, on the other hand, usually requires an instructor to teach you the positions. You could take a class or use a video. *Kathy Smith's New Yoga* video offers an excellent starting point. Most people who try yoga feel immediate results from the movements and positions. Before starting and after finishing any exercise, do some of the stretches or yoga movements. As we age, our bodies lose elasticity. These slow stretches help to prevent injury—plus they feel good.

Strength exercises require your muscles to work against resistance. This type of activity is effective in lessening the problems of osteoporosis (decreasing bone density). Also, it treats the cosmetic problems of sagging arms, flabby legs, and poor muscle tone. To strengthen your legs, engage in fast walking, hill/step climbing, cycling, cross-country skiing, and swimming. For arms, pull, push, and lift. Add weights as needed. One of the best all-purpose books for developing your routine is *Getting in Shape: Workout Programs for Men and Women* by Bob Anderson, Ed Burke, Bill Pearl, and Jean Anderson. If you need more structured motivation, you might enjoy *Fitness After 50* by Walter Ettinger, Jr., Brenda Mitchell, and Steven Blair.

For those who could use weights but do not want to buy and store them, the "slowdown" technique can create a rigorous workout without equipment. For example, if you do squats for your legs, do them slowly. Sink gradually (up to several seconds), hold it for a couple of seconds, then unhurriedly rise. The effect is the same as holding weights across your shoulder.

Endurance helps your cardiovascular system. Consider that your triglyceride level (tied to stroke and heart attack) is mainly determined by your activity (or lack of) once you pass age seventy. You increase endurance when you build up your strength routine both in duration, as well as the pace. If your breathing presents a problem, do two shorter routines rather than one long one. Strive for activities that make your heart pump, and continue that level for at least twenty-five minutes. Do your routine three times per week.

When attempting to develop the best routine for you, you will find examples of endurance regimens under the category

Given the importance of physical fitness, long recognized as the key to longevity and quality of life, I recommend various sports and fitness regimens. I've taken up golf myself. It has been a good source of meeting people, as well as providing me with many hours of passing my time. Bicycling is my other avid sport.

RETIRED PROFESSOR
Ohio

of aerobics. Check out books, magazine articles, classes, videos, and television workouts for ideas.

Calculate Your Target Heart Rate

To measure the aerobic or endurance level of your exercise program, a popular method is to use a target heart rate. A maximum heart rate is established based on your age. (Take the number 220 and subtract your age.) With that maximum in mind, you want to discover an exercise target rate that will be well above the do-nothing rate, yet is still safe (well below the maximum). To calculate the target, measure your resting heart rate (while lying or sitting down and being calm). If you are unsure, do it a couple of different times. Subtract the resting rate from the maximum rate to find your personal range. This number is too high to be safe, so multiply it by 0.6 or 0.7. (Use 0.6 if you are starting an exercise program and 0.7 if you have been exercising regularly.) This provides a safe boost that you can add to your resting heart rate to find your target. This target heart rate is one you would like to reach and maintain for twenty to thirty minutes while exercising.

Example: a target heart rate for a sixty-five-year-old sedentary person might be 121. The calculations are: Take 220, minus 65 to reach 155 (a maximum rate). This person's resting rate was 70. So, 155, minus 70 yields 85 as the personal range. To be prudent, take 0.6 times 85, which is 51 (a safe amount to raise the resting rate). Add this safe boost (51) to the resting rate (70), and 121 becomes the target heart rate.

Note: If you have had or suspect a heart condition, check with your doctor to obtain a graduated exercise program.

Benefits of Exercising

One classic study in the 1960s examined a class of seventy-year-old men completing a one-year exercise program. These men ended the year with the bodily reactions of men thirty years younger! Since that study, many research activities have confirmed that exercise at all ages increases one's ability to function. A study of ninety-plus-year-olds placed in an exercise program found they gained more than a 100 percent improvement in their conditioning! Though exercise is not the fountain of youth, it is crucial to those who desire to maintain good health.

·

Notes for the Seriously Out-of-Shape

Start Moving

If you are so overweight or have had such minimal activity that you dread even the thought of an exercise program, lighten up. You stand to benefit the most from a change in routine—the trick is to make it a win-win situation. Do not expect a miracle; rather, imagine your ideal physical self as you might appear one year from now. To get there, start with one change today. Take a few minutes during the day to consciously raise your activity level. For instance, take a stroll after dinner. Congratulate yourself after your activity and let your body feel good.

Continue each day with either a slightly longer walk or a different activity. At the end of each session, reflect on your behavior and pat yourself on the back. Think how wonderful it is that these activities are helping you feel and look better. As you slowly develop this day-to-day rhythm, add to your program a small change in your diet. For example, during the first week, cut down on your intake of margarine, butter, or oil. During the next week, reduce dairy products or sugar. In the third week, add more fruits and vegetables.

Reinforce Your Can-do Attitude

As your new program continues, reinforce your can-do attitude. When you backslide (a day of bad diet or no activity), do not wallow in guilt. Instead, pick up where you left off. It is doubly effective if a friend or spouse joins you in this endeavor; you can reinforce each other when the going gets tough. If you are a visual person who likes feedback, you might make a large graph. Weigh in as you begin your fresh approach. Dot in the weight on the vertical axis. Mark off fifty-two weeks along the horizontal axis, then dot in your ideal weight at week fifty-two. Connect the beginning weight and your ideal with a straight line. Once a week, at the same time each day, weigh in, and then mark your weight on your chart. You will probably see that you can stay under that straight line without too much extra effort. If a week goes by without weight loss, that's okay. You are heading in a gradual yet positive direction. For additional help, you might contact former U.S. Surgeon General C. Everett Koop's nonprofit group, Shape Up America!, 6707 Democracy Blvd., Suite 306, Bethesda, MD 20817; www.shapeup.org, or the commercial site by NetHealth, www.obesity.com. Always check with your doctor before adopting a specific plan.

Rest and Relaxation

Even if you have never had difficulty falling asleep or getting adequate rest, be aware that your body changes. People older than sixty wake as many as 150 times per night (compared with 5 times per night for younger adults). Such a sleepless pattern can result in a loss of energy and even depression, without a conscious clue about the cause. If you find yourself caught in this pattern, you may want to investigate sleep aids. Of course, one of the most successful techniques for ensuring adequate rest is to exercise during the day. Another effective aid is several hours' exposure to sunlight, which helps prime the body for nighttime sleep. Deep breathing can serve as a relaxant. The old "warm-milk-before-bedtime" prescription often works. You can plan an evening activity that compels you to leave the house and jump into a new routine before returning home ready to sleep. You might try a minimal dose (three mgs) of melatonin, because your body's pineal gland produces less and less as you age. (Often, before it helps you sleep, melatonin must be taken several days before it raises the level in your body. Check with your doctor before you take any chemical sleep aid.) Remember, don't force sleep. Go to bed only when you feel tired.

Also, check Chapter 3, "Social and Emotional Changes," for ideas to lower or eliminate stress. And, if you are on-line, count sleep links at www.sleepnet.com.

Proper Nutrition

Many human maladies can be directly attributed to poor nutrition. What is wonderful about this knowledge is that we can correct many problems and prevent others simply by altering what we eat. All retirees will discover that their nutritional needs have changed. Physiological changes, plus variations in daily activities combine to present an altered set of requirements. The RDA (Recommended Dietary Allowance) was not aimed at an aging population. Only recently have the standards begun to address those needs. You will also notice that the term RDA is now being changed to Dietary Reference Intakes (DRI), which will include recommended and maximum levels, with separate numbers for age groups such as fifty to seventy and those older than seventy.

The amount of available information on nutrition has exploded over the last several years. How can one make sense of it all? Start with the common guidelines agreed upon by the American Cancer Society; American Diabetes Association; American Dietetic Association; American Heart Association; Centers for Disease Control; National Heart, Lung and Blood Institute; and the U.S. Department of Agriculture: Health and Human Services. Some of their nutritional tips include:

- Eat a nutritionally adequate diet consisting of a variety of foods.
- Reduce your fat consumption, specifically saturated fat and cholesterol.

- Increase your consumption of complex carbohy-drates and fiber.
- Reduce your intake of sodium.
- Achieve and maintain a reasonable body weight.
- Consume alcohol in moderation, if at all.

Another resource for healthy eating is The American Dietetic Association, 216 W. Jackson Blvd., Suite 800, Chicago, IL. 60606-6995; its Nutrition Hotline, at 1-800 366-1655; or for those on the Internet, www.eatright.org. Notice, however, that each of these organizations' "fact sheets" is paid for by a company or group with a vested interest. Of course, always check with your doctor before adopting any new diet.

Since you may find yourself losing your appetite as you age, you must be vigilant about eating the most nutrition per calorie. That means loading your diet with fresh fruits and vegetables. Try eating a few hundred calories of nothing but fresh fruits and veggies—the volume will amaze you. To that fruit and vegetable base, add grains and legumes to further increase your low-calorie volume. You'll soon discover why, through the ages, most cultures have relied on such dishes as beans and rice or flavorful stews to stay healthy.

Retirement is a perfect opportunity to broaden your repertoire of food. It can be good for your body and mind. Learn to cook new dishes. If you have never cooked before, now is the time to begin. Anyone who can read can learn to cook. Go to your public library or local bookstore and grab some cookbooks. Let your imagination run wild. Play games, for example, try nothing but new recipes for one month straight. If you and your friends hold dinner parties, agree to prepare dishes no one has ever tried. If you are part of a couple, try dividing the chores. Each person could develop their own specialties.

You might look for Leslie and Robert Cooper's *Low-Fat Living Cookbook* (excellent recipes), Sunset Books' *Complete Book of Low-fat Cooking* (not the easiest recipes, but lots of options), or even Donna Weihofen and Christina Marino's *The Cancer Survival Cookbook* (for specialized needs). The Internet has a wealth of recipes and sites to give you fresh ideas. Search for "healthy recipes." For example, you may surf to www.digitalchef.com; www.advocate-health.com/fitness/health_recipe/healthyeat.html, or www.healthyideas. com.

Eat Well and Regularly

Eating well and regularly must be your top priority. Beware of common excuses: "I'm saving money"; "I don't have any interest in food"; "My teeth/dentures bother me"; "I can't get out to shop"; "I'm too depressed"; "It's boring"; "Food just doesn't taste good"; "I hate to eat alone"; "I don't have the energy"; or "I don't know how to cook." There are easy remedies for each of these excuses. To revitalize your interest, take a class or check out, borrow, or purchase an easy cookbook. For less preparation make six snacks a day instead of three full meals. Get your teeth in shape by eating crunchy foods.

By all means, do not forget your best possible drink—water. Your thirst "trigger" is not as effective as you age. You must consciously replenish necessary water. Drink at least one to two quarts per day. It will keep your skin more elastic (fewer wrinkles), help the kidneys resist bacterial onslaughts, and promote a full feeling—with zero calories.

Meal Planning and Shopping

Healthy retirement meal planning begins with shopping. Compared to other peoples of the world, American consumers rate lucky in the wide array of products available. These consumables can overwhelm us at times—especially at the grocery store. Here are a few tips to make grocery shopping more pleasurable and economical—and more nutritious.

Think of yourself as a detective following the trail to the best buys. (If it is more fun for you, put on a Sherlock Holmes cap or a Colombo raincoat with a magnifying glass in your pocket!) The point is: Adopt an attitude that turns a mundane experience into a rewarding one. At the same time, take the responsibility for obtaining the most food value for your money and giving necessary feedback to store management. For example, if that pound of fish was tasteless and spongy, the department and store manager should know. How else will they discover there is a problem that needs correcting? If you cannot find a product you want, let the management know so it can be stocked. You are the reason they are there.

When you enter a grocery store, search for the best values in fresh meats and produce. Generally, the freshest items are those in season. When these products are in great supply, they usually cost less. When you buy the unusual at its lowest price, it gives variety to your diet, as well as your life. For example, if you find fresh fish and tropical fruits on special, plan a Caribbean dinner. What fun! Depending on the items you choose, you can plan main dishes and accompaniments for two to three days. It is economical in time, as well as money to shop approximately twice a week. Also, the grocery store receives deliveries at least twice a week. Find out which days the fresh produce arrives and when the meats and fish arrive. In other words, show some shopping savvy.

If the store has a bulk-food area for items such as pastas, beans, nuts, and spices, stop here. Study the storage bins. If the products are tightly stored so as to not be overly exposed to air or to one another, you can often obtain fresher products for less money than prepackaged ones. Be sure to compare prices to make sure.

Try products over brands. Sample the various brands and trust your judgment. Often, you may find a superior product in a house label, something that is particularly true on canned vegetables, frozen juices, or staples, such as peanut butter. Remember, if you are buying vegetable oil that is 100 percent canola, it is 100 percent canola no matter what brand you choose. Give yourself the freedom to try any product once, then make up your own mind.

Learn to read the ingredients labels. One rule of thumb is: If you cannot easily pronounce the ingredients, do not buy the product. For that reason, you may reject most convenience foods except for condiments, such as light salad dressings or an occasional dessert, like frozen yogurt. Often, convenience foods such as frozen pizzas and dinners contain more preservatives than real food value, not to mention high levels of fat and sodium. (If your time constraints dictate a frozen entrée or fast-food purchase, always skip the extracrunchy chicken and fish selections: the coating contains loads of fat.) It has become tricky to buy wheat bread with assurance of valuable nutrition. When you read the label, whole-wheat flour may have been replaced with bleached flour (stripped of the healthy bran and wheat germ) as the main ingredient. Shop with patience. If you look hard enough, you will usually find a desirable product.

In addition to talking to department and store managers, write letters to manufacturers or call their hot lines. These manufacturers are not mind readers; they need their customers' input. For example, Campbell's Soups makes soups with 200 percent of an adult's daily need for salt (sodium chloride). Because so many consumers, nutritionists, and doctors complained about the health hazards of too much sodium, Campbell's now makes a lighter line. These companies want to make money. That is possible only if they produce products people will buy. Vote with your wallet—what you will and will not buy. Follow up your vote with a call or letter to emphasize the point. You can make a difference.

Besides looking for in-season specials, search for markdown items. Often, they include day-old baked goods or items reaching a manufacturer's suggested shelf-life date. Evaluate each item individually. For instance, fresh produce loses food value as it ages so you may have to buy great quantities to garner the same nutrition. If you think the product is still good and you have an immediate use for it in mind, buy it.

Use coupons only for products you like. If you are not careful, you can devote your life to cutting and organizing coupons. Be selective so they do not take more time than they are worth.

The last word concerns roadside stands (produce, crab shacks, etc.) and specialty shops. You can find some of the best tips here—someone willing to share how to choose a ripe papaya, steam a crab, brew the best cup of coffee, or use millet. Support knowledgeable entrepreneurs. You may even find a bargain in the process!

When you prepare your food, learn to cook without oil and fat. At the very least, use only a small amount of olive or canola oil. Sautéing with water or wine, stir-frying, poaching, steaming, baking, broiling, roasting, pressure-cooking, and microwaving are all methods that retain nutrients without adding fats.

A Word about Fat

Americans have heard for years that their diets contain too much fat—specifically saturated fats. Major health groups recommend a diet that includes no more than 30 percent of your calories from fat. Translated into specific amounts this means if you are eating 2,000 calories per day, no more than 600 of those calories should come from fat. To convert to a weight, remember the number nine. One gram of fat equals nine calories. So, 67 grams of fat means the maximum 600 calories. It is not always easy to lower fat intake, especially if you choose a processed food or eat in a restaurant. When choosing among products with fat, lean toward those with monosaturated fats (olive oil and canola oil). Steer clear of any fat substitute, because it may well leach the important nutrients and cancer-fighting substances your body needs.

When you follow the above guidelines and incorporate exercise into your daily life, weight control isn't a problem. If too many pounds are a source of concern, look honestly for the culprits. What are you drinking (alcohol and nonalcohol)? You can easily add several hundred empty calories through your liquids. If you use processed foods (packaged, canned, or frozen), check the fat grams and the sodium levels. Remember that the per-serving rating is often underestimated. (One small can of tomato sauce is three-and-a-half servings.) Regularly snack on small amounts of healthy items. Healthy snacks reduce the tendency to overeat at mealtime.

A simple way to improve your diet and avoid too much fat is to "modify" your basic recipes. Over time, most people develop personal favorites they eat regularly. These constitute the majority of everything they consume. Usually there are between fifteen to twenty-five dishes. Look at each of these favorite recipes and modify the ingredients to make the dish healthier: Cut the fat and enrich the seasonings. Your health depends on what you typically eat, not on the occasional treat.

Supplements

In the last several years, the supplement business has exploded. Research in gerontology consistently adds new information to our understanding of the aging process. For example, it appears that free radicals attack cells in a way that leads to permanent damage and aging. Free radicals are molecules that have lost an electron due to oxidation. Free radicals are present inside and outside our body (specifically in cigarette smoke, car exhaust, air pollution, and wherever oxidation occurs). These free radicals are useful when our body employs them to fight infection. Generally, however, the body must repair cellular damage caused by free radicals— and it succeeds 99 percent of the time. As we age, the repair process becomes less precise, and the damage can escalate.

Antioxidants, substances that can give up an electron and thus neutralize a free radical, can help the body prevent and repair free radical damage. Our challenge as we grow older is to supply enough of these antioxidants to our body. The key is knowing which antioxidants to supply and how much is enough.

Ideally, we could take care of the free radical problem by altering our diet. For instance, we could increase the volume of foods high in antioxidants, such as broccoli, fish, garlic, soy products, tea, and tomatoes. We could also avoid foods that are easily oxidized into free radicals, such as corn and safflower oil, margarine, and dried eggs. Many doctors and researchers feel we cannot absorb enough antioxidants purely through diet; they suggest supplements.

Major organizations, such as the FDA and the American Heart Association, take the conservative position, insisting that not enough data is available to firmly recommend any regimen of antioxidants. These two groups suggest a broadly balanced diet until more research is done. Let's summarize the trends from other researchers who feel more positive about increasing the intake of antioxidants.

Antioxidants

One of the antioxidants touted as most potent is vitamin E. Studies have shown that it lowers LDL cholesterol oxidation dramatically. (Cholesterol comes in low-density lipoproteins [LDL] and high-density lipoproteins [HDL]. LDLs deliver cholesterol through the blood system; HDLs remove cholesterol. It is important to not have too many LDLs for the HDLs to remove.) Another study found that 250 mgs of vitamin E daily significantly lowered the risk of heart attack and stroke. Also, the vitamin appears to lessen colon cancer, relieve arthritis, postpone cataracts, and retard brain and blood aging. Vitamin E is contained in leafy greens, nuts, whole grains, broccoli, brussel sprouts, kale, and cabbage. The most preferred dose, 400 IU, however, cannot be obtained easily through food alone. We are left with taking a supplement. Since vitamin E is oil-soluble, take it with a meal, which means you'll ingest enough fat to help absorb the vitamin.

Another powerful antioxidant is vitamin C. Research indicates it has an impact in preventing some cancers, raises HDL, and lowers LDL cholesterol, stimulates the overall immune system, helps male fertility, lowers the risk of chronic bronchitis, strengthens gums, and prevents cataracts. The Alliance for Aging Research suggests adults must ingest 250 to 1,000 mg per day. It is possible to obtain that much vitamin C by consuming lots of fresh vegetables and fruits. Most researchers suggest taking supplements to ensure adequate amounts. (There is no evidence of toxicity, even at 10,000 mg per day.) Several scientists recommend taking two 500 mg tablets twelve hours apart.

Beta-carotene appears to block cancer. It also lessens clogging of the arteries and stroke possibilities, as well as stimulates the immune system. Carrots, pumpkin, and sweet potatoes are the leading food sources of vitamin C. Ten- to fifteen-mg supplements are recommended but must be taken with a little fat. Three small, spread-out doses are far more effective than one big dose. If you are a cigarette smoker, be aware that a few studies suggest that beta-carotene supplements can actually be harmful.

The Other Necessary Vitamins and Minerals

Beyond these three antioxidants, various resources suggest extra amounts (more than the Dietary Reference Intakes [DRI] minimum) of B vitamins, calcium, chromium, coenzyme Q-10, magnesium, selenium, and zinc. There are special subcategories of antioxidants, such as flavonoids (particularly those found in green tea) and carotenoids, which are thought to be of value in preventing some types of cancer. If you want to supplement, check the labels of multivitamin and mineral tablets—many include all the recommended antioxidants (though in smaller doses than many advocates recommend). One mineral you need less of as you age is iron. So avoid large amounts of iron in a multivitamin, especially if you eat an iron-fortified cereal.

I take a lot of supplements but I couldn't tell you what they are. I put them in rows of six and take a different six each day! Six is my lucky number.

MINNESOTA RETIREE

Those interested in supplementing their diet should check their library for periodicals such as *Nutrition Action Newsletter* by the Center for Science in the Public Interest, 1875 Connecticut Ave. NW, Suite 300, Washington, DC 20009-5728; www.cspinet.org, or other health magazines. And always check with your doctor.

Additional Protection

Once you have adopted regular exercise and a healthier diet supplemented with useful antioxidants, your next healthy choice is to protect yourself from harmful habits. Two powerful actions you can take are to decide to not smoke cigarettes or to be around people who do. No single item in our culture has a more negative health impact than cigarettes. As former U.S. Surgeon General Jesse Steinfeld once said, "Imagine four commercial airplanes with 250 people aboard each, crashing every day in our country and killing everybody aboard. That is how many people die prematurely from smoking cigarettes every single day in our country—more than 1,000 people!" One hundred times more people die from the legal use of cigarettes than from the combined effects of cocaine, heroin, and other illegal drugs. Second, use alcohol in moderation. Regular amounts of alcohol, particularly red wine, appear to be helpful; too much leads to loss of physical and mental functions.

Environmental Control

Look at your geographical location. Does it have a high pollen count or, if in a high humidity area, an elevated level of mold spores? Both of these conditions aggravate hay fever and allergies. How is the quality of the air and water in your area? You can exert some control over water quality by using a filter. If you discover a lot of uncontrollable, negative environmental situations where you live, consider a move. At the very least, let your desires for a clean, healthy environment be known to local officials through telephone calls and letter writing.

Stress Reduction

Perhaps the most important step you can take to improve your overall health is to minimize stress. Stress destroys our well-being and opens us up to many serious illnesses. If you are someone who carries around a string of "worry beads," learn to put them aside—except for a few minutes that you can dedicate to worrying each day. During that time, you can take on your family's, friends', even the world's problems, and really worry about them. When your few minutes are up, put all the worries away until tomorrow's session!

Discover a daily relaxation technique that works for you—and practice it. This type of relaxation employs a conscious mental effort to focus your attention inward and relieve stress. While lying down in a chaise lounge to "relax" can be healthy, deep relaxation requires a concentrated effort. Programs that teach and strengthen relaxation techniques include self-hypnosis, meditation, yoga, and most types of martial arts. You can locate basic relaxation programs in books, on cassettes and videotapes, or on-line at www.oasisnet.org/institute/about/muscle.html, and www.nwreiki.com/ol_prog/b_relax/relax-int.htm. (Find a sample relaxation exercise in the next chapter, "Social and Emotional Changes.")

Prevention

Be the best you can be. Try to incorporate 180 minutes of aerobic activity every week into your life. That is thirty minutes per day, six days a week. Hopefully, you can achieve this by doing something you enjoy. Add to that routine strength, flexibility, and endurance activities. Watch your body fat count, and eat healthy. Avoid smoking, and use alcohol moderately. Throughout the day, keep your stress level low. All of these healthy behaviors require your time, not your money. In return, you will feel better and look better, and have far fewer health problems—not a bad prognosis. You are in control.

Accidents

Accidents occur at any age and primarily at home. Keep clearly written, large emergency numbers handy. (If you have a medical ID number, keep it in the same place.) Create or buy a basic first aid kit with large Band-Aids, 4 × 4 inch and 2 × 2 inch gauze pads, tape, burn ointment (or aloe), antiseptic, petroleum jelly, a pack for ice, safety pins, stretch bandage, small scissors, Q-Tips, moist towelettes, and a small towel. Take a first aid course and receive certification in coronary pulmonary resuscitation (CPR). To sign up for classes, and contact your local Red Cross chapter. Find it in your local phone book or search on-line at www.redcross.org.

Top Concerns of Retirees

No matter how careful you are and how healthful you eat, medical problems will arise. Catching them early leads to a much higher chance for a successful outcome. This means regular checkups, including common tests, such as blood pressure, and specific diagnostics, mammograms for women, and prostate checks for men.

Ten health conditions, mentioned by Wesley Smith in *The Senior Citizens' Handbook*, affect most retirees (personally or among friends and family). Several are common, like arthritis, while others are rare, and frightening, like Alzheimer's disease. Plenty of information exists to help you find the best course of action, if and when you face one of these health problems. In alphabetical order, following are quick summaries and contacts for additional material.

Alzheimer's Disease

This dementia-type disease has a poor prognosis. *Always* obtain a second opinion, because there are many treatable conditions whose symptoms mimic Alzheimer's. The person who has this must make many life adjustments, but advance planning will make it easier. For information, contact the National Alzheimer's Organization, 919 N. Michigan Ave., Suite 1000, Chicago, IL 60611-1676; 1-800-272-3900; www. alz.org.

Arthritis

There are two types of this painful condition—rheumatoid and osteoarthritis. While joints can be replaced, there is no cure. Promising pain treatments include glucosamine and chondroitin as described in *The Arthritis Cure* by Jason Theodosakis, M.D. Contact the Arthritis Foundation, 1330 W. Peachtree St., Atlanta, GA 30309; 1-800-283-7800; www. arthritis.org.

Cancer

There are many types of cancer, with widely ranging prognoses. A strong positive attitude, plus chemotherapy, radiation, surgery, or a combination is the usual treatment. Contact the National Cancer Information Center, 1-800-4-CANCER; www.nci.nih.gov, the American Cancer Society, 1-800-ACS-2345; www.cancer.org, or, for women, the Society of Gynecologic Oncologists, 401 N. Michigan Ave., Chicago, IL 60611; 1-800-444-4441; www.sgo.org.

Diabetes

This illness is generally managed through diet and insulin (taken orally or by injection). For information, contact the American Diabetes Association, Customer Service, 1660 Duke St., Alexandria, VA 22314; 1-800-DIABETES; www.diabetes.org.

Heart Disease and Heart Attack

Individuals can do much to prevent these problems via proper diet and regular exercise. For information, contact the American Heart Association, National Center, 7272 Greenville Ave., Dallas, TX 75231; 1-800-AHA-USA1; www.americanheart.org.

Hypertension

The most favored preventive regimen for this condition includes less salt, controlled diet, exercise, and, medication. For information, contact the American Heart Association, National Center, 7272 Greenville Ave., Dallas, TX 75231; 1-800-AHA-USA1; www.americanheart.org.

Incontinence

Exercise, medication, catheters, or, as a last resort, surgery are used to treat incontinence. For information, contact the National Association for Continence, 1-800-BLADDER; or Simon Foundation for Continence; 1-800-23-SIMON.

Loss of Hearing

This common feature of aging demands a regimen to keep the ears clean of wax and then, possibly, hearing aids or surgery. For information, contact the Better Hearing Institute, 5021-B Backlick Road, Annandale, VA 22003; 1-800-EAR-WELL; www.betterhearing.org.

Loss of Sight

Schedule regular checkups and wear glasses. Eye surgery has also opened up new possibilities. For information, contact the American Optometric Association, 243 N. Lindbergh Blvd., St. Louis, MO 63141; (314) 991-4100; www.aoanet. org, or National Eye Institute, 2020 Vision Place, Bethesda, MD 20892-3655; (301) 496-5248; www.nei.nih.gov.

Old Age

Aches, pains, and ailments seem to increase with older bodies. You must find medical care that respects and understands the needs of aging people. According to the American Dietary Association, of the 128 U.S. medical schools, only two have geriatric departments. Less than 1 percent of all doctors and nurses have received training dealing with the special needs of older adults.

To acquire more information (your most valuable tool), go to your public library or contact the National Health Information Center (NHIC), P.O. Box 1133, Washington, DC 20013-1133. The NHIC maintains an excellent hotline for referrals at 1-800-336-4797. Computer users can check out the government's web site at www.healthfinder.gov. Here, you will find a great set of links to health and medical information available on the Internet. For example, you can link to Med-Line (millions of articles from more than 3,800 periodicals) and search for free, thanks to a 1997 ruling. If you seek policy and programs on aging, you will find the complete bibliographic database at www.ageinfo.org/bibinfo.html. For a slightly different focus, with the emphasis on staying healthy (but with links to medical resources), check out www.well-web.com. For a healthy, consumer-oriented approach, contact the nonprofit People's Medical Society, 462 Walnut St., Allentown, PA 18102; (610) 770-1670; www.peoplesmed.org and its publications, *People's Medical Society Newsletter* and *Vita-Health*. Join with thousands of others in discussing specific health concerns at www.betterhealth.com, a constantly improving site started by two doctors.

As you deal with all these aches and pains, one thing you want to be careful of is too much "bed rest." As Dr. John H. Bland writes, "Clearly, confinement to bed is an anatomically, physiologically, and psychologically unsound practice." Request that your doctor get you up and moving as quickly as possible.

Diminished Capacity

For many of the debilitating conditions you may encounter, you can learn compensating behavior. Taking responsibility for this inevitable reality can make your life more enjoyable. For example, hearing loss affects one-third of the people older than sixty-five. Denying the problem makes situations worse. If you or an acquaintance experiences hearing loss, immediately communicate that loss with others so you can develop ways to minimize the problem. You might position furniture closer together, establishing more direct conversation. Whenever possible, soften the room to cut down echos, eliminate distracting noises, and carefully attend to reading others' lips. Hearing aids are imperfect tools, but you may find they help a little. Investigate all types, not only the most cosmetically desirable. You are trying to hear better. If you find yourself straining to hear the unhearable, leave or change the situation.

Eyesight

Your eyesight may worsen with age. More than half of those older than sixty-five have a noticeable loss in vision. You can upgrade your glasses. (Prices are down and options have increased.) Also, you can de-clutter your world to make it easier to spot items. When reading or researching, look for larger-print books. When experiencing dramatic light changes, allow yourself extra time, because our eyes are slower to adapt as we age. If you suspect something is seriously wrong with your eyes, schedule a checkup with an optometrist or, if you suspect disease, see an ophthalmologist. For those with financial problems, the National Eye Care Project of the American Academy of Ophthalmology (AAO), P.O. Box 7424, San Francisco, CA 94120-7424, has a help-line number to refer callers to local ophthalmologists who will volunteer to provide needed medical care. Call 1-800-222-EYES or explore www.eyenet.org. Another excellent resource is The Lighthouse Inc., National Center for Vision and Aging, 111 E. 59th St., New York, NY 10022; 1-800-829-0500; www.lighthouse.org.

Taste and Smell

Other senses change, too. If you find taste and smell declining, adjust your seasonings or switch to a different drink. Our sense of taste diminishes with age, since the tongue's taste buds become less sensitive. The "sweet" taste buds are particularly affected. However, try to not add extra sugar. Future research might find extra sweetener correlates with the rise in blood sugar, which is considered part of "normal" aging.

Touch

You will probably also discover your sense of touch has changed. Pain awareness decreases, so be extra careful around hot items (even hot water out of a faucet). If you have unsure balance, use a cane. In other words, we cannot always have perfect body functions, but we can use our brains to develop alternative strategies that minimize the impact.

Incontinence

The one chronic condition that may cause great embarrassment is incontinence. Many more women are affected than men (due to childbirth and estrogen loss). More than half of the cases of incontinence can be either cured or greatly improved. The Kegel exercise (frequently squeezing the muscles that cut off urine flow), medical devices, or prescription drugs can help. Call the National Association for Continence, at 1-800-BLADDER, or Simon Foundation for Continence, at 1-800-23-SIMON.

Life Can Still Be Good

Do not worry over possible "problems." As an eighty-five year-old retired teacher tells us, "My life has been good and is good now. I have kind friends and family—I wouldn't change a thing." She is somewhat crippled by osteoporosis, is a diabetic, has high blood pressure, but "life is good." Your health may fare better or worse, but life can still be good.

Memory Loss

Another concern as we age is memory loss. In reality, most memory is stable with age. The basic, or core memory, that includes all the incredible number of simple skills we have learned stays almost completely intact. Similarly, our verbal or semantic memory of knowledge and facts changes little. Our automatic memory and reactions do not appear to change. What psychologists call episodic memory may show problems. Think of episodic as short episodes, as in meeting a person (and learning his name) or putting down your glasses. These episodes call upon short-term memory. Unfortunately, these cells are the first to die—so it may be hard to remember what we had for lunch, since the knowledge never registered in the brain's memory banks.

Short-term Forgetfulness

Once you recognize the difficulty of a task such as remembering names, you can pre-prepare or use aids to help. Everyone has some difficulty in name recall, so try not to overreact. For other types of remembering, learn to put out reminders as soon as you think of something. (For example, if you are supposed to take an item to some event, place it near the door.) Use calendars to remind you of appointments, then check them off as they occur. Set an alarm clock or timer for more specific reminders. Create a map for your hidden treasures.

As an overall tonic for the mind, consider some of psychologist's B.F. Skinner's ideas from *Enjoy Old Age: A Program of Self Management*. If you find your memory is causing you to lose the thread of your thought, focus on simply making one point at a time. Ben Franklin once said, "By my rambling digressions, I perceive myself to be growing old." To think clearly about a problem is no easy task, but it is worth the effort. Keep essentials (paper, pencil, tape recorder, typewriter, and word processor) around to record your thoughts as you have them. To keep stimulation alive, develop small groups of friends and acquaintances for discussion of ideas. (Several retirees have shared that this discussion time is crucial. They recommend talking about topics more complex than the weather—subjects such as philosophy or science. If there is no one handy, you can substitute chat rooms and discussion groups on the Internet.) When feeling overloaded or confused, take time to let your mind relax. Do not allow yourself to be forced into a bad decision. You should also encourage yourself to engage in novel thinking. Push your thoughts into variations, and then evaluate them for any merit.

Finally, realize that confusion or forgetfulness might be caused by factors other than aging. Medication or the interaction of several medicines, dehydration, lack of certain nutritional elements, such as sodium and potassium, chronic infections, vascular disease, hearing or vision problems, hormonal imbalances, malnutrition, depression, or other emotional trauma—can all create confusion/forgetfulness. Even a less structured day may generate problems. A tightly structured day puts you into a routine, with little room for confusion. Retirement does not offer such structure, so you must create it if you desire it. Look for easy adjustments. Preventing forgetfulness can be as simple a solution as organizing information by your phone or at your desk, keys and umbrellas by the front door. Repetition will help you to remember.

Keeping Your Mind Active

Other ways to keep your mind active include traveling, taking education excursions, enrolling in courses, or enjoying quality television and movies or videos on a variety of subjects. Exercise your brain!

Take time to push your mind. For example, when you have a problem (being tired of cooking supper, for instance), whip out a legal pad and jot down solutions. The first ten or so may come fairly quickly, then push that mind of yours. Try to think creatively, which generates a modifiable, workable alternative. Work on your mental flexibility, too. Try to see connections or lessons between situations that do not seem related. Find the commonalities. For example, what does an ant colony have to teach you about family reunions?

If you tend to talk around a problem without solving it, practice getting to the *point* of the conversation. Write down your quandaries and ask yourself questions. (How can I get around this obstacle? What is stopping me? How can I reward myself?) Learn to relax, shut out distractions. Concentrate. Finally, ensure that you have organized your thoughts and plans and broken down what needs to be done in manageable steps, so you can finish and feel good about your accomplishments.

Gerontologist Edgar J. Munter states, "Even at eighty, your brain can learn at the speed of a thirteen-year-old's, and that's damn fast!"

The common fear that seniors become senile has been grossly exaggerated: Dementia is diagnosed in only about 1 percent of all sixty-five-year-olds! A nun of the School Sisters of Notre Dame died at the age of 102. She was considered to possess one of the highest mental functions of the order. An autopsy revealed a brain riddled with the protein plaques of Alzheimer's—yet she never revealed a symptom! The brain responds to new and varied interests, plus active stimulation.

The Right Doctor

In the medical realm, the most important action you can take is finding professionals who will work for you. Remember—*you* are in charge of *your* health. Look for an available doctor who is willing to explain conditions and various treatments, who is willing to accept consultations and second opinions, who charges reasonable fees, and who shows a competent, compatible attitude on preventive medicine—nutrition and exercise. Talk to your doctor. (It is okay to ask: "Would you go over that again?" "What are the risks?" "What are the costs?" "What are the side effects?" "I'll let you know tomorrow." "I'd like another opinion." "I don't understand the reason for this prescription." "Will this affect my other prescriptions?")

If a young or middle-aged man does not recollect where he laid his hat, it is nothing; but if the same inattention is discovered in an old man, people will shrug their shoulders and say, 'His memory is going.'
SAMUEL JOHNSON
British author

Finding appropriate and affordable health-care assistance has become one of the more difficult problems in modern American society. Following a series of strokes, Dr. Elisabeth Kübler-Ross described her experiences in *The Wheel of Life: A Memoir of Living and Dying.*

All my sensibilities as a physician were mortally offended. Was this modern medical care? The decisions made by someone in an office who's never seen the patient? Had paperwork replaced concern for people? As far as I'm concerned, the values are all out of whack. Today's medicine is complex, and research is costly. But, the heads of big insurance companies and HMOs are making millions of dollars in annual salaries. At the same time, AIDs patients are unable to afford life-prolonging drugs. Cancer patients are denied treatment because it is called "experimental." Emergency rooms are being closed. Why is this tolerated? How can anyone be denied hope, or be denied care? Once upon a time, medicine was about healing, not management. It must adopt that mission again. Doctors, nurses, and researchers must recognize that they are the heart of humanity. . . . They need to make helping their fellow man—whether rich or poor, black, white, yellow, or brown—their highest priority.

The questions all of us (including the medical profession) must answer are: "What have you done to help?" and "How much service have you rendered?"

Where to Look

You are searching for good medical assistance. But where? Doctors may operate on their own and/or be part of a system such as a Health Maintenance Organization (HMO). They may be on the staff of a public-health or a not-for-profit institution. They may believe in drug and surgery medicine only, or incorporate holistic or alternative medical practices. It's confusing. Remember that most people have never seen the inside of a hospital. (It's a recent invention.) There is nothing

Some people think that doctors and nurses can put scrambled eggs back into the shell.
DOROTHY CANFIELD
FISHER
Author

sacred about our current medical state of affairs. Indeed, the United States, for all of its high-technology medicine, ranks an abysmal twenty-third among the world's countries in longevity. Without a national health-care system, it is even more critical that you step forward and take charge of your life. Your task is to decide how you want treatment (and what kind you'll accept) *before* you need it.

If you are unsure of what is available in your area, try the Eldercare Locator. Set up in the early 1990s by the National Association of Area Agencies on Aging, it provides information about community services, including health. Call the Eldercare Locator at 1-800-677-1116 weekdays, 9:00 A.M. to 8:00 P.M. (ET).

For other referral and information possibilities, contact the American Academy of Family Physicians, 8880 Ward Parkway, Kansas City, MO 64114; (816) 333-9700; www.aafp.org or the American Osteopathic Association, Public Relations Department,142 E. Ontario St., Chicago, IL 60611; (312) 280-5800; 1-800-621-1773; www.am-osteo-assn.org. For hospital research, contact the nonprofit Center for the Study of Services, 733 15th St. NW, Suite 820, Washington, DC 20005; 1-800-475-7283; www.checkbook.org, which publishes several review-type publications, including a definitive one on hospitals. Also, check with the American Hospital Association, 1 N. Franklin, Chicago, IL 60606; (312) 422-3000; www.aha.org.

You might decide on a doctor-for-fee (that is, one or more doctors in a private practice who bill you or your insurance company directly). This doctor might be part of a clinic, use alternative medicines, or be a nurse-practitioner (with doctor backup).

How do you choose? Narrow the field to a handful of possibilities. Take recommendations of friends. Similarly, you can discover candidates' credentials by their own admission (often advertised in the Yellow Pages) or by contacting local medical societies. Certification and accreditation alone do not make someone a good professional (though they can rule out quacks). Ultimately, you must interview the person or group you are hiring to be your medical provider. Keep in mind Kübler-Ross's admonishment that you are looking for a healer, not a manager or someone interested in creating his own personal fame and riches.

Before interviewing, one technique is to reflect on your medical history. Pick your most frequent problems (or ones you think might be concerns in your future). Set up a consultation. (There may be a charge.) Then, ask the professional how he or she would approach such a situation. You should be searching carefully for individuals who share your feelings about prevention, proper diet/exercise, and minimum drug or invasive therapy. Also, be sure to find professionals who listen to you. Look for a nondefensive attitude. For example, does the doctor encourage second opinions on serious conditions? Develop your own criteria. It is crucial you find someone in sync with your beliefs.

Treatment

When you go to your doctor for treatment, be prepared. That means you've written down all your questions before your appointment. Include notes on your symptoms, as well as a list of medications you currently take. During the consultation, try to speak simply with one sentence-statements, "I have a pain in . . ." Listen carefully to the answer. When you are asked a question, answer only what was asked—do not ramble. Use your notes to pinpoint your symptoms. Do not hesitate to repeat an answer or question. Write down the doctor's responses and advice or take a friend to help you recall what was discussed, or a tape recorder to record the session. Ask for details about various treatments. Do whatever it takes to make sure you understand.

The great secret of doctors, known only to their wives, but still hidden from the public, is that most things get better by themselves; in fact, are better in the morning.

LEWIS THOMAS M.D.
Author

Surgery One of the most common medical treatments is surgery. As we age, this invasion of our body becomes riskier due to our diminishing capacity for recovery. You must be careful before agreeing to surgery—especially elective surgery. Learn your doctor's position. Ask questions.

- Why is the body not performing well?
- What are the risks with or without the surgery?
- How will the recommended surgical procedure provide correction?

- What's being removed? (Will any function be lost or any imbalance be created?)
- What would life be like without surgery as opposed to life with surgery?
- What are the alternatives? Can I modify lifestyle and diet or take nutritional supplements and drugs? What is the prognosis for each action?
- Will additional surgery be required?
- What are the odds of complications?
- What is the medical profession's success record?
- What is the doctor's win-loss record?

Caregiving

There is a strong possibility that during your retirement you will be thrust into the role of a caregiver. As one widow shared, "I never saw myself as a nurse or even doing 'nursey' things, but when it's someone you love, you surprise yourself." A young retiree found that he was suddenly a caregiver for his mother, then for his father. He suggests that you not lose your common sense. For example, when he needed something that would make drinking easier, he discovered covered cups and bendable straws in the children's section of the grocery and discount stores. Again and again, he found devices designed for toddlers that helped him with his parents when they had difficulty with manual tasks.

When you become a caregiver, you become part social worker. Contact your state agency on aging (see Appendix B, State Resources), call the Eldercare Locator, at 1-800-677-1116, or contact AARP to obtain a list of all the local services for seniors. You will probably find support groups or, at least, helpful tips through the senior centers, hospitals, or clinics. For a fee you can employ a case-management worker to help, which is similar to hiring a general contractor when building a house. There are numerous options in most communities, from lendable equipment (often from the American Red Cross) and homemaker services to congregate meals and a plethora of in-home aid. The more you can do, the more personal (and less expensive) the treatment. Do your research, however, so you can call for backup when you need it. There is even a newsletter called *Caregiving* from Tad Publishing Company, P.O. Box 224, Park Ridge, IL 60068; (847) 823-0639; www. caregiving.com. If you are on-line, check the comprehensive list of support groups at www.cmhc.com/selfhelp.

Medicare

Once you have decided on a medical practitioner, you are faced with the runaway costs of medical treatment. When your car needs servicing or breaks down, you take it in and pay for the service. We are accustomed to having items repaired that are not under warranty. When it comes to our bodies, though, we panic if 100 percent of the costs are not covered. Yet, in spite of a strange, complex system, the principle is still the same: You are paying for a repair or maintenance check. To help with the payments, insurance companies issue policies—on which they make a profit.

Social Security, with its Medicare component, was not designed to be an all-inclusive health-insurance program. It was designed to give people sixty-five and older assistance with medical bills. If you are frugal, take care of yourself, and are reasonably solvent, it may be all the assistance you need. You may also want to explore additions/alternatives, such as medigap insurance or an HMO. Before you do, carefully evaluate your Medicare coverage.

The best source for Medicare information is—surprise—the government overseer, the Health Care Financing Administration (HCFA). Order its publications, "Your Medicare Handbook" and "Guide to Health Insurance for People with Medicare," by contacting HCFA, Office of Beneficiary Relations, 7500 Security Blvd., Baltimore, MD 21244-1850, www. hcfa.gov or www. medicare. gov. In addition, there is an overall Medicare Hotline, at 1-800-638-6833. See Table 2.1, page 60, for a list of regional offices.

Table 2.1 Health Care Financing Administration (HCFA) Offices

City	Telephone	States Covered
Boston	(617) 565-1232	Conn., Md., Mass., N.H., R.I., Vt.
New York	(212) 264-3657	N.Y., N.J., P.R., V.I.
Philadelphia	(215) 596-1335	Del., D.C., Md., Pa., Va., W.Va.
Atlanta	(404) 331-2044	Ala., Fla., Ga., Ky., Miss., N.C., S.C., Tenn.
Chicago	(312) 353-7180	Ill., In., Mich., Minn., Ohio, Wisc.
Dallas	(214) 767-6401	Ark., La., N.Mex., Okla., Tex.
Kansas City	(816) 426-2866	Iowa, Kans., Mo., Nebr.
Denver	(303) 844-4024	Conn., Mont., N.Dak., S.Dak, Utah, Wyo.
San Francisco	(415) 744-3602	Ariz, Calif., Guam, Hawaii, Nev.
Seattle	(206) 615-2354	Alaska, Idaho, Ore., Wash.

Medicare, Part A

With the booklets in hand, analyze your benefits under Part A and Part B. For most Social Security recipients, Part A is free and covers hospital, nursing facility, home care, hospice, and blood work. How much is covered will change as the law changes, but as of this writing, most of the first sixty days in a hospital (except for $764 "coinsurance") is covered. Also included are the first twenty days in a skilled-nursing facility, most of home health care, almost all of hospice, and all but three pints of blood. Coverage diminishes with longer stays in hospitals or nursing facilities. Before you consider supplemental insurance, become familiar with these limits. Add to your Medicare jargon the term *hospital reserve days*. As mentioned above, Part A covers the first sixty hospital days. If you need more days, you can draw on a one-time reserve of sixty days. So, if you are in for seventy-five days (an incredibly long hospital stay), you use Part A's sixty days and you draw on fifteen reserve days (leaving you with forty-five reserve days). After you have been out of the hospital sixty days, Part A will again cover the next sixty days, but your reserve is still only forty-five days.

Medicare, Part B

Part B is an optional coverage for doctor fees, lab services, and outpatient hospital or ambulatory surgical procedures. Optional means you must choose to be covered and you must pay a premium (currently $43.80 per month). If you elect to add Part B, then all clinical work, plus 80 percent of your medical services, outpatient, and ambulatory services are covered (less a $100 deductible). Check for the current rates and limitations before considering additional insurance. Each state picks an insurance carrier to handle all of this Part B paperwork. (See Appendix B, State Resources) If you have questions or disagree on a claim, contact the carrier.

Another term to add to your jargon stack is *assignment*. If your doctor accepts assignment of Medicare, it means you won't be charged more than the 20 percent gap that Medicare does not cover under Part B. If the doctor does not accept assignment, he can add another 15 percent on top of what Medicare approves. If you are shopping for a doctor or trying to predict what additional money/coverage you might need, assignment is an important factor.

For-Fee Care

Be cautious about what you sign regarding medical care. There have been recent moves to enact legislation to allow doctors to offer you a contract to provide for-fee care. If you sign this contract, you give up your right to have Medicare pay or help pay for the procedure. There is no limit on what the doctor can charge. The law states that you must be informed, but "informing" may not clarify the situation for a confused patient.

Beginning in 1998, Medicare added more preventive coverage. For women, yearly mammograms, Pap smears, and pelvic and breast examinations are covered. For those with diabetes, glucose monitoring and education are included. For all, colorectal-cancer screening, bone-mass measurement, and flu and pneumococcal pneumonia shots are paid.

Medigap

Once you know what is covered, you might consider supplemental insurance, called *Medigap*. Brace yourself, because much of the marketing of these policies revolves around fear. You will be inundated with the horrible financial consequences a medical catastrophe might bring. Use your common sense. Don't fall victim to scare tactics. The question is, Do you need it? If you are covered under a former employer plan or a pension plan, probably not. If you are diligent enough to save and earmark money to cover the gaps yourself, possibly not. If you decide to join an HMO, definitely not. (If you quit the HMO, you might pick up a Medigap policy.)

If you decide you must purchase Medigap insurance, your best option is to pick from one of ten standard Medigap policies within six months of enrolling in Part B. (Persons living in Massachusetts, Minnesota, and Wisconsin have different options. Contact your state insurance agency.) During these first six months, you cannot be turned down or charged higher premiums because of poor health. After the six-month period, you can still purchase a policy but only what (and at what cost) the insurance company is willing to sell to you.

What Is Covered

The ten plans are called Plan A through Plan J. They all offer the basic gap insurance of covering your coinsurance payment for hospital days sixty-one through ninety and all hospital expenses beyond day ninety, covering your coinsurance for the hospital reserve days used, covering the three pints of blood, and covering the coinsurance of Part B (the 20 percent medical or 50 percent mental health). The other plans beyond

Plan A offer additional coverages (with premiums to match).

Each state has an insurance office that provides free counseling. Call before you purchase. (See Appendix B, State Resources.) You should also check with the National Insurance Consumer Helpline, at 1-800-942-4242.

Use Caution Before Buying

Be cautious about buying supplemental insurance. Compare several policies before buying, because there are huge difference in price/value. For example, if you have Internet access, check out www.quotesmith.com. Comparing the policies for one state reveals premiums from $300 per year for a Plan A to $3,500 per year for a Plan J. Within each plan, there are up to 100 percent differences between companies. None cover all the contingencies. Ignore scare tactics about high costs. (The average hospital stay is one week, and Medicare covers up to sixty days per benefit period. If you are out of the hospital for sixty consecutive days, then another benefit period starts with another sixty days of coverage.) Do not buy multiple policies, since coverages overlap. Never pay cash. None of the policies are affiliated with the federal government. Also, many organizations, such as AARP, do not offer their own policies but simply advertise policies for various insurance companies. Compare them for pre-existing exclusions, indemnity payments, elimination periods, co-payment plans, and renewability clauses. Demand at least a thirty-day "free look" at the policy.

Medicaid

Medicaid is a joint federal-state medical assistance program to assist people with low or no incomes. Low-income seniors may qualify for a Medicaid program—either the Qualified Medicare Beneficiary (QMB) program or the Specified Low-Income Medicare Beneficiary (SLMB) program. The QMB income limits are no more than $678 monthly for an individual or $905 for a couple. Plus, there can be few assets. The SLMB income limits are no more than $809 for an individual and $1,081 for a couple. These figures change with inflation, and Alaska and Hawaii have higher limits. If you or someone you know might qualify, application must be made for Medicaid at your state's local medical assistance or social services office. Call your state insurance office for help. (See Appendix B, State Resources.)

Managed Care

To cut your costs, you might consider managed care, such as an HMO. You must be under Part B (and continue to pay those premiums). Under managed care, you receive all of the Medicare benefits, plus additional services—all with little or no paperwork. But how can you find one dedicated to quality care and overall patient health and not solely to making more money? If you are leaning toward this approach, obtain a copy of Ellyn Spragins's authoritative *Choosing and Using an HMO*.

A major hurdle in your selection process is that Medicare HMOs are newcomers to the medical field and are generally run by for-profit groups. The budget bill of 1997 provides additional choices, including private fee-for-service insurance plans, private contracting with doctors, medical savings accounts, and new HMO relatives (point-of-service plan, preferred provider organization, and provider-sponsored organization). Again, since all of these options can be confusing, contact your state insurance office for free counseling.

Finding Information on HMOs

To help you take charge of your decision, consider some of Spragins's suggestions for assessing the quality of an HMO. First, insist on full accreditation by the National Committee for Quality Assurance (NCQA). This rating overemphasizes the HMO's organizational skill, but it is a good first step. Reports are available from NCQA, at 1-800-839-6487, for a small charge or free at its Web site, www.ncqa.org. If possible, investigate at a library other cross-comparison data, such as the

Health Plan Employer Data and Information Set (HEDIS). (It is expensive.) Also, you can view the HEDIS criteria at the NCQA Web site. Any HMO that wants your business will supply you with its information that has been compiled by some objective source. Another accreditation body to survey is the Joint Commission on Accreditation of Healthcare Organizations (JCAHO), www.jcaho.org. If you are interested in a Medicare HMO, the Health Care Financing Administration (HCFA) has the oversight responsibility. (See the phone numbers listed previously in the discussion about Part B.)

Criteria Used for Evaluation

Once you have found one or more qualified HMOs, develop some personal criteria to evaluate their results. Spragins uses the following eleven guidelines as leading indicators of excellence since they emphasize prevention and stability:

1. A fifteen- to twenty-year history in your region
2. Full accreditation and reporting on FACCT (Foundation for Accountability) measures
3. Not-for-profit status with doctors on staff or in a group
4. Low heart-bypass and angioplasty rates
5. Relatively few caesarean sections
6. High cervical- and breast-cancer screening rates
7. High diabetic retinal–testing rates
8. Excellent follow-up after hospitalization for a mental disorder
9. Available doctors who accept new patients
10. Highly satisfied doctors with less than 10 percent turnover
11. Highly satisfied members, with low turnover

You might delete and add your own concerns, but try to insist on a holistic approach that includes many free screenings. Prevention and early treatment, after all, are much preferred to the alternatives. Also, look for staff experts on aging. Another good sign would be if the number of board-certified doctors exceeds the 60 percent national average. If you do not like your primary-care physician, you must be allowed to shift to another of the HMO's doctors. Appointments should be readily available. Do not become too enthralled with the promise of a high drug benefit; rather, look for an integrated, electronic patient drug system that minimizes drug interactions and inappropriate prescriptions. Finally, if you plan to travel for extended periods of time, check the HMO's limitations on receiving medical service elsewhere.

If you decide to enroll (or if you are already part of a plan), contact AARP, at 1-800-424-3410, to order its publication *9 Ways to Get the Most from Your Managed Health Care Plan* (D16615).

A Word about Fraud

Become a vocal advocate for a more meaningful, responsive, and responsible health-care system in America. As Malcolm Sparrow writes in *License to Steal*, "Fraud in the health-care system has been, and remains, *out of control.*" He suggests not supporting across-the-board cuts or simplistic solutions, because they only make the fraudulent operators more careful, while penalizing legitimate concerns. Patients can take control. Scrutinize all medical charges, whether covered by Medicare, insurance, or you. Question everything that appears exorbitant. Report suspected errors to the doctor or clinic, then the responsible government agency, or insurance carrier. Do your part to stop abuses of the medical insurance system.

Drugs

One of the most dangerous drug problems this country faces may be the overmedication of seniors. Almost half of older Americans take multiple medications every day. You are in charge of what you put into your body, so be fully informed of the effects of any prescription!

The magic pill does not exist. All of us have probably yearned for a simple tonic that would give us more energy, help us lose weight, raise our sex appeal, or make us live longer. We want answers and cures for all our ailments. To fill that demand, an immense pharmacological cornucopia exists, producing massive profits for producers, sellers, and distributors. The lone watchdog agency, the Food and Drug Administration (FDA), has produced little research on the long-term effects or interactive complications that each of these drugs might manifest. If you understand these severe limitations, you will be a better, if more cynical, consumer.

Getting More Information

Check with your local library for drug reference works, such as *The Physician's Desk Reference.* If you have access to the Internet, you will find a wealth of information available. The standard drug reference is maintained by the U.S. Pharmacopeia, www.usp.org—so named since the first list of drugs with instructions for preparation, called a pharmacopeia, appeared in 1546 in Nuremberg, Germany. Its searchable database, which offers medical consulting and sharing possibilities, is available at www.mediconsult.com. Also, look at www.intelihealth.com, the Mayo Clinic's www.mayohealth. org (under Medicine), *McCall/Family Circle*'s www. healthanswers.com, and, if you are on Compuserve, GO HEALTH.

Work on your own health model rather than a medical-school model. Remember, any drug that may help you can also harm you. Before taking a prescription, ask questions.

- What condition is the medication designed to help?
- What is the medication (brand name and generic name), and how does it work? What should it do?
- What are the alternatives to the drug?
- What could I be doing with nutrition or exercise that might improve my condition?
- What are the specific instructions for use, and how long must I take it? Do I take it orally, apply it

topically, or in an ear or eye, or other? With meals? How much and how long?

- How will I know it is working?
- What should I do if it doesn't work?
- What are the possible and predictable side effects? Are there possible permanent effects? How can I lessen them?
- What experience have you had with this drug? Has your knowledge come from testing, experience, or pharmaceutical reps?
- Have all of my current medications (with possible interactions) been considered? How about food, caffeine, and alcohol? Must I avoid driving?
- Are there less expensive medications that will have the same impact?
- How do I store it? Can I obtain a refill?

If your doctor prescribes medications, make a daily chart. Try to acquire written information on each. Hopefully, you received good answers when you asked about interactions with other drugs you are taking, but be doubly cautious if you decide to also take an over-the-counter product. Over-the-counter drugs are still drugs. Check your medicine storage area and throw away old medicines.

For the lowest prices, ask for generic drugs rather than brand names. The July 1995 issue of Money magazine found the best prices for generics from Health Care Services (for members of the National Council of Senior Citizens, 8403 Colesville Road, Suite 1200, Silver Spring, MD 20910-3314; 1-888-3-SENIOR; www.ncscinc.org).

Long-term Care

Once you understand your personal system with Medicare and supplemental insurance policies, and join an HMO or use a fee-for-service doctor or clinic, you still have decisions to make. You will likely encounter one more frightening possibility: nursing homes. You may have to decide on one for a parent, your spouse, or yourself. Nursing homes are anxiety-producing because of their costs. Currently, these facilities can charge at least $100 per day and these numbers are growing at 10 percent per year (much faster than inflation). So, when faced with a new $40,000-plus yearly expense, no wonder most people grow concerned. Plus, 40 percent of all those over sixty-five (54 percent of all women) will probably enter a nursing home. To calm things a bit, most (75 percent) nursing home stays are less than one year. For example, once the patient has recovered from a broken hip, they return home. Only 7 percent remain as residents for more than three years. These numbers lower the odds—and, hopefully, the anxieties—significantly.

Paying for Care

In case of long-term care, Medicare offers some help. The first 20 days in a skilled-nursing facility are covered. For the next 80 days, Part A pays costs above $78.50 per day. Nothing is paid after 100 days.

One way to "pay" for a nursing home is to use the Medicaid assistance program. To qualify, you must have limited assets (less than $4,000), and your spouse must have few assets and little income in their name. Each state has its own limits on these categories, so you must check with your state's Medicare office if you think you might qualify. It is not an easy or pleasant road to travel the Medicaid way, but it is there as a last-ditch safety net.

If you can afford three years in a home (you have $100,000 or more in liquid assets), think hard before purchasing a long-term care policy. Few can comfortably afford long-term care insurance. Premiums for a newly retired couple easily surpass $3,500 per year. If you feel you must have long-term care insurance, select a high-quality company that has been issuing this type of policy for more than five years. Next, request from your library the October 1997 issue of *Consumer Reports*, and read it carefully. These are expensive policies and the consumer must be highly selective. (They are among the most difficult policies to understand, and the various companies' "truth-in-selling" record is poor.) Find out how much the premiums have risen during the last several years—a far better alternative is if the policy has a guaranteed, renewable, fixed premium. Since companies can raise premiums differently from state to state, make sure you are given the figures for your state. As for coverage, if today the policy covers half of the nursing home cost, how much will that be in ten years? (In other words, does it have compounded inflation protection?) Does it offer a life-time period of nursing care? How about home care (an expensive alternative to a nursing home)? There should not be a requirement for a hospital stay before coverage begins. Check out the policy's restrictions. How does it define assisted living? Which rest home(s) can be used? What type of care is covered? Finally, examine several specimen policies side-by-side before deciding. Never pay cash.

Long-term Care Insurance

Recently, newspapers and other periodicals have published "articles" about long-term-care insurance written by insurance agents, the self-proclaimed "experts." These thinly veiled advertisements are filled with misused statistics, emotional phrases, and scare tactics. Be skeptical.

One seventy-five-year-old financial adviser tells us he recommends that people take the same amount of money they would pay for a long-term policy and put it into a special savings account. Since most nursing home stays, if required at all, are less than four years, the odds are favorable that his clients will come out ahead.

Other Available Options

Look at other options for long-term care, such as skilled home health care (which may be covered by Medicare). You may discover adult day care and day health centers in your community. If needed, you can probably hire a case-management worker (public or private). You may find a wide range of in-home services, such as chores and homemaker services, skilled medical and therapy workers, friendly visitor services, Meals on Wheels, emergency electronic buttons, transportation services, protective services, and even telephone contact. Plus, there may be the availability of congregate meals at central locations and senior centers.

Checking Out Nursing Homes

If the nursing home appears to be the most viable option, search out the best one. Is it licensed? Find out the levels of care offered. Check out the number of residents, nurses, aides, social worker visits, types of physician assistance, and backup. Ask how problems are solved (such as medication difficulties). Look at the rules, administrative procedures (for example, off-hour situations), the owners and managers, and their track record. Obtain a complete accounting of all costs and possible increases. Talk to the residents. For more items to check, see the nursing home section in Chapter 6, "Here or There Decisions."

There is no absolute solution; every situation presents its own challenges. Until the United States rises to the challenge of a comprehensive health policy, you are left with poor choices. Consider as many options as possible. Then, if the need arises for a long-term care arrangement, you are more likely to make a good decision.

Hospice

When you or someone you love has a terminal illness, contact your local hospice. They provide full services needed to allow the patient to remain at home and in as little discomfort as possible. Also, hospice staff members help others understand the experiences of a dying person. If you have difficulty finding a local hospice, try the National Hospice Organization, 1901 N. Moore St., Suite 901, Arlington, VA 22209-1714; 1-800-658-8898; www.nho.org.

Summary

For your personal good health and well-being, take time to brainstorm, then examine all your health-care options. Put your own positive, preventive program into action. Proper diet, regular exercise, and low stress go a long way toward minimizing your medical needs. Explore all your community's resources *before* you need them. Choose your helpers and institutions as if your life depends on that choice.

CHAPTER 3

Social and Emotional Changes

Retirement brings a shift in focus—from a task-directed existence to a more inner-directed life. This tendency has been dramatically illustrated to us by an eighty- six-year-old friend. In his preretirement period, he was an attorney serving as general manager for one of the world's top newspapers. In addition, he worked on the staffs for establishing the North Atlantic Treaty Organization (NATO), the Environmental Protection Agency (EPA), and for preventing inner-city race riots. He married and had five children. He exhibited the epitome of the Protestant work ethic. Sudden changes in this high-speed, high-success track forced him into early retirement, derailing him to the point at which he dissolved his marriage, causing him to contemplate suicide. Through the help of a therapist, he rebuilt his world, eventually becoming a Gestalt therapist. He explored Buddhism, massage therapy, and other alternatives to our structured Western society. In short, he switched from a left-brain (logical, analytical) existence to one more directed by his right brain (intuitive, feeling). Not all retirements reflect such a dramatic shift, but healthy, intelligent, and emotional individuals accept and grow with changes produced by retirement.

No one can tell you how to achieve the perfect retirement. Relish the finding by several studies that people sixty-five and older are the happiest people in the world. Those who are unhappy appear to have fallen into a "give-up" mode. You can find many excellent role models among retirees. After all, longevity favors those with strong interests.

Retirement is a fantastic opportunity. You move into a world in which you are the main creator of the roles you want to play. You have time to practice and perfect these roles. You will face your own psychological patterns as never before. First, discover how to lessen the possibility that negative emotions will control your life. Next, look at using your time to develop a better perspective. Examine the specific situations facing retirees, such as loneliness, close relationships, familial roles, and special sources of stress. Then figure out how you want to manage these challenges.

Emotions

Emotions are essential to human behavior. From ecstasy to depression, our outlook on the world is shaped by our feelings. What many of us ignore is how strongly our thoughts and beliefs control these emotions—thoughts and beliefs we can control. Retirement brings many changes to your environment and your routine. Subsequently, you experience unfamiliar situations and emotions. It is important to understand these emotions and how to rationally manage them.

Gaining Stability Over Emotions

All humans have choices when confronting the power of their emotions. On one extreme, people can give into their emotions, be blown about like a rudderless ship, and blame the world, their parents, or companions for their problems. At the other extreme, individuals can try to repress, ignore, or denigrate their feelings. A healthy, highly effective way to gain more stability over your emotions is to take control of your thoughts. The underlying belief of this approach is that imperfect humans living in an imperfect world can learn to more objectively understand their situations. Once these conditions are understood, people can improve their emotional state, maintaining lower stress and finding greater happiness. That is not the only or perfect answer. Obviously, powerful chemical influences within our bodies can create emotional states. (Observe anyone who is overmedicated by legal or illegal drugs.) This rational approach simply provides safe techniques that are useful in most day-to-day scenarios.

The Effects of Irrational Thinking When most of us experience a strong emotional reaction, our typical response is: "He or she made me . . . ," "It's awful that . . . ," or "They should have . . ." With all these explanations, we assume that emotions are caused by external events. In reality, with our beliefs we create all our emotions. Psychotherapist Albert Ellis simplified this process to an A, B, C, D pattern. An action (A) occurs: One of your children does not call as promised. You have an emotional consequence (C), such as being hurt ("They don't care about me") or becoming highly anxious ("Suppose something's happened?"). Our tendency is to think that A (the lack of a call) caused C (the hurt or worry). In actuality, C was created by our beliefs (B) ("They should call"). If we believe the child was deliberately avoiding us, we are hurt; if we believe a horrible accident occurred, we worry. These beliefs are often irrational. (What is the probability of an accident?) These irrational beliefs create high stress and harmful emotions. Ellis suggests you dispute (D) your irrational beliefs, substituting more rational thoughts. Your child was occupied at the time for the call or maybe he or she forgot. These more rational beliefs lead to a less-stressful emotional state (minor annoyance) and allow you to consider appropriate action (pick up the phone and call your child).

An action or event does not create emotional consequences; your belief or perception of the event does. If your belief is irrational, learn to dispute it with your own common sense, and bring that dangerous emotional reaction back in balance.

Think about your tendencies or thinking patterns as you read about the more common types of irrational beliefs. At one time or another, all of us have thought irrationally. Instead, we should maintain rational thoughts (and their appropriate emotional reactions) as our default behavior.

Awfulizing The tendency to think, "Ain't it awful?" when in actuality little is truly awful. We take an unpleasant event and make it terrifying. An occurrence such as learning a burglar ransacked your house may be inconvenient, a real nuisance, or an unwelcome intrusion, but it is not awful.

Polarized Thinking To see the world as right or wrong, black or white, or good or bad. This tendency leads to poor emotional reactions for even common events.

Overgeneralization A frequent human tendency to go far beyond what the evidence suggests. Working off one or more specific instances (such as encountering an inconsiderate teenager), we overgeneralize when we think, "The youth of today are totally inconsiderate." This irrational thought is a basis for bigotry and bias.

Mind Reading A highly problematic, irrational belief of granting ourselves psychic powers. You engage in mind reading when you make judgments about why someone acted a certain way. ("She didn't come to the picnic because she doesn't like my spouse.") Inferring other people's motives is a guaranteed way to create unnecessary social and familial problems.

Catastrophizing Turning unpleasant events or situations you dislike into "horrible" or "unbearable." This leads to obsessing rather than frankly facing the unpleasantness and either changing it or accepting it.

Personalizing Believing that external events are directly pointed at you. If you regularly practice this irrational belief, symptoms of paranoia will soon appear. Believe it or not, all that happens in this world does not revolve around you.

Blame A moralistic stance rarely supported by reality. One seeks not only to identify who may be the cause of a problem, but also to condemn them. (A person's poor behavior does not make them a rotten person.) Blaming is often a symptom of someone who avoids personal responsibility. A corollary is to self-condemn yourself: "I did something stupid, therefore I'm stupid."

Avoidance Dodging difficult situations or relying on something "greater" than ourselves (the experts or the supernatural) for decisions. Thinking for yourself and acting less dependently is a sign of growth.

Shoulds Overuse of the word *should* in your thinking. Whenever you hear yourself considering, "They should have . . ." you can almost guarantee that it is an irrational belief. Ellis cajoles, "You shall not should on yourself."

Fixation Mentally replaying an irrational belief and/or a terrible event over and over again. This behavior can be the basis for emotional trauma. You may need a therapist to help you desensitize your fixation. (There is a high success rate.)

When you experience a strong negative emotion (anger, hate, despair, panic, terror), try to sort out the beliefs that led to your reaction. Your beliefs and thoughts trigger the emotion. Rational thoughts produce mild emotions, irrational thoughts create overly strong, destructive emotions.

For more information on how to work with your emotions, check your library on these subjects: cognitive behavioral therapy or rational-emotive behavioral therapy. You might also contact the Albert Ellis Institute, 45 E. 65th St., New York, NY 10021; 1-800-323-4738; www.REBT. org. An excellent self-help book is *A Guide to Rational Living*, 3d ed, by Albert Ellis, Ph.D. and Robert Harper, Ph.D.

Realize that it is a common tendency as we age to have a growing fear of change. First, we lose job and career status. Next, we observe the landscape about us being changed. Friends and family and our relationships with them change. Crime appears to increase, while we feel more isolated. A few years ago, the well-educated readers of a magazine responded in a poll that they felt crime had dramatically increased over the past few years and they were in far more danger. In reality, crime had decreased and they were in less danger. Work at keeping your thoughts rational, and your emotions will certainly follow.

Stress

Gain a Rational Handle on Your Emotions

I'm seventy-five and I've been widowed five years. I'm happy to do what I want when I want. My children experienced a few surprises after my husband's death—for example, I refused to put up another Christmas tree, then without consulting them I moved to this retirement community and took a trip to Russia.

RETIREE
North Carolina

No matter what you choose to do or what befalls you during retirement, one disruptive emotional state you must minimize is stress. The essential first step in handling such feelings is to gain a rational handle on your emotions as previously discussed. Learn to spot any self-deprecating; stop negative thought patterns; create rational responses, even rebuttals.

Regularly Practice a Relaxation Technique

The second step is to regularly practice a relaxation technique. As mentioned in Chapter 2, effective techniques are taught and practiced through yoga, self-hypnosis, martial arts, and meditation. Systematic practice allows people to lower blood pressure, as well as grow calmer more quickly during a highly stressful event.

As a brief introduction to this type of exercise, look at a typical approach to relaxation as shown in Exhibit 3.1, page 79. As you practice relaxation, you will find the meditative state easier and easier to obtain. You may be able to selectively relax parts of your body while other parts are on full alert. This technique has been highly successful for competitive athletes, allowing adrenalin to flow to the desired muscle groups.

Wisdom

Before shooting for the wisdom of the ages, you might set your sights on creating positive role models. First, build a persona who defies the more common negative stereotypes of retirees and older people in our society, for example, retirees

EXHIBIT 3.1 Typical Relaxation Techniques

Read through the steps below; put them into your own words, then record them on tape or have someone read them to you. The most important factor is that the instructions must be read slowly and in a calming voice. Pause for a couple of seconds at the end of each instruction. It is necessary to use the recording (or reader) since you cannot read and relax at the same time. Initially, relaxation techniques must be guided exercises until your body-mind learns what to do without the words.

1. Lie on the floor in a comfortable position and practice deep breathing. Attend to the air coming in and out of your lungs.

2. Close your eyes and listen to the tape (or the reader).

3. Focus on your scalp. Breathe, relax, and calm yourself. Feel the tension leave the top of your head.

4. Feel your eyes. Let any strain drain from them. Relax. Feel your eyes grow heavy.

5. Shift your attention to your mouth. Tighten the muscles around the mouth. Now relax them. Feel the tension flow away. Keep your attention here a moment as you grow even calmer.

6. Focus on the blood circulating in your neck. Feel the calm. Relax your neck.

7. Feel your shoulders. Sense them becoming heavier. Let them relax onto the floor.

8. Focus on your chest. Feel it slowly rise and fall as you continue to breathe. Relax even further.

9. Attend to your upper arms. Tighten your biceps. Now release them. Breathe easily as your arms grow more relaxed.

10. Feel your lower arms. Feel their weight increase as they relax and sink onto the floor.

11. Move your attention to your hands. Squeeze your fingers into a fist. Now release. Sense each finger relaxing as your hand grows heavier.

12. Focus on your lower abdomen. Sense the blood slowly circulating. Feel your abdomen relax even further.

13. Let your attention move to your buttocks. Feel their weight. Relax until your buttocks sink onto the floor.

14. Shift your focus to your thighs. Tighten the muscles, then slowly release them. Feel them grow heavy and relaxed.

15. Feel your knees. Let your knees relax and sink further toward the floor.

16. Slowly shift your focus to your calves. Keep your attention there until they feel heavy. Let them relax.

17. Focus all of your mind's attention on your feet. Feel the blood running through their veins. Sense the weight of your feet. Feel them grow heavy and sink onto the floor.

18. Continue your easy breaths as you let any tension slowly leave your body. Feel an energy source above your stomach provide calming sensations throughout your body. Sink into a quiet, meditative state.

Get rid of your regrets. You are what you are on account of what you have experienced. And rightly understood, and accepted, all experiences are good, and the bitter ones best of all. I feel sorry for the souls who have not suffered.

ELBERT HUBBARD
Philosopher

are stingy. This is an easy one to counter if you live frugally, not cheaply. Or, old people are boring. Well, boring will be used to describe you if you talk incessantly about the old days or your former job, fail to develop interests to share with younger people, repeat yourself, dwell upon your aches and pains, ramble on about your kids and grandkids, or preach rather than talk. Avoid those pitfalls. Develop interests outside of yourself. Enjoy your new life and refine your sense of humor. Choose to grow wiser.

One retiree shares a couple of easy-to-overlook tips that contribute to a happier, more fulfilling life. One is to regularly show and express gratitude—not only to people, but to the fates, nature, the creator, or anything you believe in that is greater than yourself. The second tip is to bury all animosities, hates, and grudges as soon as possible. Lighten that negative load.

Learning to Accept Yourself

Wisdom implies that you have learned to accept yourself. It sounds easy, but it requires you to reject any demand that you be different. Obviously, you may *prefer* to be different (at least in some areas), but prefer is not the same as demand. You may conclude it is in your best interest to make a few changes. Notice, however, that you are making a choice in attempting a change. Avoid saying "I have to change." Self-acceptance means you do not evaluate yourself as "good" or "worthless." These self-judgments only serve to wrest energy and focus from what you can control—your behavior and the quality of your life.

Assets to Growing Wiser

Though our bodies may become more frail, our minds will normally age less rapidly. Now you have time to think things over. There is time to read, explore libraries and museums, and seek knowledge. You can gain confidence in your grasp of totally new fields. As you assimilate this information, it

would be doubly wonderful if you could share your new per-
spectives. If you look around, you might find an outlet, such
as a newspaper column, radio show, video, or book.

You can grow wiser. Your experiences and longevity are
your assets. A wise decision implies that, first, you consider a
wide range of factual knowledge. Second, you create strategies
for obtaining necessary information you do not have at hand.
Third, you recognize the long-term consequences of various
courses of action. Fourth, you realize that any course of action
must occur in a real-world cultural milieu. Finally, you appreciate that all possible "solutions" have strengths and weaknesses. Integrated Learning Systems simplified this process for
school-age children by having the students process: "What
don't you know?" (What's the problem?). "What do you
already know that can help you solve it?," "How can you find
out more about what you don't know?," "Do it." "Is the problem now solvable?," "What have you learned about learning?"

As one French retiree shared, wisdom is a synthetic
process. As we age, we accumulate an incredible number of
successes and failures. If we synthesize well, we can see more
clearly the big picture surrounding any problem—the heart
of wisdom. Simultaneously, we are amused as the young must
reinvent the same wheel we did, making many of the same
errors. Of course, they will not listen to our sage advice. To
paraphrase Reinhold Niebuhr, the ideal situation would be to
have "the serenity to accept things that cannot be changed;
the courage to change things that must be changed; and the
wisdom to distinguish one from the other."

The Marriage Relationship

For many couples, retirement brings significant changes in
the marriage relationship. These changes are dictated by the
new roles partners assumed. In far too many cases, these roles
are not discussed or planned, which leads to real problems.
Your relationship must continue to adapt to the changing
external influences of health and money, as well as dealing
with old emotional issues (often termed *baggage*).

Potential Problems

The first year of retirement can be a real adventure. Two people who were busy and structured in various roles are suddenly thrust together for most of the day. Conflicts and challenges will arise. An acquaintance who has worked as a family counselor reports, "I've listened to many women complain loudly about having their retired husbands around too much—and about what their husbands are doing with their time." In this new, unstructured realm, power plays can develop over the smallest things. You may discover areas where you cannot work together or share. Tension can be created if one takes over what the other is doing or complains about the quality of the other's job. It is easy to see where difficulties might arise. If your relationship is fragile, the extra time together will often increase the strain. There is also a tendency toward boredom. The "I-don't-have-to-work" inertia can carry over into the marriage. You start to get on each other's nerves. An increase in belittling or carping about the other is a symptom of a relationship heading toward trouble.

Planning and Discussing Planning and discussing will help you find satisfactory ways to work around these problems. These first few weeks and months are the best time to reexamine who does what, and then make accommodations for one another's likes and dislikes. An essential factor in creating a solid foundation is joint planning. One simple yet effective method is for each person to share each morning what he would like to do that day, including ideas about what to eat at each meal. Then, as husband and wife set out on their various tasks, individually or together, they know they are on a mutually agreeable track.

Knowing the Partner's Everyday Tasks Examine the everyday tasks that consume your lives. Do both individuals know how to do the other's chores? Do both partners know how to turn off the house's water, electricity, and gas? Are both capable of replacing washers, unplugging a toilet, and flushing out a drain? Can she add gas and oil to the car and change a flat?

Can he iron a shirt and sew on a button? Can both of you cook and clean? Can both of you find names and addresses of family, friends, and repairmen? Do both of you understand your financial status and know how to handle the checkbook, taxes, and important papers? When both members are competent, you can choose specialties as well as share chores, working as a team and strengthening the relationship.

Balancing Joint and Individual Pursuits Many couples have spent years developing separate interests. Retirement may bring that divergence into sharp focus. You need to be alert for a feeling of abandonment that one or both of you may encounter. "Golfing widows" and "bridge widowers" are not uncommon. The balancing act is to determine what activities or hobbies you want to pursue, then which of these will be joint and which will be separate. The most successful couples do this as an ongoing process, insuring that neither feels deserted nor trapped.

Rebuild a Loving Relationship

Retirement is the perfect time to become reacquainted with your partner. Do you love your spouse? If so, turn that feeling into reality by exhibiting loving behavior. Monitor the messages you give to determine if they are positive or critical. With small changes, you can create the best moments of your relationship. Your expectations could be high on the enjoyment scale.

You can begin the process of strengthening your relationship by looking in the mirror and honestly trying to answer, "I wonder what it is like to be around me all the time?" If you are serious about this exercise, you will find small ways in which to change your behavior for the better. Then you can turn your attention to your partner to ask, "How can I improve life for you?" Once again, you will find that small alterations, such as more hand-holding and hugging, less criticism and anger, can improve a relationship. Learning to truly listen can revitalize the marriage. And, as one widow shared with us, "I do remember so many more times when I could have said 'I love you.' "

Active Listening Many of you may have been exposed to, and hopefully practice, the technique of active listening. If not, start now. When you hear someone talk, you often spend much of your time developing a response to what is being said—sometimes rational, often, emotional. Active listening requires that you seriously listen rather than prepare a response. After the talker has finished, the active listener reflects verbally on what was said (similar to how a mirror reflects an image). The first time you try it, you may be amazed at how poorly you understood what the speaker was trying to communicate. Words and phrases mean different things to different people. Plus, a speaker talks from a personal history the listener does not have. So, if a wife says, "I think we should go see the kids this weekend," the active listener would reflect, "You think we should drive over on Saturday?" This reflection gives the speaker the opportunity to amplify the thought, which could be, "I guess I just want to get out of the house." This response is closer to her true feelings but would have never been expressed if the husband had first responded with, "It's their turn to come here." With that nonreflective response, the couple might have been distracted, thinking, unthoughtful versus thoughtful children or some other extraneous and emotionally charged notions or topics. Learn to reflect and amplify before jumping in with your own thoughts.

In *On Becoming a Person* psychologist Carl Rogers writes, "When someone expresses some feeling or attitude or belief, our tendency is almost immediately to feel 'That's right'; 'That's stupid'; 'That's abnormal'; 'That's reasonable'; 'That's incorrect'; 'That's not nice.' Rarely do we permit ourselves to understand precisely what the meaning of his statement is to him. I believe this is because understanding is risky. If I let myself really understand another person, I might be changed by that understanding. And we all fear change. So as I say, it is not an easy thing to permit oneself to understand an individual, to enter thoroughly and completely and emphatically into his frame of reference. It is also a rare thing."

In every marriage more than a week old, there are grounds for divorce. The trick is to find, and to continue to find, grounds for marriage.

ROBERT ANDERSON
Playwright

To help each of you with your self-analyses, answer the following questions truthfully:

- Do you like to do most things with your spouse or do you prefer being alone?
- Do you wish your spouse were more affectionate?
- Are your tastes similar in entertainment, food, and friends?
- Do you plan and agree on money topics?
- Do you share your thoughts on current events? Do you share your innermost thoughts?
- Do you discuss topics beyond weather, house, neighbors, friends, and relatives?
- Does your spouse have a particular habit that irritates you?
- Do you resent being criticized? Do you criticize your spouse?
- Do you interrupt each other?
- Are certain topics hard to discuss?
- Do you and your spouse laugh a lot?
- Do you respect each other's privacy?
- Do you frequently lose your temper?

Take time to go over your responses and, if possible, share them with your spouse.

If you find lots of petty arguments developing, it might be necessary for the two of you to sit down and develop a sore-subject list. Both must agree on ways to alleviate the problems surrounding those sore subjects. In a few cases, you might want to use a referee.

Establish Intimacy There is no better time than retirement to reestablish intimacy and a quality sex life. This process begins by learning how to better communicate with one another. For most humans, information questions, answers, and dialogue are easier to start with; the feeling-emotional interactions can follow. Your goal is that you're trying to understand each other. By reliving your relationship's history, focus on why you were attracted to each other, then attempt to build on these initial feelings. Revitalize your sex life by being honest about your interests, feelings, desires, and ideas. The ability to discuss and decide how to sexually please each other is crucial. Make sex a priority. Add massage and stroking while you vary typical routines, including time and place. Take pleasure in being close and sharing moments of affection.

Singles and New Relationships

There is a strong likelihood that a retiree will spend at least part of his or her retired life as a single. At any given point in time, more than 40 percent are single. While most men older than sixty-five live with a spouse, less than 40 percent of the women live with a spouse. By age eighty-five, those numbers have dropped to half of the men, and less than 20 percent of the women. If you enter retirement as part of a couple, estrangement, divorce, or death are real possibilities—more than at any other time of your life.

The Effects of Divorce or Separation

At this point in life, separation and divorce can occur. For instance, both spouses slowly realize it is an impossible task to grow old together happily. One may sense that now is the time to escape what has become an intolerable situation. In a variation of that scenario, one grasps that she or he can now liberate themselves. (Frequently, it is the woman abandoning a submissive role.) Another typical breakup occurs when one member finds a new passion—either a new calling or another person.

No matter the underlying reasons, separation and divorce will bring a change in roles, status, and relationships with family, friends, and community. Couples often socialize exclusively with other couples. When you become single again, you may face a barrier with your former friends. (They too may feel forced to choose between you and your ex.) If you are a woman, you must struggle with a diminished sense of identity. (After all, you were known as Mrs. What's-His-

Name.) And, you face the difficulties of establishing a new identity. One acquaintance who was highly successful in this transition took a new name and relocated to a new town and state. This new person was able to create a whole new life.

Giving Yourself Positive Messages Whether you are newly single due to divorce or a spouse's death, take on the challenge of trying to feel better about yourself. Give yourself regular positive messages. This advice sounds mundane, even silly, but it requires your conscious effort. Force yourself to say something positive to yourself each time you touch a drawer or door handle. Go ahead and say, "I'm a good person" or "I like my attitude." After several days, and then weeks, of this new practice, you will find your mood is elevated.

Get into Good Physical Shape In your new life, get into good physical shape. You will feel better psychologically and you really will "glow." Update your wardrobe. You will meet new people, so be honest with yourself and them about your current situation. Reexamine your likes and dislikes, and increase the frequency of indulging those likes. Above all, find a challenge outside yourself, which demands that you give emotionally (a person who needs help, an organization, an animal, etc.). This giving builds your own sense of self-worth.

Especially if you live alone, consider an affectionate pet, like a dog. Cats may be too aloof.
RETIRED MINISTER
South Carolina

Forming Other Types of Relationships

As the baby boomers swell the ranks of the retired population, other types of relationships (other than single and married) will become more common. The social needs of an aging population will be met. Since their families have already been established, single retirees will pay far more attention to loved ones' current emotional needs. We will see an increase in romancing, dating, and coupling without a formal marriage. In most retirement centers, you can already see this increasing trend. Since far more women older than sixty-five are single than men, there will be more relationships that reflect this reality. More and more older women will date younger men. Informal (and formal) share-a-man relationships will likely pop up—especially useful for escorts to social outings, dinners, concerts, etc. Same-sex relationships will practically offer the desired companionship for travel, education, and social events. Our society has yet to acknowledge, name, and accept these new patterns, but social and emotional needs demand new solutions.

You can find your own joy and contentment. One retired widow comments, "I've tried dating, but I couldn't wait to get back home. And my experience was one of the good incidents in my group!" She says she finds more than ample social activity with her bridge club and travel group of four widows. While at home, she professes, "I'm content. I enjoy my solitude. I'm not lonely."

Remarriage

One traditional option for a single person is to seek a new marriage. When you are retired, this alternative is not as straightforward as when you were younger. Each of you has spent years developing rich personal histories, plus separate family and financial interests that often will not merge easily. For many, a long-term relationship (without marrying) is a better alternative.

Problems That Can Arise

If you are leaning toward remarriage, beware of the common motivations that spell trouble: you are infatuated (rather than in love); you are lonely; you feel pressured; it is convenient; it seems to make sense financially. None of these reasons forms any basis for a happy marriage. Realize that the most common failure of remarriage is a series of conflicts related to a previous marriage, including feelings of anger, guilt, and remorse. If one or both of you are recovering from the death of a former spouse, the previous mate may assume a saintly status. There is nothing wrong with that person's positive qualities—unless the comparison denigrates the new spouse.

Both partners in this new union must focus on each other's positive characteristics. Comparisons to previous relationships destroy the current one.

If one or both suffered through a contentious divorce, the strong and persistent emotions of anger and guilt can continue into the new marriage. Honestly assess how well you are doing at putting your past behind you. Whenever you feel the negative oozing closer to the surface, redirect positive attention to your new spouse. If that does not work, turn to a counselor for help before you allow a bad situation to develop.

Assessing Practical Issues Beforehand

There are many practical issues to address before remarriage, such as who will pay what bills? You both have assets, liabilities, family, and friends. How will all of these be handled? For instance, will you loan money to others in the family? Who will provide what kind of support to which family members? Due to these complications, many sign a prenuptial agreement which, at a minimum, specifies what happens upon divorce or death. One version that appears frequently states that each spouse retains control over what each possessed on the date of the marriage, while property acquired thereafter (including capital gains on the previously owned assets) becomes joint or "community property."

Resolving Financial Issues Financial issues must be resolved before the marriage. Discuss everything related to money. Look at each other's assets and prior commitments (loans or other obligations). Agree on common monetary goals. Set up a workable budget and decide each other's responsibilities on how to implement the plan. Property (including stocks and bonds) can be retitled either as a single owner (fee simple), two owners though not fifty-fifty (tenants in common), or shared owners (joint tenants with right of survivorship). You might decide to change all the assets to one type of ownership or you might decide ownership item by item.

Children and grandchildren may have a difficult time

accepting a remarriage—particularly if they think it negatively impacts their inheritance. This is not a pleasant fact.

Pitfalls aside, a late remarriage can be a wonderful experience. It can provide joy and companionship when they are most needed. At its best, a new relationship will open you up to new adventures, as well as to reexperiencing the tried and true in a totally new light.

Familial Roles

In spite of all the press given to deplorable situations that highlight the lack of family support in retirement institutions or senior services, most older Americans (somewhat more than 80 percent) receive some care from their families. Most older people will not, however, live with their children. Indeed, the romanticized notion that the extended family used to take care of all seniors is pure myth. We will soon find that the average woman will spend as many or more years assisting in the care of one or both of her parents as she did in caring for her children. (This is not to say that men do not help take care of their parents; the prediction is based on the fact that women live longer.) As you move closer to retirement, this new caregiver role becomes more and more apparent. In addition, adult children present their own challenges. Increased longevity means that multigenerational relationships will exist in most families.

Your Aging Parents

As you work with your aging parents, try to avoid any "old" stereotypes. Understand the patterns of aging and the difficulties that a diminished capacity might pose, if and when it happens. These are challenges, not hopeless obstacles. Provide positive expectations for your parents and be acutely aware of the negative effects of inertia and inaction. Good diet, exercise, minimal drug dependency, and an active mental life go a long way to making their lives (and yours) more fulfilling.

Next, look at your children. Do you have an adult relationship with each? At this point in the family picture, you as parent are no longer the financial, moral, and physical guardian. Old childhood patterns may remain, such as a child's feeling that he or she is a disappointment and can never obtain your complete approval. Others sense the primary parental motivation is to raise their level of guilt or shame. Among multiple siblings, there is the issue of favoritism. Now is the time to introduce yourself to your children as you would to a new friend—adult to adult. Learn to understand their choices and encourage them to share with you.

As you gain the extra time of retirement, you'll be tempted to give significant help to a grown child and/or your grandchildren. In recent years, an increasing number of children have returned home due to the rising cost of living (and the failure of real wages to keep pace), divorce or death of a spouse, unemployment or layoff, or illness. Consider that practically all the assistance you might give comes with strings attached. From the receiver's point of view, a gift attaches an obligation. Guilt often arises. After many gifts, a receiver comes to view the gifts as an inalienable right. These patterns weaken the relationship between the giver and receiver and may do more permanent damage than good. Rather than a pure gift, offer assistance. In one instance we've observed, a retired doctor used his newly refined woodworking skills to help his son-in-law with an old house renovation. They always work on the project together.

Your Relationships with Your Grandchildren

As a grandparent, you have a whole new role to perform. You have seen many variations: such as the gift-giver (spoil them rotten); the surrogate parent; the formal grandparent; the distant, rarely seen figure; the fun-lover; and the wise old matriarch or patriarch. The most important gift to your grandchild is time to listen and to attend to the child's life. Read to them. Learn tricks and jokes to share with them. Fix their favorite food. Create magical moments. Certainly, new grandchildren receive many gifts. (They are young and cute and they love stuff.) As the young grow into their preadolescent years, successful grandparents are seen as having something more to offer (a desired skill, new ways to have fun, time to help learn, or insights into the family history). Teenagers appear to respond best to mature adults (role models). At every stage, unsolicited advice is rarely welcomed by your children (the parents) or by your grandchildren.

One retired couple realized that they had no role models for grandparents. (Theirs had died early.) So, they are taking time to listen. "We're finding it important to have time alone with our grandchildren—to listen, to talk, and to appreciate. Our college-age granddaughter has shared that she tells us more than she tells her parents."

Your Wider-family Relationships

Wider family relations such as in-laws and stepchildren provide numerous other challenges. Know your limits and try to not overstep them, for example, trying to run everybody's lives. With stepchildren, spend time and share your interests. Nurturing will take a lot of time. Encourage the biological parents and children to work out their problems. Otherwise, you may become a convenient scapegoat.

Loaning Money to Family Members

Finally, look at one other family challenge: loaning money. Mature, and particularly retired, family members are seen as good candidates to approach for a loan. If you are asked, make sure you are loaning money you can afford to lose. You should also be sure that the loan is a reasonable financial deal. If this borrower has been a poor risk before or you feel you are being manipulated, do not make the loan. If your analysis shows there is a real need and you have adequate income without counting on the loan proceeds, go ahead. Draw up the loan on a standard form (from office-supply houses or family financial software) stating the interest rate and repayment schedule. Determine collateral and other arrangements for what happens if the loan is not repaid on schedule or what happens if you need the money. Put everything in writing so that all family members know this is a loan—and not a gift.

Groups

Humans like to belong, to feel needed, and to be respected. You can achieve many of these feelings by selectively joining groups. In spite of our society's scattering of family members, ever-changing casts of characters due to increased mobility, and feeling anonymous in urban settings, you can become involved with others who care.

Choosing a Group

For a low-key introduction to groups, consider various local clubs and organizations. Choose from service groups, political organizations, sporting or leisure clubs, religious or nonprofit outreach programs, art and library committees, educational volunteer programs, and environmental action groups. In our tiny county of 15,000 people, one can join more than 220 active volunteer organizations! If you're unsure of where you would like to put your time, take courses and workshops on topics that pique your curiosity. For those who hate meetings, there are other options of rewarding social activities, such as providing transportation, working with youth (scouts, literacy, sports, Special Olympics, or Junior Achievement), or serving as a reader or handyman. In short, you can find innumerable chances to participate with other human beings on meaningful projects. Being a contributing member will make you feel better in many ways.

Joining an Organization

You may help yourself socially, as one couple tell us, "People like to be constructive—so organizations are wonderful ways to meet other people with similar interests. We've made many new friends as we all work together around a common task." Another couple shared that they had no trouble blending into their new community because they became active in the AAUW (American Association of University Women), the local Chamber of Commerce, and a church. Acquaintances soon became friends.

Being Part of a Volunteer Group

If you would like to become more involved in a volunteer group, look back at your self-analysis in order to generate ideas about your favorite interests. Categorize those interests into fields of activity, including music, electronics, or travel. Search for organizations that have significant endeavors in each of these fields (educational institutions, community agencies, etc.). Finally, look at specific jobs and opportunities being offered by each. Then, take the plunge.

Friends

Friendships evolve out of common interests and experiences. Occasionally a friendship that began with a commonality (such as going to school together) flourishes in spite of a lifestyle divergence. More typical, however, is the necessity to make new friends who share your situation. Thus, the set of friends and acquaintances that was created around work and the social obligations related to work may fade away rather rapidly. Retirement has changed the commonalities.

Acquaintances are easy to establish—friendships take time to develop. Finding new friends can be a significant challenge as you age. Others have previously formulated their patterns and friends; there is often little room or time for a new entry. Frequently, retirees who travel or move to retirement centers have an easier time, since all they meet are newcomers without rigid in-place patterns. Whatever your situation, you can choose to begin new friendships.

In their personal network, most people have about ten others who are close enough to provide emotional support. This number stays remarkably constant over their lifetime even though individuals change. The healthiest people continue to maintain this network by seeking new relationships after the loss of someone close. In fact, emotional giving appears to alleviate times of sorrow.

Be Open and Adaptive When trying to make friends, include those of different ages and gender, as well as couples. Meeting couples, naturally, are the most difficult, since it takes four people to enjoy one another's company rather than only two. Also, retirement brings about new ground rules—there are far more women than men and fewer and fewer couples—so you will need to adapt to the situation. Joining groups, taking classes, showing interest, and being active increase your chances of meeting people who can become friends. Stay positive. Few people enjoy being around a whiner and complainer.

Include Pets Do not overlook "man's best friend." Dogs can provide comfort, companionship, and a reason to exercise. Several studies have linked better health, more complete recoveries after medical problems, and lower stress in people who have dogs. Depending on the animal, a pet may also add a dose of security. Any pet requires time and attention, so whether you are considering a dog, cat, or hamster, they are not appropriate for people who travel or spend extensive time away from home. And, of course, you must provide regular meals and veterinary services. For many, it is a wonderful investment. To check out the possibilities, contact your local humane society.

If a man does not make new acquaintances as he advances through life, he will soon find himself left alone; one should keep his friendships in constant repair.

SAMUEL JOHNSON
British author

Loneliness

At some point in your retirement, the odds favor that you'll find yourself alone and/or will feel lonely. The estrangement of a spouse or children, loss of meaningful friends, or death of someone you love can leave you feeling adrift. The basic advice for preparing for these disheartening events is to become your own best friend. Work on your self-analysis and modify your habits until you truly enjoy going out to dinner by yourself, taking a walk alone, or sitting and doing nothing. Once you can accomplish these feats, you will experience solitude, not loneliness. Many people never reach this point, and it shows in their interactions with others. Most people are attracted to someone who acts alive and is comfortable with himself or herself.

Social Isolation

When you are active, have passionate interests, remain a vital part of the community, possess a warm, caring family, and have several good friends, it is hard to imagine the idea of social isolation. But when you are in an institution and unable to travel or leave, it is hard to imagine not being isolated. During your retirement years, you will observe the tendency of individuals to become isolated. Your choices can minimize the negative impact of isolation.

When someone is confined to a contained facility, the opportunities for meaningful social interaction plummet. You must make the most of every social occasion and creatively devise new possibilities. First, make it a priority to become a good companion. For example, if someone helps by driving you somewhere, learn to focus on the scenery rather than the road ahead. Read, learn, and discuss new fields in art, literature, and entertainment. Also, keep in mind that almost all humans respond well when they are given gratitude, respect, and trust. Make it a point to provide all three.

Loneliness leaves its traces in man, but these are marks of pathos, of weathering, which enhance dignity and maturity and beauty, and which open new possibilities for tenderness and love. . . . Loneliness is as much a reality of life as night and rain and thunder, and it can be lived creatively. So I say, let there be loneliness, for where there is loneliness, there is also sensitivity, there is awareness and recognition of promise.

CLARK MOUSTAKAS
Author

Practice Enlightened Self-interest Fundamentally, humans are activated by self-interest. This tendency is ancient, probably genetic in nature. It means we strive to keep ourselves alive and happy. In addition, humans are motivated by altruistic or social thoughts. This inclination appears to be a wired-in predisposition, too. Thus, there is a drive to ensure that the social system survives and thrives. One who acknowledges only the self-interest aspect becomes the epitome of selfish. One who acknowledges only the altruistic component can become the whining martyr. The seemingly contradictory notions of self-interest and altruism work best when we realize that when we help others we are helping ourselves. This blending is termed *enlightened self-interest*. It also explains why humans feel so empty or disturbed when they are isolated from other enlightened, self-interested creatures.

Start a Common Interest Group Organize a small group around a common interest. A regular walking group, for example, provides social support and physical activity. You can use a hobby, game, or even a mundane chore, such as shopping or laundry, to set up steady social events.

Get a Computer Set up a computer and subscribe to an Internet provider. Millions of others will be available to converse with you (through E-mail and chat groups) about any subject under the sun. Cyberpals are simply the latest addition to the more familiar pen-pal and phone-pal groups. You might also take up a new avocation that will bring you social interaction.

Try New Endeavors No matter what your current limitations, you can probably find a satisfying endeavor. For example, at age eighty-five, Leland Effie Wilder (who had never seriously written in her life) turned her stay in a rest home into a best-seller. She has three popular novels, *Out to Pasture (but Not over the Hill)*; *Over What Hill?: Notes from the Pasture*; and *Older but Wilder: More Notes from the Pasture*, and has made thousands of new acquaintances. Another small group in an assisted living center opened a gift shop. Residents who created items could offer them for sale. It became a money-maker, but also, a social center for the facility.

Counteract Isolation

Isolation can occur at home when one does not get out of the house and participate in activities. Even when it is an effort, leave your four walls, and mingle. Make an appointment (forcing yourself into various social situations) every day on your calendar, and meet it.

Beyond human interaction, people also yearn for connections with all living creatures. One of the great appeals of gardening lies in this basic need. As one retiree suggests, "Have plants inside and outside your place. Surround yourself with life." He adds that if at all possible, live where you have a wonderful natural vista. If that is impossible, go outside in the evening to gaze at the stars. There is a reason almost all religions speak of their holy men spending many days in the wilderness before they begin to share insights. Stay connected.

At ninety, I'm still interested in local history, politics, and financial matters as well as my family. I sleep well because my conscience is clear.

GENEALOGIST
Ohio

Depression

Similar situations that lead to feelings of loneliness can lead to depression. The first year of retirement yields many discouraging moments, as people struggle to find balance in their new lives. If you have ever experienced depression, you know you are unlikely to pick up this book (or any other) to read about what you can do. Remember, however, that depression does not last forever, and there are actions you can take to escape it more quickly.

In Chapter 2, "Health and Well-Being Matters," baby steps are suggested for those seriously out-of-shape to approach their ideal weight. That same suggestion holds true for depression. For example, each evening write down three things you can accomplish tomorrow, for example, taking a walk, eating healthy meals, and telephoning someone. Congratulate yourself and mark on your list the successful completion of each item. You'll gradually increase the number and complexity of this list.

Symptoms of Depression

Depression that lasts for weeks and months is clinical. Two types exist—major depression and bipolar or manic depressive (usually appears in younger people rather than retirees). These conditions go beyond the normal sadness or temporary depression all of us encounter in life. Since clinical depression occurs in about 3 percent of retirees, make yourself aware of a few of the symptoms.

- A persistent feeling of sadness, "emptiness," anxiety, or being "down" that is generally present on most days, though it often lifts as the day wears on
- Loss of interest in life or pleasure in ordinary activities, including sex
- Decreased energy, more fatigue, feeling "slowed down" so even a simple task seems overwhelming
- Lack of confidence in yourself, often with feelings of uselessness or burdening others
- Restlessness resulting in sleep problems, such as insomnia, oversleeping, or early morning waking
- Loss of appetite or weight or the opposite: You can't stop eating
- Wanting to withdraw from people or, when around others, being snappy and irritable

- Difficulty in concentrating, remembering, or making decisions (small ones appear huge)
- Feelings of being guilty or "bad"; being punished for long-ago events
- Excessive crying
- Having recurring thoughts of death or suicide

Some of these same symptoms mimic Alzheimer's disease, which makes it even more important to recognize them. Depression, including major clinical depression, is treatable. Contact your local mental health agency or doctor.

Helpful Medications

Medications are often prescribed for depression, for example, traditional doctors opt for Prozac while herbalists prescribe St. John's Wort. If you can change your behavior and diet so that you feel more energetic and back on top of things, you may not need such chemical remedies. If you decide to take drugs, inform yourself about the research studies and know the side effects. Start with the smallest possible doses. Psychotherapy may also be used as treatment.

Information Available

If you or someone you know appears depressed, obtain a copy of *If You're Over 65 and Feeling Depressed. . . Treatment Brings New Hope* by writing to Depression: Awareness, Recognition, and Treatment (D/ART), National Institute of Mental Health, 5600 Fishers Lane, Room 14C-02, Rockville, MD 20857; www.nimh.nih.gov. You can order the free *Depression in Late-Life: Not a Natural Part of Aging* from the American Association of Geriatric Psychiatry, 7910 Woodmont Ave., Suite 1350, Bethesda, MD 20814; 1-800-573-4433.

Public-opinion polls reveal that many consider depression a reality of old age. However, it does not have to be a part of old age. And, if it does occur, it can be helped.

Bereavement

With increasing longevity, the grief of losing someone close often occurs later and later in life. Thus we are often unprepared due to our lack of experience, unlike people who lived a hundred or more years ago. Add to this phenomenon the idea that a youth-oriented culture treats the topic of death almost as a taboo. Intellectually, we know these losses will occur, for example, 75 percent of all married women will become widows (and remain widows for an average of twelve years). There is no need to obsess about death, but it is a good idea to mentally prepare for the loss of someone close to you. It will be the single most stressful episode in your life.

As one retired couple told us, "Aging has brought us greater awareness about health and about death. You gain a new perspective as your friends die. We've attended twenty-five funerals in eleven years."

Grieving a Loss

Retirees will know grief. If it is caused by losing someone you love, the grief will become a powerful succession of feelings that takes time to work through—and cannot be hurried. You have been wounded—deeply. Similar to a physical wound, healing takes time and care (to avoid infection). After all, grief is the "other face of love"—the ultimate cost of fondness, closeness, commitment, and a lifetime of shared experiences. All humans share similar challenges in dealing with their personal losses. Grieving is necessary for a healthy future.

The Five Responses to Death Most will experience the five common responses to dying—denial, anger, bargaining, depression, and acceptance. Examine how these stages occur. Initially, those closest feel stunned. This feeling of shock occurs even when the death has been expected. Soon, the numbness disappears and may be replaced by a sense of agitation, with pining and yearning for the dead person. Still in denial, you may somehow want to find them, even though this is impossible. Sleep brings vivid, disturbing dreams. Next comes the point where frequently irrational anger ("The doctors didn't do enough.") or guilt ("I didn't do enough.") arises. The agitation continues for about two weeks and may include bargaining with the supernatural, feeling remorse over things unsaid, or experiencing relief (especially if the person had been suffering). As you move into the four- to six-week period, you have less agitation, but periods of depression will set in. Often, spasms of grief feel uncontrollable. You sit for hours thinking of the good and bad times you experienced together. Slowly, the intensity lessens and acceptance begins. This grieving period is probably the hardest task you will ever face. Eventually, you will build a new life.

Helping Others in Their Grief Individuals are different; cultures are different—the reality of death and grieving is the same around the world. To help a bereaved person, simply be there. The process of recounting the same painful memories is a real and natural part of grieving. To tell the story again and again is natural and therapeutic in accepting the fact of death. You can speak the name of the one who has died—it acknowledges the loss. Understand that it is impossible for one who has not lost a long-term spouse to identify with someone who has. When a marriage of fifty, sixty, seventy, or more years ends with the death of one partner, the other faces an incredible emotional schism. Often, others who have been through a similar loss are the best sources of comfort and help.

Needing Help Through the Stages of Grief Occasionally, one can become "stuck" in one of the stages of bereavement. Experiencing endless depression, building a figurative "shrine" to the departed, or sleeping and eating difficulties are signs that outside help may be needed. You might consult support groups (at local hospitals and senior centers), counselors, mental health professionals, therapists, or doctors. Call the National Mental Health Association, at 1-800-969-NMHA for organizations in your area that can help. If on the Internet, select alt.support.grief or go to Yahoo and look for Bereavement under the medical category. Readers can pore through innumerable valuable books on the subject. The works of Dr. Elisabeth Kübler-Ross are particularly insightful. There is a light at the end of the tunnel.

One retiree recalls that when his wife of thirty-nine years was suddenly killed in an auto accident, "I shut down. For months, I mentally and physically shut down. Fortunately, my son lived in town and he called or came over every day for six months. He kept me going." When asked about the recovery, he notes, "A friend took me out to a ball game and to his church. Then, suddenly, he had marital problems and was literally out on the street. He asked if he could stay with me a short while until he could make arrangements. I guess when I had to help him became my turning point." His story emphasizes the finding that giving of yourself emotionally is one of the strongest mechanisms for pulling yourself out of a low period.

Summary

As a retiree, you will face many social and emotional challenges—many quite different from those you have previously encountered. Even if some of your contemporaries start to congeal or solidify, endeavor to stay flexible. Reality provides plenty of moments for you to apply your problem-solving talents. Also, you might want to increase your tolerance for frustration and discomfort. As one eighty-year-old shared, "Old-age is no place for sissies." And, though you are retired, building toward long-term enjoyment (rather than pure immediate gratification) remains a meaningful choice. To raise the probability of weathering emotional storms, increase your self-knowledge, truly accept yourself, build confidence in your abilities, and understand your enlightened self-interest.

CHAPTER FOUR

Work and Play Opportunities

As you consider retirement, there are several issues to evaluate. First, are you psychologically ready? Second, can you afford it? Third, if you elect to be a lord or lady of leisure, how will you spend the additional 2,000 hours each year that were once consumed by your job?

Your Goals, Your Time, and Your Life

If that perspective on your time seems weighty, try another viewpoint, which comes from former Wall Street bond trader Joe Dominguez and inspirational speaker Vicki Robin, who co-authored *Your Money or Your Life*: How much of your precious time are you willing to trade for an almighty dollar? At retirement age, more than any other time in life, you must be completely honest with yourself about what your time is worth to you. Quiz yourself by answering the following questions.

- What did you want to be when you were growing up?
- What have you always wanted to do but have not yet accomplished?
- What accomplishments are you really proud of?
- What do you find fulfilling? Is it related to money?

- If you did not have to work, what would you do with your time?

Pay special attention to what brings you fulfillment and satisfaction. How much time are you now able to spend on these activities? And, if you did not have to work, would the amount of time that you enjoy those activities change?

Sometimes we become so caught up in our everyday routines that we forget to ask ourselves what is really important to us, and to structure our lives accordingly. The exercise in Exhibit 4.1, page 107, will help you determine your values and prioritize your time.

Go through the list again, but this time be totally honest. When you have finished the second time, examine the areas that grabbed your highest scores. These are the areas with the greatest potential to bring you fulfillment and satisfaction. These areas are where you should devote your time.

Do You Want to Pursue Leisure or Continue Working?

Here's another exercise that converts your personal goals and work values into meaningful information to help you make decisions about pursuing a life of leisure or continuing to work in some manner. How true are these two statements?

1. I could easily adapt to the experience of a life of leisure.
2. I eagerly desire spending more time pursuing personal growth.

If these statements are true, they indicate a self-directed person ready for less structure in his life. How true are the next two?

1. It's important for my feeling of self-worth to earn money.
2. I really enjoy work.

Exhibit 4.1: Determining Your Values and Prioritizing Your Time

On a scale of 1 to 5, rate what is important to you: 1 is unimportant, 3 is somewhat important, and 5 is very important.

What You Value	1	2	3	4	5
Making money	___	___	___	___	___
Holding a full-time job (paid or unpaid)	___	___	___	___	___
Working for the pleasure of it	___	___	___	___	___
Doing something useful	___	___	___	___	___
Associating with congenial people	___	___	___	___	___
Being recognized in your community	___	___	___	___	___
Wielding power	___	___	___	___	___
Setting own goals, trying out own ideas	___	___	___	___	___
Tackling problems and finding solutions	___	___	___	___	___
Learning from what you do	___	___	___	___	___
Seeing results of your efforts	___	___	___	___	___
Being self-reliant	___	___	___	___	___
Helping others	___	___	___	___	___
Enjoying a variety of activities	___	___	___	___	___
Being flexible	___	___	___	___	___
Using leadership abilities	___	___	___	___	___
Achieving status in organization	___	___	___	___	___
Working for a well-known institution or company	___	___	___	___	___

If these statements reflect your feelings, chances are you should look for some type of work situation. Narrow your options by using the following guides:

- I'd like a job with flexible hours. (Look for flextime, part-time, or seasonal positions.)

- I'd like a job with variety in its assignments. (Free-lance or become a subcontractor.)
- I'd like to solve problems in my area of expertise. (Become a consultant.)
- I'd like to do what I really want, and I'm willing to do what's necessary. (Retrain to switch careers.)
- I'd like to be my own boss, try out my own ideas. (Think of becoming an entrepreneur.)
- I'd like to help others and contribute to society. (Seek out volunteer work with nonprofit groups.)

In retirement, get involved with something you've had a secret passion for (your shadow side).

RETIRED EDITOR
New York

Now, what do you think you want to do? How do you want to spend your remaining time on earth? Remember: There are 10,957 days in thirty years. Will you wake up 10,000 times looking forward to the day?

Write down what you expect to be actively involved in. Don't count pastimes such as reading the newspaper or watching television, in which you are gathering information secondhand. It's the firsthand experiences that will keep you lively. Many people list travel, continuing education courses, tennis or golf—and then they're stuck. To avoid boredom—and to avoid boring others—broaden your interests and activities. Be honest with yourself: How long has it been since you've been involved in a new interest or renewed an old interest? If you're doing little more than fantasizing about what you want to do when you have more time, your ideas may turn out to be just that—fantasies.

Whatever happens, as you make plans do not feel guilty about appearing unproductive to others. In our society, with its strong work ethic, free time can be a challenge to every-one—no matter what age. Another societal problem is that if a paycheck is not connected with an effort, then it tends to be devalued. Volunteer work for nonprofit groups is not counted in the Gross National Product. Nor is there an accepted mea-sure for productivity that results in learning (whether it is mastering the art of throwing a pot or improving your reading rate). Nor is there extensive recognition for performing good works, such as assisting a family member, friend, or neighbor.

Don't let these societal shortcomings stop you from preparing to accomplish and then achieving great things.

As you test your plans, learn to appreciate the differences between long-term goals and immediate consequences. (It is the latter that keeps you going as you find joy in whatever you do. Generally, though, it is achieving the long-term goal that makes the effort feel successful.) Give yourself permission to fail or to take a long time learning something new. For example, one seventy-nine-year-old wanted to write his memoirs. He decided he would teach himself to use a computer, though he'd never touched a keyboard (even a typewriter). He figured he had the rest of his life to learn. Four years later, we received two disks in the mail containing the work! Relax about retiring. Chances are, if you were an interested and interesting person before you retired, that pattern will continue. So go out there and give life another whirl.

Make New Discoveries About Yourself and Life

How exhilarating to discover (as reported by David Hobman in *The Social Challenge of Aging*) that in ancient China, two calendars delineated the life of every person. One calendar began at birth and recorded events through age sixty. On the sixty-first birthday, a second calendar was presented. This calendar was called *Kanreki*, meaning "second childhood." What did this calendar signify? It meant that as you grew older, society allowed you to be free—to make new discoveries, form new relationships, and take a few risks. And, if you floundered along the way, there would be no disgrace. How lovely!

With retirement, you gain more than opportunities for leisure pursuits, volunteer projects, or second careers. Most retirees affirm they have no regrets about spending less or no more time at work. But, as one lively eighty-year-old shared with us, "Playing golf is *not* enough!" What every retiree expresses joy about is the opportunity to continue to learn and grow into the human being he or she has always wanted to be. You, too, can realize this opportunity to grow, be independent,

As far as your interests go, fan the sparks to see if they flame. Scratch those itches.

RETIRED REALTOR
South Carolina

and feel free. It is up to you to claim your freedom and to chart your course for a successful retirement, self-fulfilment, and satisfaction.

Let's examine some of the options for using your time. Learning can take place while you play or work. Sometimes it is difficult to distinguish between what is work and what is play. To keep things simple, we'll define work as what you are paid to do, volunteer work as work you are not paid to accomplish, and everything else as play.

Play

It is important to refresh your mind and body, do things you enjoy, develop new interests, and become involved with things you like. Take advantage of this time in your life. Retire *to* something! Here are some activities grouped by concepts:

- rest and relaxation
- self-expression
- social activity
- continued learning
- mental activity
- contemplation
- physical activity
- travel

Rest and Relaxation

Rest and relaxation or "R&R" involves many quiet activities. Read the books you have never had time to read. For motivation, consider joining a book club. Indulge yourself with a book about a new topic. Start a collection—of baskets, black and white photographs, stamps, coins, and so on. Attend musical and theatrical productions. Visit museums and galleries. Make beer. Enjoy nearby public lands (national/ state/local parks, forests, wildlife refuges) while hiking, observing wildlife, and photographing nature. As one retiree noted, "It is only when you are exposed to beauty that you become beautiful." Let your mind soar with the best.

Self-expression

Self-expression offers an array of challenges. Write newspaper and magazine articles, short stories and books. Correspond. Hone your ability to make your points known—be it a sentiment to friends and family, a social concern to the local paper, or feedback about a product to the head of a company. Perform in the theater. Compose or play music. Create art. (Exchange one of your works of art with another artist somewhere in the world by participating in the Global Art Project, P.O. Box 40445, Tucson, AZ 85717; (520) 628-8353; www.global-art.org). Take photos (film, digital, or video). Learn a craft such as pottery, weaving, or wood carving. Refine abilities to cook, sew, or make fine cabinetry.

Gardening Let's examine one common way to express yourself—gardening. An Internet sharing includes:

I never had a garden until I was forty. As we begin to realize our own mortality, maybe we take more interest in the cycle of life and the renewal of life that spring promises.

Another friend who got into gardening says:

All my efforts and energy for months were focused on nurturing our landscape and gardens and learning and making correspondences between plants and people; learning that we cannot force on plants that which we think is good for their development, but rather that we must observe and thereby hear what the plants are saying about what is good for their growth. I have so much to learn, I expect to be observing and listening for sometime to come. . . . I am finally beginning to appreciate the reduction, fermentation and germination of futures, which is a natural product of the seasons, this now being winter, in which things are not dead, but merely in suspension, abeyance, waiting for the return of favorable growing conditions. And one thing I am trying to do is clean up all the unfinished events, piles, correspondences, etc., trying to get the slate clean before I embark on another beginning, one clean of holdovers and guilt feelings for things undone.

Another gardener shares:

I think it was there . . . looking down at the springtime burst of life in the gardens of the valley, that I began to see myself in relation to the atom, on the one hand, and the universe on the other. It was there I learned to see myself as a tiny grain of sand, of no importance whatsoever in the vastness of the universe, but, at the same time, of great importance to me.

These comments about gardening can be applied to other areas of self-expression. Listen to the sharings of artisans finding their craft later in life: "Inspired by nature, my silk painting has expanded my awareness." "Although I've been carving crystals for eighteen years, I'm still fascinated with light transmissions through glass." "Making musical instruments has become my joy. It's tangible. I can see as well as hear the results."

Social Activity

Social activity can be as simple as playing with your cat or dog or as progressively complex as interacting with your friends, children, and grandchildren, or meeting new people by joining a senior center or community center. Enjoy free activities. Become part of an interest group (books, films, investments, or various hobbies). Go to picnics and potlucks. Take aerobics classes. Consider joining clubs and organizations for their benefits to your personal health, continued learning, or social and emotional well-being. Participate! Discover the simple things that engage you and enjoy them to the utmost.

Continued Learning

Continued learning comes in many forms. Find the things that best suit you. Become acquainted with all the resources available at your local library—books, magazines, newspapers, videos, musical CDs, cassette tapes, and audio books. Set up your own research projects. One acquaintance, who loves photography, researched an early 1900's process called *autochrome* (using potato starch). Then he shared his findings in a delightful presentation at an art gallery.

Enroll in continuing education courses at local colleges and universities. (Many institutions offer discounts to seniors.) If you're learning to obtain a degree, discern which colleges offer credit based on the College Level Examination Program (CLEP). Many establishments, including foreign-language study institutes, have independent, home, and extension courses. Learning options that involve new places, new faces, and new concepts are available from, among others: Earthwatch Expeditions, 680 Mt. Auburn St., P.O. Box 9104, Watertown, MA 02272; 1-800-776-0188; www. earthwatch. org) and Elderhostel, 75 Federal St., Boston, MA 02110-1941; (617) 426-7788; www.elderhostel.org. You are never too old to learn!

Mental Activity

There may come a time when you cannot be as physically active as you would like, but no one (except you) can stop you from being mentally active. There is a wide variety of other mental activities, too. Challenge yourself with puzzles or board and card games with friends.

Change Television Viewing Habits Turn the mindless activity of watching television into a rewarding one by changing your viewing habits. Watch only worthwhile movies, news forums, or documentaries. Better yet, create your own seniors' programs at your local television station.

Getting a Computer Opens Up a New World Another option to hone mental activity is to purchase a computer. This technological wonder will open up a whole world of opportunities to you. You can play computer games. Buy a genealogy program and fill in the branches on your family tree. Put your home accounting on a money-management program such as Quicken, then use the results to do your own taxes. Track your investments on a spreadsheet. Use the computer to help you update your will or other legal documents. Enter your address book into a personal organizer program to assist you with holiday greetings. With a word-processing program, share recipes, write letters to friends and your local newspaper's editor, chronicle your memoirs, and create how-to books or the Great American Novel. The advent of the computer has helped bring the ideas and experiences of many retirees into print. One such book is Bob Wischmeyer's *Guacamole Infinity*, a humorous self-published diary recording his exploits as he took care of two youngsters. A more literary effort is May Sarton's *At Eighty-Two: A Journal*. Emily Whaley regales us about her garden in *Mrs. Whaley and Her Charleston Garden*.

Go on-line and correspond quickly and inexpensively with friends and family. Surf the Web. Check out the AARP Web site, www.aarp.org, and download its *Guide to Internet Resources Related to Aging*. You might make your next stop www.seniornet.org. Membership in SeniorNet includes a quarterly newsletter, *SeniorNet Sourcebook*, and discounts on merchandise and services. Seniors communicate with each other and participate in group discussions on topics such as health, travel, gardening, financial planning, and current events. In addition, computer training for both beginners and advanced users is available—both on-line and in various cities. Contact SeniorNet, 121 Second St., 7th Floor, San Francisco, CA 94105; (415) 495-4990. Check out the numerous other Web sites included in this book. You'll find everything from how-tos to humor. In chat rooms of your various interest, you may make new friends. One caution—computers and cyberspace can be addictive. Don't let going on-line stop your exercise program and other social outlets.

Contemplation

Contemplative arts are more difficult to describe, but important as a means to develop your spiritual life. Here are a few examples. Practice yoga or another form of meditation. Look for workshops that explore the inner self. Go on a retreat. Spend time in the desert, where you can observe life adapting to extremes. Consider it a great natural sculpture garden. Sit by a stream or waterfall, or visit the redwoods. Observe other wonders of nature. Try to allot time simply to "be," to absorb, and reflect on how you fit into the grand scheme of life. As one retiree shares, "Listen to silence; admire beauty in a mountain laurel limb." Find your center.

My wife is a WASP—work, work, work is her primary ethic. I prefer pleasure—an Italian way of looking at life—sitting at a sidewalk café, feeling the sun streaming over my body, and enjoying being alive.

RETIRED LAWYER
New York

Physical Activity

Physical activities range in degree of strenuousness and amount of necessary time to perform. Participate in sports by playing, coaching, or observing. Walk, cycle, play golf or tennis, swim, ski, ice skate, dance, bowl, ride (horses, bicycles, or motorcycles). Work out on exercise equipment. Train for the Senior Games, then Senior Olympics. Make fishing and hunting into truer sports with fly casting and archery instead of using bait and guns. Play informal games, such as Ping-Pong, billiards, shuffleboard, or horseshoes. If you need assistance with learning a new activity, check out magazine articles, books, even instructional videos.

Cleaning house and maintaining the yard may rate as light physical activity. Many people try to approach these time-consuming chores as hobbies. Unfortunately, they are repetitive and mindless. Try controlling chores instead of letting them control you. Trade housecleaning and yard-work chores with someone else—do more in less time so you have more truly recreational time!

Kenneth Soddy and Mary Kidson in *Men in Middle Life* write:

There's "the thrill of learning" something new after forty-five. . . . When undertaken in the right spirit, such activities (skiing, golfing, hiking, playing the piano) have nothing to do with dilettantism. The point is to defeat the entropy that says slow down, give it up, watch television, and to open up another pathway that can enliven all the senses, including the sense that one is not just an old dog.

The bonuses are considerable if one of the new pursuits chosen is an active one that can be done in fresh air. True, after forty we may tire faster during exercise because we can't incur the same oxygen debt, which means we can't count on stored oxygen to keep us going for long after we run out of breath. Regular exercise, rather than sudden spurts, is best, but certainly there is nothing good to be said for physical inactivity. The brain needs oxygen, and the lungs need help in providing it because the natural chest expansion lessens as we grow older. The heart muscle can use all the new and collateral pathways for blood circulation that can be opened up with regular physical activity. Well-chosen exercise can literally retard the aging process.

Those who settle back for a sedentary, indoor middle age conspire with their backaches, hernias, broken hips, and heart attacks. A sluggish heart cannot be expected to meet sudden demands any more than slackening muscles can be expected to provide the spine and vital organs with sufficient support. Once again, the more we use, the less we lose.

Taking up an active pursuit in midlife doesn't mean falling into the trap of physical competition with one's younger athletic self. The hard-won resources gained by half a lifetime of experience can be directed to other goals, other prizes.

It's all good advice since if we don't use it, we lose it.

Travel

Travel can be adventure. Having the time to travel is considered by retirees to be one of the best benefits of their new phase of life. Plan your getaways carefully. Know what you want—and don't want—on a specific trip. Otherwise, when you begin to gather information, you can find yourself deluged with options created by marketing masterminds. You will feel pressured to take all kinds of tours and cruises—which are often different from the dream trip you were planning. You can travel with your wits—and your money— about you. Plan trips that are as satisfying and as expensive as you want. Plan a trip with a focus. Visit the past, something new, or even a natural wonder. Visit small county or village museums, as well as big-city offerings.

Camping Try camping. Personally, we're big advocates of tent camping because it is simpler and lighter than alternatives. On the spur-of-the-moment, you can go almost anywhere and, in a short distance, be far from the crowds. If you're backpacking, set up a base camp. Then, make leisurely day hikes without carrying much weight. Short camping trips on which you are surrounded by the wonders of nature can be great restoratives.

New Experiences Be open to new experiences and new ways of doing things. For example, a couple of expert Caribbean sailors share accounts of "stripping off their clothes and swimming with the dolphins as we had all been created" and with bathing and doing laundry on the sailboat by "finding fresh water, filling buckets and coolers, agitating the clothes with our feet. . . . The clothes were work; the bodies fun!"

Of course, check out passports/visas, customs regulations, and insurance in new places. Try to adapt to the language and the ways of locals. Become more of a traveler and less a tourist. Take any medical precautions. (If going abroad, you may want to obtain the directory of the International Association for Medical Assistance to Travelers [IAMAT], 736 Center St., Lewiston, NY 14092; (716) 754-4883; www.sentex. net/~iamat.)

Look for Adventure Take a risk! You might want to investigate Mary VanMeer's top-rated monthly newsletter, *The Over-50 Thrifty Traveler*, P.O. Box 8168, Clearwater, FL 33758; 1-800-532-5731; www.thrifty traveler.com.

Additional Travel Tips Here are some additional tips for obtaining the most experiences for your money:

- Consider all your transportation alternatives: personal car, rental car, RV or travel trailer, bus, train, and boat. (Many car rental agencies offer senior discounts.)
- Pay less for airfares and cruises by booking early or late (on fire-sale basis). Some foreign airlines offer senior discounts. Join a seniors' travel club to take advantage of additional savings.
- Besides lodging in motels and hotels that offer senior rates, consider camping or staying in youth hostels, Elderhostels, and bed and breakfasts. Campus housing, Ys, and truck stops offer alternatives. You can rent condos and villas, or swap apartments or houses.
- Combine travel with an educational pursuit or learning new skills. You can attend "camps" that provide instruction in activities from painting to learning computer programs. Sponsors include colleges and universities, alumni associations, cultural institutions, special-interest groups, such as the Audubon Society, Sierra Club, and the Smithsonian Institution. Another popular choice is Elderhostel. College dormitories provide room and board for participants, who take classes and join in field trips.
- Adventure travel includes dude ranching, scuba diving, white-water rafting, bicycle touring, mountain climbing. . . . There are working vacations on farms, ranches, and archaeological digs. There are other sites for scientific studies. Check with Earthwatch or your nearest science museum for what are called *volunteer vacations*. In these arrangements, retirees provide their time and expertise to volunteer projects either in the United States or abroad. These projects allow participants to contribute while enjoying travel, cultural, and scientific exchanges. Keep in mind that in many cases volunteers must pay their own way— including the costs of transportation, housing, and meals. Other adventurous ideas include following in

someone's footsteps, such as botanist John Bartram or explorers Lewis and Clark. Adventure travel definitely offers new alternatives to current routines.

- If you are looking for a travel partner or partners, there are services that match travel companions. Long established are the Jurgens, who publish a bimonthly newsletter *Travel Companion Exchange*, P.O. Box 833, Amityville, NY 11701-0833; (516) 457-0880; www.whytravelalone.com. This matching allows singles to take advantage of the lower (per person) double rates. Several recreational vehicle organizations arrange convoys to special destinations. Some senior organizations offer planned tours to members. Travel agencies, motor clubs, and discount travel clubs can also book you on tours. (Try not to prejudge. Some tours are worthwhile and offer competitive pricing. Examine offerings, compare options, and determine how closely the tour comes to your dream trip before signing up.)

- If you want to travel free, guide your own group tour. Or, you can present lectures and slide programs, or perform host services on a cruise.

- Obtain the most up-to-date travel information from the various bureaus of travel and tourism (states and countries). Numerous travel newsletters are loaded with current information (such as those by *Consumer Reports* and Arthur Frommer). Magazine articles, books, and videos can be helpful, too!

Listen, however, to an arresting thought shared with us by a still-working senior citizen: "Traveling around the world is the antithesis of what seniors need to do—which is living frugally." He adds that if you are spending your capital on pleasure (rather than on earning dividends or interest), he thinks you are making a mistake. It is up to you alone to decide what is best, and to plan accordingly. Carefully consider your plans.

Leisure Time Changes as Baby Boomers Age Here are a few other interesting thoughts on the subject of play. A trend, as

America's baby boomers age, is that leisure time will change with them. Activities will become more active and more adventurous, physically and intellectually—in short, more intensely satisfying. Peter Dickinson offers these additional observations on leisure in his book *The Complete Retirement Planning Book*:

- Effective use of leisure time appears most inhibited by lack of education.
- Advertising appears to sap all quality use of leisure. Go for quality rather than quantity.
- Free yourself. Examine where you fit in and know what you want to do.

Develop Your Interests Before Retirement

Again, it is imperative to be in touch with yourself, your interests, and desires. Different forms of play offer many viable options to help "re-create" you, to assist your continued growth physically and mentally. You may find that the current "in" thing being marketed on television, radio, magazines, newspapers, or on-line is dissatisfying. So be prepared to break away from the crowd and follow your bliss. Only you can determine how best to spend your time.

A word of caution: If you have not had time to develop your interests during your working years and you plan to do so after you retire, you are at risk of making a difficult transition and, perhaps, experiencing a regrettable retirement. Generally, people who have not cultivated their interests during their middle years are not able to do so after age sixty-five, either. These people end up being bored and disappointed. So, get involved—now—in those activities you find interesting!

Volunteer Work

Albert Einstein stated, "There is no higher religion than human service. To work for the common good is the gentlest creed." You can volunteer for others as did Mother Teresa in India and Albert Schweitzer in Africa. On the subject of volunteering, Jimmy and Rosalynn Carter say:

> For us, an involvement in promoting good for others has made a tremendous difference in our lives in recent years. There are serious needs everywhere for volunteers who want to help those who are hungry, homeless, blind, crippled, addicted to drugs or alcohol, illiterate, mentally ill, elderly, imprisoned, or just friendless and lonely. For most of us, learning about these people, who are often our immediate neighbors, can add a profound new dimension to what might otherwise be a time of too much worry about our own selves.

Interestingly, while you are helping others, you are helping yourself. One study reported that 95 percent of the participants who volunteer show a decrease in chronic pain and an increase in optimism. What's more, volunteer work helps you focus on what is truly important to our society and world. As one retiree points out, "I strongly feel the planet needs us retirees to continue to work—not for a paycheck but to pay for the space we take up."

Many Volunteer Opportunities Exist

Volunteer opportunities abound: medical organizations (such as Red Cross, hospitals, nursing homes, mental health clinics); violence-prevention organizations (for example, Humane Society, National Coalition Against Domestic Violence, Parents Anonymous); environmental groups (Earthwatch, Audubon Society, Sierra Club, Greenpeace, Nature Conservancy); garden clubs; youth groups (Girl Scouts, Boy Scouts, Big Sisters, Big Brothers); public schools and youth camps; museums of all types; volunteer programs in federal parks (National Park Service, National Forest Service, Bureau of Land Management, Army Corps of Engineers); public service programs (Service Corps of Retired Executives [SCORE], Active Corps of Executives [ACE], Peace Corps, Corporation for National Service,

Since leaving the White House we have had a chance to revive a number of our old interests and pursue some new ones, a process that we hope will continue for the rest of our lives. There is no way to know how many years we will have to spend together, and we want to make the most of them. In addition to having a good time, we have taken on some challenging projects, but our tendency has been to move toward the simpler activities that we can share with each other and our friends—and enjoy now and for a long time to come.

JIMMY AND
ROSALYNN CARTER

AmeriCorps, Volunteers in Service to America [VISTA], Retired and Senior Volunteers [RSVP], Foster Grandparents Program, Senior Companions Program); political groups (League of Women Voters, Democratic party, Republican party, various candidate campaigns); senior associations (AARP Volunteer Talent Bank, senior centers); and other local civic, political, religious, and charitable organizations.

Take Responsibility for Finding Your Niche

Take responsibility and fill responsible posts. Survey the field and spot something you feel good about. To do this, broadly evaluate your likes and dislikes, your abilities and limitations, as well as your motivations. Next, categorize your likes into fields of activity, such as agriculture, medicine, religion, art, music, communications, etc. Consider the organizations that make substantial efforts in your areas of interest (educational institutions, community agencies, national associations, religious groups, etc.) Finally, look at the specific jobs offered by each organization in light of your dislikes and limitations, as well as your schedule. Remember: The organization wants the match to be good, too.

Perhaps you find no organization that fits. Start your own. One acquaintance found his city was not engineered for easy bicycling—and he wanted to pursue his new hobby. So, he began to work through the bureaucratic maze of planners, engineers, and elected officials who establish how the roads are built. In so doing, hundreds of other cyclists joined him, and he found himself as spokesman for a new action group.

Convince an Established Organization to Fill a Need

Perhaps you can convince an established organization to meet a need. Following an early retirement, one upstate New York couple floundered for a few years trying to find a direction. Escaping harsh winters, they headed south to a small town.

The husband was appalled to find little music instruction available for the elementary school students. He also discovered the local American Legion Post in the doldrums. First, he joined the legion, became active, and was soon chosen commander. He convinced the post that a major mission would be to upgrade local music programs. His son had attended the North Carolina School of the Arts, so he used that connection to bring faculty and advanced students to his rural county. The School of the Arts students performed on Sunday afternoon in rotating church facilities (the churches fed the performers), stayed overnight, then performed again in the schools on Monday. Passing the hat and other donations offset all the costs. These performances quickly grew to thirteen or fourteen per year at no expense to the legion. Now that the students were seeing what music could mean, the retiree cajoled the post to raise money to buy violins so every child who desired might learn by the Suzuki method. Two years later, there were more than 130 violins and lessons, which continued year-round.

Leave safety behind. Put your body on the line. Stand before the people you fear and speak your mind—even if your voice shakes. When you least expect it, someone may actually listen to what you have to say. Well-aimed slingshots can topple giants. And do your homework.

MAGGIE KUHN
Founder,
Gray Panthers

Additional Ideas

What is your passion? What are your strengths? Can you share any of them with your community? Here are some additional volunteer ideas:

- Work for different agencies on an "on-call" basis.
- Assist in fund-raising.
- Write an article or design a brochure.
- Create a display or special exhibit.
- Lead tours.
- Give a talk or lecture.
- Conduct a special project in an assisted-living facility—such as planting a butterfly garden, teaching an art or craft class, or leading an exercise session.
- Deliver meals to the homebound.
- Help construct a Habitat for Humanity house.
- Read to preschoolers.

- Instruct in an adult-literacy program.
- Be a "hugger" in the Special Olympics.
- Answer hot-line/help-line phones.

Most older people perform productive work. As detailed in the MacArthur Foundation Study, only 2 percent report no productive work, while 80 percent report more than 500 hours per year and 40 percent report more than 1,500 hours per year. These amounts of good works are substantial.

Take this chance to make a difference in your life and in others. The underprivileged don't need handouts; they need opportunities and tools that offer more control over their own destiny. They don't want caseworkers; they want coworkers. Be a Veronica Maz, who made a few rooms into The House of Ruth, a homeless women's shelter. Take time to teach another adult to read in a literacy program. Or, help build a Habitat for Humanity home alongside a needy but hardworking family. The number and type of volunteer opportunities are almost infinite. Find where you can make the biggest difference.

For example, one retiree, after deciding to move to a small, economically depressed mining town in Minnesota, found that there were few fathers living and working there. She and her husband had raised three boys; she knew the importance of positive role models for young boys. She organized a Big Brothers group and found mentors for all twelve of the community's single-parent boys. She raised money to send the neediest to summer camp. Finally, she gave practical counseling to each of the single moms. One person can make a difference!

Rewards of Volunteering

The rewards of volunteering are numerous. Besides accomplishing something worthwhile and providing purpose, there are opportunities to:

- Give back what you've been given in your lifetime.
- Work with altruistic organizations.

- Perform interesting assignments.
- Learn new skills.
- Do what you do best.
- See the results of your efforts.
- Make new friends.
- Add meaning to life.

Volunteer "pay" includes feeling purpose, fulfillment, and satisfaction; improving one's health and self-esteem; staying active and being involved. Feeling useful does not demand a paying job. (When volunteering, however, keep up with your expenses; they may be tax deductible.)

Combine Opportunities

Finally, combinations of playing, volunteering, and working often function well together—performing volunteer work and working part-time; practicing a craft and going to school. The options are yours. Try not to be influenced by friends or neighbors. This is a personal balancing act. After the flurry of activities at the beginning of retirement, you'll have many hours of time to fill. Knowing that the most successful retirees are those engaged in lives full of meaningful activities, make your preparations now for what your future could hold.

For-Pay Work

You may need to work in your golden years to make financial ends meet or to maintain structure in your day and life.

Former President Jimmy Carter describes how it was before Social Security:

> In earlier days . . . retirement was just not a factor in people's lives. There was no form of Social Security, and everyone was expected to be active and productively employed until they were incapacitated. Anyone who was "able but unwilling" to work was subject to ridicule and scorn, and those who

Helping others becomes more and more important. We think solutions to many problems (poverty, housing, etc.) may come from grass roots organizations such as Sojourners and Habitat for Humanity.

RETIRED COUPLE
North Carolina

Personally, I've seen the following problems in folks upon retirement: difficulties with time management (both too much and too little) and volunteering oneself "to death," leaving no room for further personal growth (which I guess is a problem of excess).

EARLY RETIREE
Georgia

were truly lazy, who habitually sat around the stove at the filling station or general store talking or playing checkers, felt it necessary several times a day to blame their inactivity on some imagined physical ailment.

Except for nurses and schoolteachers, women labored in homes, yards, or field, and with advancing age simply chose less strenuous activities. Women of a great-grandmother's generation would sit in a chair by the fireplace in winter or on the porch in warm weather, long skirts down around their ankles, carding wool or cotton, churning milk, or shelling peas. The men who were storekeepers, clerks, mechanics, cobblers, doctors, or lawyers pursued their relatively sedentary careers for a lifetime. Those employed in more arduous jobs on the farms or railroads or in logging and sawmilling usually spent their later active years doing light farm work, or took jobs at stores or filling stations.

Indeed, in America where one disadvantage of aging is being pushed out of your job, your need to continue to work may do you a favor psychologically. You may be able to postpone dramatic changes in your income, productivity (and, consequently, self-esteem), relationships with coworkers, or daily routine. So, consider the following work options.

Do You Want to Continue Working at the Same Job?

If you look forward to going to work each day and feel challenged by the nature of your job, you may want to consider staying. You would be assured of continued relations with your work associates. And you could save more money before retiring.

Do You Want to Change the Way You Work?

Consider sabbaticals, phased retirement, job sharing, flextime, part-time, or seasonal alternatives.

You know you want to continue working, but you think you want a change. Where do you start your job search? To speed you on your way, look for options on the Internet, as well as in books, magazines, and newspapers. Research librarians are helpful at unearthing appropriate information. Another avenue is to seek assistance from a career counselor.

Women often find their first jobs after their husbands retire. This may provide self-esteem, social and intellectual stimulation, social contacts, confidence about bringing home a paycheck, or a way to escape. Be aware that this role reversal can produce problems. (Where does her money go? She's never home!)

Consider Job Preferences In his 1981 book *The Three Boxes of Life: And How to Get Out of Them*, Richard N. Bolles identified the three boxes as playing, learning, and working. For working, he categorized jobs into those that deal with data or information; those that deal with people; and those that deal with things. Consider your job preferences. (For example, you favor a position dealing with people rather than information, or vice versa, or, perhaps, you lean toward an occupation dealing with things and few people.) Various skills include those with your hands, body, senses, intuition, logic, words, numbers, leadership, helpfulness, persistence, and creativity. Rate what you feel are your top five skills. Obtain feedback from others, particularly work associates. Now look for careers using your best skills that are compatible with your job preferences.

Job Satisfaction Predicting the future is always chancy. Predicting future job satisfaction is less dicey, if you analyze what you liked/disliked about previous assignments, and then determine how those results fit into the career you're considering. Areas to rate as high/average/low include: pay, people contact, work associates, variety of tasks, use of skills, responsibility, challenge, creativity, autonomy, positive influence on others, and positive impact on environment.

Turn an Avocation into a Career A surefire way to find a job you enjoy is turning an avocation into your next career. For example, a retired engineer who worked all over the world took excellent photos of people and places. Now with the assistance of a digital scanner, computer, and color printer, he is creating his imagery anew. He is uncertain how monetarily rewarding the endeavor will be, but he hopes to do better than recouping his expenses. Another example is the avid hiker we met on a mountain trail. In winter she loves to cross-country ski so, in her eighties, she has started teaching skiing on a part-time basis.

Age Discrimination Despite laws prohibiting age discrimination, finding a satisfying job is not always easy for an older person. Some futurists thinks this scenario is likely to be doubly true for baby boomers, who will be retiring in unprecedented numbers and then competing for jobs.

If you're looking to change jobs or careers, it is a good idea to plan how you will make it happen. Test the position. Make sure it is available and is as satisfying as you imagine.

Tips to Finding a Satisfying Job

If you want to remain in (or jump back into) the work arena, here are some pointers to assist you in searching for your ideal job.

- *Assess yourself*—your interests, job-type preferences, skills, work-environment needs, limitations (for example, inadequate transportation, health problems, or training need). Prioritize your five best skills in business terminology. (If you were a homemaker, look at your experiences from the standpoint of having a thirty-year-long job that included scheduling, budgeting, planning, designing, and decorating.) Think of specific knowledge you possess, specific tasks you can perform, and specific people/social skills you can use.

- *Analyze the job market.* Scan your newspaper's business sections for new and expanding businesses. Check the Yellow Pages for companies with employees who do what you do. Professional and trade association publications can provide contacts. Obtain the local chamber of commerce's directories. Look for world and national trends becoming local opportunities. (Check what's hot in an area of the country that has always been among the first with the latest trends, for example, New York City or Los Angeles.)
- *Network!* Inform friends, relatives, social and business acquaintances, former employers and coworkers, as well as members of your professional, religious, alumni, and other organizations that you are looking for a specific type of employment.
- *Be organized to market yourself.* Carry an index card with employment-related data—your Social Security number, your last three employers' names, addresses, phone numbers, and dates of employment. Prepare a well-written, well-designed résumé. Tailor it to emphasize those skills and attributes you would like to use in your new job. (There are numerous books on how to write a résumé.) Write inquiry letters. Be on time for appointments, and dress appropriately for interviews. At interviews, offer a firm handshake, speak positively, and make eye contact. Be willing to learn new skills (for example, computer training). Follow up with thank-you notes and phone calls. Continue to be self-directed (in touch with your goals) instead of becoming a number at a job-placement company.
- *Be aware that technological innovations involving computers and on-line networks have created more flexible working arrangements.* Work can often be accomplished at home and transmitted via modem, saving you time and energy. Using the computer and its power may help you land the job you want.

Counteract Stereotypes When you approach today's marketplace, you may encounter stereotypes. Arm yourself with facts. According to the American Association of Retired Persons (AARP), older workers:

- Possess work experiences that give them mature judgment; good basic skills in math, spelling, and writing; proven social abilities that allow them to cooperate, collaborate and negotiate, as well as specialized job knowledge. Older workers are capable decision makers and problem solvers.
- Have learning capacities to perform new tasks as needed. Intelligence and memory remain constant for most people until age seventy—for many, even longer.
- Exhibit productivity rates as high as in other age groups because of self-management skills and beliefs in a full day's work for a full day's pay.
- Care about the quality of their work. Older workers are loyal, dedicated, reliable employees with a strong sense of responsibility to contribute.
- Can adapt to change—in family, work, and the world. Older workers have adapted to deadlines, crises, and plans gone awry. They've learned coping mechanisms at home, on the job, and in the world. They're survivors.
- Have fewer accidents on the job than other age groups. (Older workers may need to modify their work environments to prevent falls.)
- Have equal or better attendance records than other age groups. Older workers stay an average of fifteeen years on a job.
- Have the same or lower health and benefits costs than other age groups.

U.S. Department of Labor facts (USDHEW Publication # OHD 77-200006) includes the following:

- Studies show no significant drop in performance and productivity of older workers. Many older workers exceed the average output of younger employees.

- Job analysis indicates that relatively few jobs require great strength and heavy lifting. Labor-saving machinery makes it possible for older workers to handle most jobs without difficulty.
- Workers older than sixty-five have a good record of attendance compared with other age groups.
- A high proportion of older workers are flexible in accepting change. Adaptability depends on the individual. Many young people are set in their ways; many older workers adjust to change without difficulty.
- Pension and insurance costs need not stand in the way of hiring older workers. Costs of group life, accident, health insurance, and workmen's compensation are not materially increased by hiring older workers. Most pension plans provide for benefits related to length of service or earnings, or both. Small additional pension costs, when incurred, are more than offset by the older worker's experience, lower turnover, and quality of work.

Read the above points again before you look for a job. Knowing these facts and being able to tactfully correct misinformation when you hear it is important to finding or creating the job you want.

Do You Want to Own Your Own Business?

There are many good reasons to start your own business: desire to be your own boss; aspiration to work at something you feel good about; belief in an idea. Be sure you understand what is motivating you and what you want to achieve.

Self-employment demands careful consideration. People take an avocation that has been a hobby and turn it into a business. Personally, we know several retirees who have begun successful second careers as writers. The question remains: Can you start a successful company? Analyze your business concept with as little emotion as possible. This

As I sat alone one day on the courthouse steps shortly before retirement, sixty-five and single, I pondered what I would do to occupy my time, to continue to exercise my brain, and to be of benefit and interest to others. . . . When I opened the envelope, removed the letter and a check for $400, I knew my second career had begun. . . . Writing opened new vistas through joining the area writing clubs, participating in seminars, and attending writing conferences. I've made a

analysis is doubly important if you are creating a "little" business. Small operations often have less room for error than large ones.

Step No. 1 Your first step could be to contact the U.S. Small Business Administration (SBA), at 1-800-827-5722 or www. sbaonline. sba.gov and request or download its publication *The Facts About . . . Starting a Small Business.* Study it.

Step No. 2 Research your market and how your business idea fits into it. Answer the following questions: What price are most people willing to pay for my product or service? Is that price higher or lower than my competitors' prices? Can I justify a higher price with better quality or service? Can I offer something my competitors cannot? How will I sell my product or service—wholesale, retail store, or catalog? Where will I do business? What is the scope of the business—local, regional, national, or international?

Step No. 3 What is its future? Learn everything you can, then adapt your business ideas to what you learn about your potential market!

Step No. 4 You're not ready yet, though. What are the legal ramifications—licensing, zoning, etc.? Educate yourself. Decide whether to buy an established business or franchise (with fewer unknown variables) or start from scratch (with more allure). You might set up a cottage industry (work from your house). Be willing to obtain professional services as needed—for example, a banker, realtor, insurance broker, lawyer, accountant, or advertising/PR agent. Pick a business name. Become a legal entity—be a proprietorship, partnership, subchapter-S corporation, or full corporation.

Step No. 5 How much business sense do you possess? Write a business plan and set goals. Do not underestimate financing requirements—you will need enough money to operate for one year without making any money. Test your market. Effectively manage your business—materials, services, employees, income, expenses (including insurance, taxes, and employee-benefit plans). As a business owner, you will wear many different hats as you make decisions to purchase, hire, fire, advertise, and plan future expansion.

Step No. 6 The profile of a successful entrepreneur includes: confidence, self-motivation, creativity, innovation, problem-solving skills, organization, forward-thinking, decisiveness, responsibility, control, risk taking, ability to learn from mistakes and others, patience, cooperative attitude, high energy, and contagious enthusiasm. Perhaps one of the most important characteristics of the successful businessman is the ability to know when and where to obtain advice. Check out books from your public library on starting and running a business. Use the SBA's volunteer group, SCORE (Service Corps of Retired Executives). Contact the National SCORE Office, at 409 Third St. SW, 6th Floor, Washington, DC 20024; 1-800-634-0245; www.score.org. If you need additional help in any area, from management to technical, check with the closest SBA Small Business Development Center (SDBC) to discover what it may be able to provide for free. (Call the SBA for a location in your state.)

Know Why You Want to Continue Working

For those who need the paycheck or the structure, work can provide a schedule for daily living, a sense of purpose and productivity, physical and mental stimulation, and opportunities for social contact. Many people enjoy the busyness their jobs and work situations offer. They feel work offers the best opportunity for them to stay engaged in life. These people may want to continue working.

What You Enjoy Can Lead the Way One couple turned misfortune into an advantage. Almost at retirement, he was laid

host of new friends and we support and help one another. . . . The only problem with my second career is not insufficient stamina nor an inadequate supply of creative juices nor even subjects about which to write—it's knowing when to knock off each day. . . . As you can see, I love my second career. It's emotionally and financially rewarding, and offers something that is even more valuable—a feeling of fulfillment. Isn't that what retirement is all about? . . . Although minor adjustments may be required in the mental computer, I suspect that everyone can realign their life, set new goals, and go forward with a second career.

TAYLOR REESE
Author

off as the company went bankrupt; his pension fund practically disappeared. His next job was with a company that downsized the plant a few months after he had been hired to run it. The two of them took a hard look at what they enjoyed. He liked to invest in stocks and bonds; she enjoyed working with people one-on-one. They established a small business in which he works as a low-key financial adviser, while she assists people with their medical claims. It provides engagement, fulfillment, and a reasonably steady income.

The MacArthur Foundation Study   The MacArthur Foundation Study finds that complexity in the job environment stimulates independent thinking and action. Additional training fuels the mind. Level of education and degree of self-mastery (a "can-do" attitude) predicts who will be most productive in or out of the workplace, the study reports.

Will Additional Income Affect Taxes and Social Security?

If you decide to continue to work in one form or another (working part-time, freelancing, consulting, beginning a second career, or starting your own business), know how your additional income will affect your taxes and any Social Security or pension plan payments. At the time of this writing, as far as Social Security payments are concerned, you can earn up to $14,000 annually without losing any benefits if you are sixty-five to seventy. (If you earn more than that amount, your Social Security benefits are partially reduced, but you will receive credits that raise the benefit once you stop work or pass age seventy.) After age seventy, you can earn as much as you want. Your earned wages are subject to withholding for income tax, Social Security, and Medicare even if you are receiving Social Security benefits.

In general, the federal income tax laws apply equally to all taxpayers regardless of age. However, certain provisions give special treatment to older Americans. Taxpayers sixty-five or older benefit from a higher gross income threshold for filing a federal income tax return. (You are considered sixty-five on the day before your sixty-fifth birthday.) Taxpayers who qualify and meet the age requirements may benefit from credit for the elderly or the disabled; exclusion of gain on the sale of their home; or an increased standard deduction. (For more specific information, refer to IRS publication #554. Call 1-800-829-3676 or explore www.irs.gov.) Hopefully, you work to enjoy more out of life than pay income taxes!

Interestingly, in 1990 the U.S. Department of Labor began reporting that paychecks had become the second greatest source of income (after Social Security) for Americans between sixty-five and seventy-four.

Summary

Many people retire *from* something: a boring job, a demanding boss, or an uncaring company. These people may not know what they are retiring *to*. Other people think they are missing out on something. There is so much being written about how to retire without missing a beat or a dollar. The advertisements show gracefully aging couples playing golf or tennis—actively enjoying their retirement village home. Consequently, after a few months these new retirees may become restless. The trick to a successful retirement is to know yourself—your talents and your aspirations. So instead of being buffeted about by forces outside of yourself (whether they be family members, societal pressures, or marketing campaigns), make plans and become involved with what you want to do during your "golden years."

In future years, you will find less linear thinking about retirement and life in general. In modern times, life has been school, job, then retirement—or learning, working, then playing. Retirement is becoming more integrated. You may continue working in some way, performing volunteer work, taking a class, and, of course, playing.

Get in touch with yourself, then find the best vehicles (forms and combinations of play, volunteer work, or for-pay work) to help you achieve personal growth and fulfillment. Feeling productive is important. Choose endeavors that interest and challenge you. Set up a support group that will offer suggestions and reassurance. Then go for it.

As the ancient Chinese did, give yourself a new calendar. With that retirement calendar, quit counting the hours, days, and years. Give yourself permission to try new outlets to transform your life into the one you want.

CHAPTER FIVE

Financial and Legal Issues

The number one topic among retirees is money. When you hear the term *retirement planning*, you can bet people are talking about how to make and invest money. This is not surprising, since finance has become the dominant force in our society. Most retirees, however, experience added pressure because they are depending on income not related to their daily life. We're no longer "working for a living." For better or worse, all of us must understand where we stand financially and what our relationship is with money. Each member of a couple or family must grasp economic reality.

In many families, money and legal matters have never been openly discussed, and financial planning has not been a crucial issue. Retirement may well change all that. The amount of discretionary time skyrockets (which can have either good or bad monetary implications) and steady pay for your work disappears. You will be inundated with well-orchestrated campaigns designed to sell you something (from products to "expert" services). There are many sad stories of retirees who have floundered because of poorly executed plans. With planning, your story can be a happy one.

You are in charge of your financial well-being. To improve your economic health (and your financial security), you can take several steps. The earlier in life you take these steps, the better the results. And, it is never too late!

1. Take in more than you spend—ideally, at least 10 percent more.
2. Whatever you decide to purchase—buy low, sell high.
3. Never put your money into something you do not fully understand.
4. Understand the difference between quality of life and standard of living.

There are many ways to ensure a financially viable retirement. You do not have to have a guaranteed pension; you do not have to have a million dollars saved; you do not even have to have Social Security. All three of the above certainly help, but many options and possibilities are available. Consider a pensionless couple in their early eighties. Recently, they shared with us that they had never worked in positions that offered retirement benefits, and they had not saved more than $5,000 before they reached age sixty-five. They had been able to buy some land ($50 down and $50 per month). Then, over the years, they built a small house and kept adding to it. A few years ago, they sold the house and the thirty acres, bought another house for cash, and had enough left over to invest. That profit, Social Security, and a little income from wooden bowls he turns on a lathe provide more than enough for their happiness. As you can see, there are many avenues and combinations to consider.

How do you feel about money? Though somewhat unusual to consider money and feelings, you probably have deep beliefs about it and its purpose. Envision yourself as first fantastically rich—and then dirt-poor. How does the presence and absence of money impact your self-image? Are you more lovable, important, powerful, or more secure with money? We often pretend money is not so important, but deep down we may feel otherwise. A little self-analysis may help bring about a more balanced notion of the role you want money to play in your life. Discuss your conclusions with your spouse or partner. Try to understand each other's position. When couples seek counseling, money is considered a "problem" in more than 50 percent of the cases. Yet almost all have more than adequate income to cover their needs. Their beliefs and attitudes toward money lie at the core of their unhappiness.

One common factor found among all types of contented retirees is an awareness of their financial situation. Interestingly, this awareness is one of the key factors in a study of millionaires detailed in *The Millionaire Next Door* by Thomas Stanley and William Danko.

Calculating Expenses

Your first task in developing your awareness is to know where your money goes as it passes through your fingers (or checkbook) each month. If you are already tracking these expenses, this step will be easier than for those who have not yet begun.

Before you skip this section and start searching for how to make more money and invest more effectively, think! Do you want to invest in a company that has little idea of what its costs are? If you do, you are practically guaranteed a poor return on your investment. You expect a business to be on top of its expenses. Don't the most important expenses of all—your own—need the same kind of scrutiny and analysis? Nobody cares as much about your money as you do. Forget the "experts." It is your money. Find out where it is going.

Look back over your check stubs and credit-card receipts. For cash expenditures, you will have to do some educated guessing at first. Assign each expense to a category. Listed in Exhibit 5.1, page 140, are some possible categories. (You probably won't need many of these, or you may have to add a category.)

When you have totaled the figures for each category from the past several months, identify the biggest surprise. Look for places where you are spending more than you thought and areas where you are spending less. You will find many of the categories are somewhat discretionary (entertaining, groceries, etc.), while others maintain fairly fixed amounts (mortgage, property taxes, etc.). Remember: You are trying to obtain a solid understanding of how your money flows through your hands.

If you have a computer but not a personal finance program, now is the time to purchase one. Intuit's Quicken,

I recommend people strive to overcome this compulsion to accumulate more money. Instead, die broke.

RETIRED LAWYER
New York

Exhibit 5.1: How You Spend Your Monthly Money

Category	Amount	Category	Amount
Alcohol—beer/wine	_____	auto	_____
Auto cost (new or used)	_____	life	_____
Auto expenses		Investment fees	_____
gasoline	_____	Job-related costs	_____
maintenance	_____	Loan interest	_____
registration/tags/inspection	_____	Medicine	_____
Bank charges	_____	Mortgage principle	_____
Books, papers, magazines	_____	Mortgage interest	_____
Cable television	_____	Natural gas	_____
CDs and tapes	_____	On-line fees	_____
Charitable donations	_____	Personal care (hair, etc)	_____
Child care	_____	Pets	_____
Clothing	_____	Rent	_____
Computer equipment	_____	Restaurants	_____
Cultural events	_____	Sporting fees	_____
Dentist	_____	Sporting gear	_____
Doctor	_____	Sporting events	_____
Dry cleaning	_____	Tax preparation	_____
Education fees	_____	Taxes—federal	_____
Electricity	_____	Taxes—state	_____
Entertaining	_____	Taxes—local	_____
Garbage	_____	Taxes—property	_____
Gifts	_____	Taxes—Medicare	_____
Groceries	_____	Taxes—Social Security	_____
Home maintenance	_____	Telephone	_____
Home improvements	_____	Toys and games	_____
Homeowners dues	_____	Travel	_____
Hospital	_____	Vacation	_____
Insurance costs		Video rental	_____
property	_____	Water and sewer	_____
medical	_____		

Microsoft's Money, or one of several other products will make your tracking much easier over time. If you are computer illiterate, there are many reasonably preprinted tracking forms (such as Dome's *Home Budget Book*) available at an office-supply or large discount store. Or, you can devise your own system. Once you have your system in place, it takes only a few minutes once a week to keep everything on course.

Calculating Your Net Worth

List All Assets

The second step in your financial self-analysis is to identify all your assets (see Exhibit 5.2, page 142). You are interested in those items you own that could be turned into money. They include cash, money in your checkbook, certificates of deposit, stocks, bonds, real estate, vehicles, boats, furniture, clothes, etc. Take the time to list your assets, and make a best guess of how much each could bring you if you had to sell each. If you had to sell something, such as a television, it will probably fetch a much lower price than what you paid. On the other hand, 100 shares of IBM may be worth a lot more than your purchase amount. You want today's value on all your assets. Keep this list handy.

List All Liabilities

Next create a list of all your liabilities—the money you owe to someone else. Include mortgages and other loan amounts, credit-card balances, taxes, and any other obligations you have outstanding.

Liquid and Illiquid Assets

When you subtract your liabilities from your assets, the difference is your net worth. For retirement purposes, that

Like most retirees, I'd
spend more money, if
I had more money.
RETIRED TEACHER
North Carolina

Exhibit 5.2: Typical Assets and Liabilities

Assets	Liabilities
Liquid	Mortgage
cash	Other loans
checking and savings accounts	Credit-card accounts
money market funds	Taxes
U.S. Treasury bills, notes, bonds	
municipal and corporate bonds	
stocks	
mutual funds	
IRAs	
Keoghs	
loans to others	
Illiquid	
house	
real estate	
vehicles	
household goods	
clothing	

amount should be as high as possible. This number, however, can be somewhat misleading. If a high percentage of your assets is in instruments such as stocks and bonds, then you can sell quickly at predictable prices. These items are termed *liquid assets*. These have the advantage of returning a regular stream of cash (dividends or interest) to augment your income. On the other hand, if most of your assets are in items such as real estate, furniture, clothes, etc., then you would have a much harder and slower time converting their value to money. These items are termed *illiquid assets*.

Take a Look at Your Illiquid Assets

Take a closer look at your illiquid assets. As an exercise, examine every item in one room of your house. Classify each into one of four categories: essential for my survival; unessential but adds great enjoyment; a luxury I could live without; or clutter. Pay particular attention to that last class—clutter. As you conduct this personal inventory, recall how little money you could obtain if you tried to sell most of these assets. Ponder how many items belong in the clutter classification. It is a critical lesson for most of us to learn before we begin implementing a retirement financial plan. We do not need to add more clutter—especially expensive clutter. Indeed, we benefit from de-cluttering our lives.

Creating a Retirement Budget

Now that you know where your money goes each month, what assets you own, and what liabilities you owe—you can look to the future. What are your priorities for your retirement? What do you want to accomplish? What do you want to be doing? Start now affixing price tags to these tasks. As in a well-run business, you do not start a new venture without having some idea of what it will cost.

Develop a Budget for Each Venture

For each venture you want to undertake (new hobby, travel, relocation, education, volunteer work, etc.), develop a budget. If you plan to focus on photography, for example, how much do you think you will spend each month on film and processing? You cannot be perfectly accurate in this task, but give it your best shot.

Combine Current with New Expenses

Next, combine your current expenses with those new expenses for your retirement projects. In most cases, the total expenses will be less than what you have been spending while working. For example, won't your current clothing expenses drop once you're retired? How many vehicles do you need now that you don't drive to the office each day? Category by category, create your projected monthly expenses for retirement. Some work sheets simply advise to take your nonretirement expenses and multiply—by 0.6 for a "minimal" retirement, by 0.8 for a "normal" retirement, by 1.0 for extras, such as extensive travel. You can be more accurate by carefully thinking about what you'd like to do in retirement and how you'll do it.

Income Sources

Investments

Now, let's focus on what's coming in. First and foremost is your income from your *current assets*. Before retirement, you might have put your money into stocks or other growth investments. After retirement, if you need monthly income, you may reallocate some dollars to investments that pay regular dividends or interest. Total your interest and dividend income, rental income, royalties, and any other income you expect to receive on a regular basis.

Pension Plans

The next stream of income, for those who qualify, might be a pension or other type of retirement plan (IRA, Keogh, etc.). If it is your own self-directed plan, fine. Skip down to the IRA section. If you are part of a company plan, however, keep reading. First, you need current information about your plan. To obtain *Your Guaranteed Pension*, contact the Pension Benefit Guaranty Corp., 1200 K Street NW, Washington, DC 20005-4026; (202) 326-4000; www.pbgc.gov. Also, you may find useful *What You Should Know About Your Pension Rights* from the Pension Welfare and Benefits Administration, U.S. Dept. of Labor, 200 Constitution Ave. NW, Room N-5619, Washington, DC 20210; 1-800-998-7542; www.dol.gov/dol/pwba.

The basic knowledge you need to learn about your pension starts with the type of plan (defined plan, defined contribution plan, etc.). Obtain your plan administrator's name and phone number. You should receive the summary description, annual report, and survivor coverage data. Know if you are vested or when you will be. Know your years of service and if you can take early retirement (with reduced benefits). Determine at what age you can retire with full benefits. Think about whether you want to receive a lump sum or monthly installments for life. (Obtain a tax implication fact sheet from your plan.) Will your Social Security benefits be deducted from your pension benefits (called Social Security offset)? Does your plan include cost-of-living adjustments? You and your spouse must decide whether to decline in writing the "joint and survivor" option. Are your benefits insured by PBGC (Pension Benefit Guaranty Corporation)? This information is covered in greater depth by the publications mentioned above. All of the answers must be made available to you by your plan.

IRAs

Most self-directed retirement plans (Keogh, 401K, and IRA) fall into the category of tax-deferred plans (except for the relatively new Roth IRA). Once you pass the age of fifty-nine, you can withdraw from them without penalty, but you must pay tax on all that you withdraw. (The tax has been deferred, not forgotten.) If you have a Keogh, 401k, or tax-deferred annuity plan, you can usually roll the amount over into an IRA without penalty. Naturally, most individuals like to keep as much in their IRAs as possible, since they still can accumulate dividends, interest, and capital gains on a tax-deferred status. Once you reach age seventy, however, you must start withdrawing or pay a stiff penalty in addition to the taxes. The amount you must withdraw to avoid the penalty is based on a life-expectancy table. Obtain the IRS Publication 590 (IRAs) by calling 1-800-829-3676 or download it from www.irs.gov. If you have the tax-free Roth IRA, then you may withdraw at will (since you paid tax as you contributed).

Everybody needs to take a 10 percent discount. The world would be a better place.

RETIRED

PHOTOGRAPHER

New York

Social Security

Social Secursity comprises a significant income stream for many retirees. Unfortunately, the high number of soon-to-be retirees jeopardizes the viability of the current system. You can roughly calculate what you might draw from Social Security (if there are no future changes) by asking for a Request for Earnings and Benefit Estimate Statement. Call 1-800-772-1213 to request this application or fill it out on-line at www.ssa.gov. Generally, you will be able to take a reduced Social Security benefit at age sixty-two or the full benefit at sixty-five. Recent legislation postpones full benefits to those born from 1943–1954 until age sixty-six. The full benefit age does depend on your date of birth.

Adding It Up

Now, you have compiled (or guesstimated) the three income streams of retirees: interest or dividends from savings and investments; pension annuity and/or withdrawals from individual retirement accounts; and Social Security. Add the numbers together to attain a rough retirement income. Compare it with the projected expenses you've calculated. How close are you? The ideal target is to have at least 10 percent more coming in than going out.

In addition, you might want to try various computer-driven retirement planning aids. T. Rowe Price's Retirement

Planning Analyzer is fairly complete. Call 1-800-638-5660 (approximately $20) for a copy. The Optimal Retirement Planner, at www.dp-net.com/orp, uses several mathematical formulas to provide the best scenario.

Your Plan

If you are like many people, the above calculations do not offer a feeling of great security. The projected expenses often exceed the projected income. Even if you are currently in the black, future inflation or unknown or escalating expenses could change the situation. You must improve your plan in order to gain a better financial balance.

Decide What's Necessary

The first step in refining your expenditures is to decide what's necessary as opposed to what's nice. Now you see the reason for including all involved family members in these exercises, because what's essential to one may be considered frivolous by another. As all of you plan for the future, try to focus on the kinds of activities, types of feelings and the personal rewards you want. Don't focus yet on what you must buy to achieve those goals. For example, a few years ago we wanted to see Alaska. Since we had time, there was no need to rush through this immense state. By researching and talking to Alaskans, we found we could visit the inland passage islands in spring, the mainland in summer, and drive back to the Lower 48 in early fall. By using the state-run ferries before the start of tourist season, we were able to take our van and stay a couple of days on each island. The transportation cost for our seventeen-day "cruise" for the two of us and our vehicle totaled less than $400. A similar itinerary advertised by a cruise line cost more than $3,000 each—without our van and the time to really visit each port. The cruise line included a complimentary bottle of champagne. For the price difference, we figured we could purchase a better bottle of wine and experience a much more realistic view of the inland passage. When you have time, you have options.

Think Broadly

Another tip learned from many contented retirees is to think broadly. To continue with the Alaska example, if all we'd looked for was the cheapest package to Alaska, we'd have cut off the opportunities (and savings) of the combination we chose. Your goal must be improving the quality of your life (rich experiences, peak moments), not raising your standard of living (spending more). And, you typically pay extra for "convenience."

When you think of starting a new retirement venture, take baby steps. Try to figure out how to experience the new undertaking without paying exorbitant amounts. You can rent or borrow equipment (bicycles, tents or RVs, boats, golf clubs, tennis rackets, skis, etc.) to give it a trial run. Not only will you have a better idea of how much you will enjoy the new activity, but you will also know what to look for when you do buy a necessary item. The experience may even change your plan. For example, staying in a condo on a golf course convinced us that we did not want to live there. The machinery used to manicure the golf course was too noisy for our sensibilities.

Predicting Your Monetary Needs

Refining and predicting your monetary needs is easier, of course, if you're not planning a move or other big changes during retirement. For those organizing new ventures, a little research provides educated estimates. Finally, try to live on your projected income (with your projected expenses) for a couple of months. Determine the accuracy of your plan. (Think of it as a test market study in business.)

Augmenting Your Income If you need to augment your income, open yourself up to a variety of ideas. Is there something (part of your house, for example) that you can rent? Can you take a part-time job? Perform a service for pay? Make and sell something? Turn a hobby into income? Find seasonal work? Consider what you have, what you like doing, and where you are, then start looking for opportunities. After all, the Colonel Sanders story is true. Take one older, minimally educated man with a chicken recipe. Add a willingness to ask for only a small percentage of increased profits. Stir in a lot of persistence (he was turned down by restaurant after restaurant). Finally, he became a multimillionaire. Even without his millions, you get the idea.

Your Tracking System

Knowing Where Your Money Goes

The first activity of this chapter, categorizing your monthly expenses, becomes the basis for your system to keep up with your money. For those who are already tracking, look for ways to ensure accuracy by all members of your household who use it. For those who don't track expenses, now is the time to begin. (It's only important if you want to be financially solvent.) You can track by putting receipts in agreed-upon boxes or baskets, then adding them up, entering amounts in a ledger, or using a personal-finance computer program. As long as it works for you and you are diligent in keeping it up, it is a good system. You might find, as many have, that creating a graph or chart makes visual what you do day-to-day (and shows of you're headed in the right direction).

Cut Costs

Next, look for ways to cut costs. Don't forget that Wall Street loves the cost cutter (stock prices usually soar). The reasons are obvious: You have control; lower costs are equivalent to tax-free savings; you have a lower dependency on higher income; the process is incredibly freeing! Think back to when you started out in the world. Perhaps you had a basic car and a few possessions. You could take off at a moment's notice for a fun excursion. You could see out the rear window! Since those days, all the clutter you have accumulated ties you down. Simplify and find better ways to use your time than spending money.

Buy Wisely

Become a materialist instead of a consumer. Learn to truly value the few material objects you use and refuse to consume disposable items. If you care about the country's future, you can cast no stronger vote than by buying and not buying specific objects and services. In a free-market society, companies respond more quickly to economic trends than to political activity. Use your intelligence and values to purchase what is best for you—and the planet.

Saving on Expenses

Frugal is good; cheap is not. Learn the difference by using such diverse resources as *Your Money or Your Life* by Vicki Robin and Joe Dominguez, *The Tightwad Gazette* by Amy Dacyczyn. On this theme, PBS produced two remarkable shows, *Affluenza* and *Escape from Affluenza*. Sort out what makes sense for you and your lifestyle.

Note that for every $1,000 per year you can save on expenses, you gain the equivalent of having another $30,000 in an interest-bearing savings account ($30,000 at 5 percent yields $1,500 before subtracting federal, state, and local taxes).

To make the most of your cost-cutting time, use this strategy. Pay particular attention to any of your upcoming big purchases. Revisit your budget categories and rank them from the highest expense to the lowest. Then, concentrate on the top group to see where you can lower costs (often significantly). For example, if you need to carpet your house (a big item on the expense list), allot extra time to look at options—perhaps a nearby mill that sells roll ends at less than wholesale. Don't be cheap; be frugal.

You are looking for a vehicle. Buy new or used? What brand and model? Look for the most reliable, efficient choice, with the fewest options. If you prefer new cars, see how much you can save on a "partially used" version (demo, dealer loaner, short-term lease return, last-year's model, etc.). Even when factoring in depreciation, you can often save hundreds to thousands of dollars. With a little research and a lot of thinking, it is not too difficult to save a bundle over what you might have purchased. Learn to roll the amount of a new car payment into a "new car fund," so next time you can buy with cash rather than paying hundreds of extra dollars of interest.

Investigate *Consumer Reports*. Computer users can check the current bargain price for many high-ticket items at the Center for the Study of Services' Web page, at www.checkbook.org. This kind of homework can enhance your life without breaking your budget. You can employ the same strategies when thinking about insurance, medical care, prescription drugs, etc.

We encourage people to periodically check their service providers (for example, AT&T as a long-distance carrier) to make certain they're receiving the best deal. On auto insurance, we advocate carrying an umbrella policy that covers expenses beyond collision. Such a policy costs us about $150 per year.

RETIRED COUPLE
Illinois

Buying Insurance

When it comes to insurance, many retirees buy policies through AARP. Before you do, understand that AARP markets selected policies from standard insurance companies—it does not provide insurance of its own. In return for allowing these companies to use its mailing list, AARP receives 2 to 3 percent of the policy premiums, which in 1994 amounted to $146 million! Analyze these policies as you would those of any insurance company—compare and compare again. When *Money* magazine looked at the AARP-marketed policies in its July, 1995, issue, it found a few mediocre offerings (homeowners and auto), two poor ones (long-term care and life), and a couple of pretty good choices (Medigap and hospital-surgical). In other words, be a smart consumer.

Life Insurance On life insurance, do not take out any new policies upon retirement. Instead, find out the monthly premium of any policy you are considering. Then create a mandatory savings draft into your money-market account for the same amount. (And, increase the amount each year—as the insurance company would.) The odds are excellent that your estate will accumulate more money by using that technique than from receiving the proceeds from the insurance policy.

Reduce Interest Payments

How much are you spending each month on interest (mortgage, car loan, credit card, etc.)? This debt expense must be one of your first targets for reduction. Your goal is to have others paying you interest (savings)—not the other way around. If your mortgage is two or more points above the current interest rates and you intend to stay put for at least three more years, investigate refinancing the mortgage. (One retiree says that though he waited too long to refinance, he is now saving about $800 per year with the lower interest rate.) First, pay off all credit cards. Next, pay down your mortgage as fast as you can.

Live Below Your Means

In short, don't live your life to impress others. Stay out of debt, and live below your means. Carefully define what you desire, then use your creativity. Use your extra time to learn how to do things for yourself—repair, fix up, build, cook, keep books, do taxes, invest, or paint. You can always hire experts or purchase ready-made items, but try it yourself first.

In one year you will make more than a thousand purchase decisions. It's likely that on each item, you could have saved a little without sacrificing your quality of life.

Some other money-saving ideas include: Retire your life insurance; cut his and/or her hair; make gifts of time and creativity rather than money; share newspapers and magazines with friends; freeze food in season; order prescriptions from a large discount drug company; use coupons; sell your car; shop your insurance needs; quit smoking; move to a less expensive place; swap services with others; avoid convenience items; rediscover tent camping; have potluck dinners; and select hobbies that are cash-neutral or -positive rather than cash-negative.

You might want to take a look at the successful *Unbelievably Good Deals and Great Adventures That You Absolutely Can't Get Unless You're Over 50* by Joan Rattner Heilman, now in its tenth edition. On-line sources for living well while acting frugally include: a site with lots of links, www.best. com/~piner/frugal.html; the home of *One Income Living in a Two-Income World*, http://members.aol.com/DSimple/index. html; the Simple Living Network's www.slnet.com; the free www.stretcher.com; and, mainly for subscribers, Mary Hunt's www.cheapsk8.com. If you like to play what-if scenarios (Do I buy or lease? How much do I need to save? What are the recommended amounts to pay down on debt, or invest?), try out the financial calculators at www. financenter.com.

An E-mail comment from a new retiree in new Mexico generates this tip: If you soon plan to sell an asset such as a house, do not be cheap on your fix-up and repairs. Frugal is always good, but cheap, shoddy work can cost you when it comes time to sell.

Robert L. Veninga sums this up well in his book *Your Renaissance Years: Making Retirement the Best Years of Your Life*: "... a successful retirement is not contingent upon great wealth. But a successful retirement is dependent upon living as if you are wealthy."

We both had learned early on of the danger of buying things on credit. We limit our credit cards to two and use only one most of the time. We pay them off each month. That way we don't have to pay any interest.

RETIREES
Florida

Investments

Savings

Savings might be considered the salary you are willing to pay yourself. What is your self-worth to yourself? The sooner you consider yourself worthy of a salary, the more you will benefit later. A yearly $2,000 savings/personal salary put into an IRA

A favorite true story is of a master sergeant who retired from the air force in the late 1960s. He joined in the 1940s without a dime in his pocket. In his new career, he got "free" housing, food, clothes, and a salary. He sent some money back home to his folks, took a bit to spend on himself, and, with assistance from astute superiors, set up an account with a stockbroker—to invest half of his take-home pay. He had no idea what stocks or blue chips meant, but he did know that saving (paying himself a salary for the future) seemed the right thing to do. During his twenty-year career, he sent half of his pay to his broker. He never owned a car (he always used public

starting at age twenty-five would easily be worth $270,000 at sixty-five; the same amount at age forty-five would be worth only $71,000 at sixty-five. Regular, steady savings are fundamental to a successful future. Unbelievably, fewer than half of America's working adults systematically save for retirement! Who do they think will take care of them?

Staying with the personal-salary metaphor, think of what to do with your bonuses, which come in the form of receiving gifts or inheritances, selling something of value (real estate, a business, vehicles), or winning the lottery. Reserve part to pay the taxes due, save most of it, and keep a little for something special beyond the usual expenses. A special $5,000 "windfall" can be blown away quickly or it can be allocated, for example, $1,500 to taxes, $3,000 to your future, and $500 to a special treat. If you choose that allocation, the $3,000 saved will pay you a minimum of $150 per year for life.

Investing Your Savings As your savings grow, you need to invest them in several places. First, there should be enough ready cash to handle six to ten months of normal living and small emergencies. Ready cash works best for you in a money-market account. Typically, the money market pays higher interest than a simple savings account.

Categories of Investing Basically, there are two categories of investments. The first is where you "lend" your money or, at least, let others have use of it for their own purposes. In return for that, they pay you interest. The second is where you "purchase" items you think will increase in value, for example, stocks, real estate, art, and other collectibles. Always remember that no place is completely safe for your money; there are only varying degrees of risk.

Interest Income

Banks, S&Ls, and Credit Unions For interest-paying investments, start by exploring banks, savings and loans, and credit unions. You will find savings accounts, certificates of deposits

(CDs), and money-market deposit accounts. The advantage to their products is that your deposits are usually federally insured, which give you good security. The disadvantage is the low interest rates these institutions pay.

Brokerage Accounts In recent years, brokerage houses have begun to offer accounts and instruments that look and sound similar to those offered by banks. At most brokerages, you can have check-writing privileges, different money-fund options, CDs, and a host of other interest-paying choices. The advantages are often higher interest rates than the banks offer and are more flexible alternatives. The disadvantage is the lack of federal insurance, though practically all brokerages maintain private insurance to a much higher amount than the banks.

U.S. Treasury Investments Next, examine the offerings of the U.S. Treasury. You can choose from Series EE Savings bonds, treasury bills (thirteen weeks to one-year maturity dates), treasury notes (two-to ten-year maturity dates), and treasury bonds (thirty-year maturity dates). Minimum amounts range from $25 for the EEs to $1,000 for the four to thirty-year obligations to $5,000 for the three-year-or-less maturity dates. The great advantages of these investments are safety, low or no commissions, ease in selling, and interest may be free of state and local income tax. The disadvantages are low rates. Intermediate-term treasuries are generally preferred by conservative investors. You can buy direct from the Federal Reserve Bank, through your bank, or through a stockbroker.

Ginnie Maes Also, you can "lend" your money by purchasing Ginnie Maes (GNMAs). These are pools of mortgages backed by the federal government. They pay slightly higher interest than the Treasuries because of an unsure maturity date. (For example, if interest rates drop, homeowners refinance. You are paid off. Suddenly, you have cash instead of the GNMA.) You buy and sell these through a broker.

Municipal Bonds Similar to treasury bonds, you can loan your money by buying other types of bonds. For example,

transportation), lived on military bases all over the world, and, by his own account, had a rich, fulfilling career. When he retired at age thirty-eight (with a military pension), those systematic investments in such companies as IBM and Xerox had put his net worth at more than $1 million!

you can buy from other governmental units (municipal bonds) or businesses (corporate bonds). Generally, municipal bonds have the sought-after advantage of being tax-free. Often, their lower interest rates have better take-home results for people in the upper tax brackets. (Retirees, however, must consider whether this "extra" income will force them into paying more tax on their Social Security income.) The bonds are rated for financial strength because they are not insured. The higher-rated bonds pay lower interest, but there is less chance of them becoming worthless.

Corporate Bonds Similarly, corporations issue bonds, which, too, are rated financially (by Moody's and Standard & Poor's). The ratings are similar to report cards: AAA, AA, A, A-, etc. By the time the rating hits B, it is considered a "junk" bond. Again, the higher the financial rating, the lower the interest, but the safer the investment. You can buy these bonds through a brokerage house. Find current rates for various ratings and length of maturity in the *Wall Street Journal, Barron's,* or *Investors Business Daily.*

International Bonds Finally, you could purchase international bonds. When interest rates are low in this country, they may be higher in others. Be cautious, because you not only have to evaluate the risk (without a financial rating system), but currency fluctuations can change the bond's value.

Advantages and Disadvantages of Bond Investments The strength of investing in bonds is, first, you can choose how much risk you take versus how much interest you receive. Second, they will probably offer higher rates than treasury or bank offerings. The disadvantage is the difficulty in buying and selling. Because there are so many possibilities (thousands of issuers and many maturity dates), it takes an astute bond trader to find you the best deal when you are buying and the best price when you are selling. If you are going to hold them for a long time (or until maturity), this difficulty is minimal.

The buy/sell skill is important because bond prices fluctuate and the quotes come in two types: bid and ask. (The difference is called the "spread.") To confuse you further, the price (what someone is willing to pay for a bond) changes opposite of interest rates. So, if interest rates suddenly increase from 6 to 10 percent and a certain bond pays 6 percent, no one wants to spend as much for the 6 percent one. They can easily purchase a new 10 percent bond. Of course, the converse is true, as the holder of an 8 percent bond is happy when interest rates drop to 5 percent, since that 8 percent bond is now more valuable to a potential buyer. To buy and sell bonds regularly requires that you find a competent brokerage house with bond traders who know how to work the spread for you. You might consider a bond mutual fund. (See the mutual fund section beginning on page 162.)

Annuities You can also "lend" money to an insurance company in what is known as an *annuity*. These instruments are often sold with death benefits, reflecting the insurance heritage. They return your money plus interest to you via monthly payments for a fixed period of time, monthly payments for life, or in a lump sum. Calculating their worth requires some effort, because fees and commissions are subtracted from the total rate of return. Advantages are that they pay reasonable interest (with some tax-deferred advantages). The disadvantages are their lack of liquidity and complexity compared with many alternatives. If you consider one (they are actively sold because of high commissions to the salespeople), check out the insurance company's rating in the *Annuity Shopper* or in one of the lists from A. M. Best (at many libraries).

Stocks

Common Stocks

The next option for where to put your savings is purchasing items you believe will increase in price (land, art, gold, silver, stocks, etc.). Unlike lending your money, there are no promises of a certain income, such as 6 percent. Indeed, there is the possibility of loss. In return for taking this risk, there is the possibility of much higher monetary gain than with the interest producers. For example, the common stocks that comprise Standard and Poor's 500 have yielded an average gain of 13 percent per year from World War II to 1997 (much higher than any interest-paying option). Thus, the most recognized purchase for many is common stocks. You buy a small part of a company and hope that, over time, it does well. If so, its profits rise (as does the price of the stock when others seek to buy it). Some of the stocks will regularly return a small amount of money in the form of a dividend. The dividends are paid, however, only if the company is profitable. Of course, there is no guarantee it will continue paying that dividend.

Preferred Stocks

When you begin to investigate common stocks, you may notice another type of stock called *preferred stock*. Large companies often issue this in addition to their common stock. Preferred stock actually resembles a corporate bond. The dividend is high (in line with interest rates), and the price of the stock tends to vary inversely with interest rates (again like a bond). Unlike common stock, the preferred stock price won't increase dramatically if the company does well. If you are still intrigued by preferred stock, focus on preferred that can be converted to common.

To make more money in common stocks than you would by simply using one of the above interest-paying instruments requires a bit of homework. The potential return is worth the effort, but first consider whether you have the time and interest to devote to this type of investing. Many people get cold feet at this point and think they can avoid personal exertion and still reap big rewards by either hiring a financial adviser or by putting their money into a mutual fund. Letting the experts play with your money may work to your benefit. Remember, they are paid if you win or lose. No one has as much interest in your money as you. You can learn enough to be as good or better then these outsiders. (The average expert does worse than random picking.) At the least, learn enough to understand what these managers are doing with your money—and why.

How to Buy Stocks

To buy stock, rely heavily on what you know. You are trying to predict the future. What will people be buying and using six months, a year, and five years from now? What companies do you think are on the right track? Stick with familiar items and easily understood businesses (a tactic used by the richest investor of all, Warren Buffet). Once you have several companies in mind, start your research. You are trying to buy low, which means you are searching for good buys in companies you think will do much better in the coming months. You also want to diversify. That is, you try to buy companies that do different things. That way if one of your predictions does not come true, you have other possibilities for gain. No "expert" ever predicts correctly 100 percent of the time. A great track record is to pick six winners, two so-so, and two losers out of ten. To shoot for all winners is absurd.

Think Long Term Another key to success (besides diversification) is time. Over a twenty-year period, carefully chosen stocks tend to do well (better than any other standard investment). If you must have results next month or within two years, the stock market may not be the way to go. It fluctuates (often wildly), so the safest way is to think long term. A healthy sixty-five-year-old retiree could easily live twenty or more years—more than enough time to benefit from long-term investments.

Research the Companies With those concepts in mind, head to the library (or Internet) and start researching your companies. Great resources are the *Wall Street Journal, Barron's,* and *Value Line.* You might start by reading in *Value Line* what your company really does. (It may surprise you.) Or, look at the numbers—the stock's current price, its yearly high and low. (Is it at a low price now?) The first ratio you will need to learn is price-to-earnings or P/E. It means the current price of the stock, divided by the company's most recent earnings (profits). So, a $15 stock that earned $1 profit per share has a P/E of 15. If the earnings rise to $1.50 per share, than the P/E is 10. If the company loses money, there is no P/E. As you ease into this number way of talking, you will find that P/E is valuable as an indicator of how good a buy the company might be. Companies with high P/Es are considered pricey (high price compared to low earnings). They may be worth it. There may be reasons: Last year was an off-year; a great new product is coming out next year, but the company is paying for the research and development now. No P/E, or a high P/E (more than twenty), should raise a red flag for more careful scrutiny.

Buy Low, Sell High

Understand that the herd mentality is based on emotion. When the market is booming (a bull market), there is a feeling of excitement, and the herd wants to buy and spend. When the market dips or crashes, there is a feeling of doom and the herd wants to sell. Notice that these trends translate to buy high, sell low—a great way to lose money. You are looking for the opposite track—buying when a stock is at its low point and selling near the high mark. You can never know those exact points (perfect timing is impossible), but internalize the philosophy. You do not want to buy and sell with the herd.

Learning About Stock Investments

Books have been written on how to pick stocks, and hundreds of "systems" have been promulgated as surefire winners. Find good companies with good products at good stock prices, hold on to them, and you will do well. Below are some of the best sources to help you learn about stock investments:

- *The Only Investment Guide You'll Ever Need* by Andrew Tobias.
- *The America's Finest Companies Investment Plan* by Bill Staton; The Staton Institute, 300 East Blvd. B-4, Charlotte, NC 28203; 1-800-779-7175; www.statoninstitute.com
- The American Association of Individual Investors (AAII), 625 N. Michigan Ave., Chicago, IL 60611; 1-800-428-2244; www.aaii.com
- The Motley Fool Web site, www.fool.com

Every brokerage house (Charles Schwab, Merrill Lynch, etc.) has a wealth of free booklets covering every phase of investing, with special emphasis on stocks. (After all, commissions on buying and selling are how they make their money.) You can also learn more by joining others in an investment club or by taking a continuing education course on investing.

Often, blue-chip stocks (large, established companies) with steady dividends are better bets in a down-market than the smaller, more growth-oriented companies. Beware of hot tips and other such advice.

Choosing a Broker

When you choose a broker or brokerage house, be a smart shopper. Does the person you are dealing with make his money from a commission (off your buys or sells) or is he paid a salary? Naturally, there is a temptation to recommend a certain buy or sell if you are obtaining a commission. This practice does not mean you cannot find quality, honest, commission-based brokers. You must select carefully too; commissions vary widely. If you intend to be active in the stock market, pay close attention to a broker's commission schedule, and ask how much valuable information might be provided to you for free. (This component is critical for intelligent picking of stocks.) For more information on how to select a brokerage house and broker, contact the National

Association of Securities Dealers, 1735 K Street NW, Washington, DC 20006-1500; 1-800-289-9999 (public-disclosure hot-line); www.nasd.com.

Exercise Caution

Be cautious about anything more complicated than basic buying and selling of common stock. Such devices as puts and calls (naked and covered), options, selling short, etc. may be pitched to you. People can make money using these mechanisms. Since they are more like gambling than investing, the real winners are always the brokers. When the promises of fantastic money and "sure" profits sound too good to be true, they are. Never consider attempts to sell to you over the telephone. The second caution is the temptation to invest in commodities. (Didn't you always want to own some pork belly futures?) To quote money guru Andrew Tobias on commodities, "If you speculate in commodities . . . you will lose money. In fact, it is even possible to lose more than you bet."

Mutual Funds

Professional Managers

To navigate in the wide world of investment possibilities, people often turn to professional managers, who create mutual funds. Many individuals give money to this professional, who in turn purchases various amounts of stocks, bonds, etc. If the choices are good, the mutual fund's value rises with the prices of the purchased investments. Of course, the opposite is also true. If prices fall, the mutual fund falls. One thing that will not fall is the management fee you pay to the professional every year (from 0.15 to 2 percent). In other words, if you bought the same stocks and bonds, you would beat the fund because you would have no management fee. Also, keep in mind that more than 75 percent of the stock mutual funds *underperform* the market. The key to successful investing using mutual funds is finding a manager who is worth his or her fee and who can beat random picking.

No-Load Funds

The thousands of funds can be divided into two camps: those that charge no commission for you to buy or sell them (no-load funds), and those that have either a front-end commission or a back-end sales charge (if you sell before holding a few years). There is no compelling case to look at anything except the no-load funds. (They have performed as well or better than their loaded counterparts.) The funds categorize themselves by what the manager generally buys and sells—aggressive growth, small caps, international, junk bonds, gold, etc. These categories help, but they overlap and create gray areas.

Advantages of Fund Investing

Funds can be a good alternative to straight investing. You seek to diversify into areas you know little about (for example, small biotechnology companies); you want some bonds but do not want the hassle of bond trading; you would like to invest on the potential of a certain index (such as Standard & Poor's 500) increasing. There are specialized funds for all these possibilities and more. Remember the tricks: Know your prediction for the future (for example, you think Europe will rebound next year) and pick a solid fund manager (in this case, a great European stock picker).

Flexibility of Buying Funds

Buying into a family of funds offers flexibility. You can switch from one to another as your predictions of the future change (from balanced to aggressive growth because you think a boom is coming). When you switch funds, however, you will probably also be acquiring another manager. Many brokerage houses allow you no-cost switching between families of funds, allowing you even greater flexibility.

Do Your Research

Intelligent buying of funds requires research. (Do not put your money into something you do not understand.) *Morningstar Reports* is a publication devoted to analyzing and grading mutual fund performance. Most of the personal finance magazines (*Money, Kiplinger*, etc.) carry mutual fund ratings. These ratings act as guides, because they tell you what happened previously; they cannot predict the future. After you pick a few highly ranked funds for careful scrutiny, you must determine if the manager has changed and if the fund has altered recently (grown too fast or switched its focus). Either of these conditions could make the past performance irrelevant. Try to discover how much, if any, of the manager's own money is invested in the fund. Be leery if the manager will not put his money into his own fund.

Illiquid Investments

You can invest by purchasing land, buildings, oil-well partnerships, gold, silver, art, and collectibles—and hope their value escalates. The same premise holds true: Buy low, sell high. Seriously consider these options only if you have real knowledge in the field. Include calculations of any maintenance fees (taxes on real estate, storage fees, or special insurance) as they eat into your possible gain. It may be hard to sell these assets when you are ready. There is also risk in assuming that these same assets will increase rather than decrease in price. The most fundamental of these purchases are those that do double duty—real estate that is also your home, art that decorates your rooms. These are useful investments and the promise of monetary gain is sec-

Our retirement financial strategy is based on investing in income property. Investment property, while not being as fast-growth as the stock market over the past decade, provides better income stability and is inflation-proof (rents follow cost of living).

TRADE CONSULTANTS
Newly retired

ondary. Others that work well are situations in which you are active in the purchase and management—for example, buy an old building and rehabilitate it or build a house on raw land.

Savings Allocations

Diversification

Most advisers recommend that you keep your money diversified, which provides a safety net, in case the future changes dramatically from your predictions. For example, to grow money fast, it makes sense that you allocate a lot to growth stocks and keep a little cash. If the stock market suddenly dips, however, not only will you not grow money fast, you will actually lose money—at least, on paper. (You do not actually lose unless you sell at that lower price.)

Stock Dividend Reinvestment If you think long term, one of the best things you can do for yourself in the stock market is called dividend reinvestment. Go with a broker who allows you to participate in dividend reinvestment with no commission. (Called DRIPs, you can participate directly with the company or through your broker.) Each dividend you receive is used to automatically purchase new stock. For example, if Sprint Corporation is paying a 25-cent quarterly dividend, and you own 100 shares, then the $25 is used to buy as much stock as it can on that day, perhaps .33 shares. You now own 100.33 shares. As time passes, this buying and compounding becomes significant, especially when the company raises its dividend. You still pay taxes on these dividends, but the overall compounding effect is well worth it. While you put no more cash into your investment, the effective dividend yield starts to rise (because you own more and more stock). If the overall market takes a nosedive (but your companies are still profitable), do not worry. Now, at this lower "sale" price, the dividend is buying you even more shares of stock. When the market rebounds, those fractional shares will also rise.

Buying Double of a Stock Another technique to diversify (and to relax about when to sell) is to buy double of a stock. Find one you like, at a good price. Buy 200 shares—all at once or 100 now and another 100 a few weeks later (the price may continue to fall). Either way, within a month or so, you own 200 shares. Set a target price for what you would like to see this stock hit in a year or two. If it hits that price, then start monitoring carefully until you think it is as high as it will climb. Sell 100 shares and look for another investment. The other 100 shares remain in your account and grow. If you sold too early (stock keeps rising), you feel all right since you still own 100 shares. If the stock stagnates or dips, that's okay, too. You use the profits you made off the sell of the first 100 shares. Either way works.

Allocating More to Money Market and Bonds You may not want as much of your savings in stocks (including stock mutual funds), if you think the market is unsteady or if you need the income to help with day-to-day expenses. In those cases, you would allocate more to money market and bonds. You might still want to have some of your savings in stocks (especially dividend-paying stocks) to take advantage of possible growth.

Examine Your Savings Distribution Once a Year Once a year or so (perhaps on your birthday or New Year's Day), examine your savings and how they are distributed. Rethink your predictions for the future to see if you need to make modifications. Always have some readily available cash. Will inflation skyrocket? Real estate often does well during inflation. Will inflation be under control or will deflation occur? Bonds do well, as does cash when it comes to stagnation and deflation. Will we continue muddling along the road to prosperity? Own well-chosen stocks so that you too can participate.

How to Hire a Financial Adviser or Planner

If you feel you must employ a financial adviser or planner, realize that this individual is someone who sells advice. You want to find the best for your money. Some advisers charge a fee for their service; others charge by taking a commission from what you buy and sell; others use a combination fee/commission. You must know how the adviser charges for his services. Advisers and their plans can vary greatly. Always ask to see sample plans. You are looking for a planner who listens carefully to your situation and develops a clear, easily understood course of action, and spells out timetables, responsibilities, and risks.

The more you know about your finances, the better your odds are of finding and working with a quality planner. For many, a consultation with a quality financial adviser/planner is well worth the fee. Contact the National Association of Personal Financial Advisors (NAPFA), 355 W. Dundee Rd., Suite 200, Buffalo Grove, IL 60089; 1-888-FEE-ONLY; www.napfa. org who represent fee-only (rather than commission-paid planners), or the Institute of Certified Financial Planners, 3801 E. Florida Ave., Suite 708, Denver, CO 80210-2544; 1-800-282-7526; www.icfp.org. (Certified Financial Planners have received training in insurance, taxes, retirement, estates, and investment planning.)

Quality of Life

As mentioned, the overall goal of retirement financial planning is to aid you in improving your quality of life, not necessarily raise your standard of living. Our society has become so obsessed with money that we, the individual members, have a difficult time defining our wishes, dreams, and plans without using money as the primary ingredient. Retirement is the time to create a high quality of life without depending on money. A simple meal shared with a companion served with a spectacular sunset in the distance reflects great quality of life. If you prepared the meal and found the place, the monetary cost is minimal. Sparkling water, beautiful music, loving people, or a smile from someone you have helped all add to the quality of life—at no cost. Travel, great music or literature, pursuing a new hobby—all of these are available by investing your time and creativity, not your money. Focus on these wonderful opportunities and redefine your life, from "how much" to "how."

And for those with the will to believe in the possibility of the simple life and act accordingly, the rewards can be great.
DAVID SHI
Author and
university president

Financial Summary

That's it—enough to get you started, at least. Let's reiterate:

1. Take in more than you spend—ideally, at least 10 percent more.
2. Whatever you decide to purchase—buy low, sell high.
3. Never put your money into something you do not fully understand.
4. Understand the difference between quality of life and standard of living.

Important Legal Papers

The basic challenge for all who reach retirement is to put your affairs "in order." You will face legal issues (some familiar, some new), and you'll have far better chances of a positive outcome if you have prepared.

Preparing a Master List of Your Records

First, make a master list of your records and contact people/institutions. Pretend you are managing a business (your life) and suddenly someone must take over for you. What does your stand-in need to know in order to function? Below are some items to include in your list. Add or subtract particulars to fit your situation. Update the list about once per year.

- List each family member with birth date and Social Security number.
- Identify locations of birth certificates, marriage license, divorce decree, passport, vaccination (and other health records), powers of attorney, living will, vehicle registration and title, deeds, and titles.
- Create a list of any paid advisers (including address

and phone number), such as stockbroker, tax pre-
parer, accountant, life insurance agent, financial planner, and lawyer.

- Detail location of will plus name, address, and phone
  number of executor.
- Detail location of trust(s) plus name, address, and
  phone number of successor trustee(s).
- Specify safe-deposit box(es) location, name of owner,
  how to access, and contents.
- List your income sources with a phone number for
  contact.
- List your bank accounts with account number and
  contact.
- List your brokerage account(s) plus any stock and
  bond holdings in your possession.
- Detail your employee savings, retirement, stock, or
  pension plans.
- Detail any other monetary accounts you manage
  (children's trusts, etc.).
- Specify real estate holdings with location of deeds,
  tax records, mortgages, etc.
- List each credit card and loan with account number
  and contact.
- Detail location of your tax records.
- List each insurance policy (life, health, and casualty)
  with number, limits, and who to contact.
- Specify funeral preferences and location of burial
  plot, columbarium, etc.
- Detail any other important records.

Legal Concerns

Retirement is a terrific opportunity to take more complete
control over your affairs. In a hectic world, it is easy to turn
to an expert rather than learn to act for yourself. As in the
financial realm, an avalanche of legal information is available
for those who want to understand their options.

Social Security

Legal concerns that impact retirees more than the general population revolve around Social Security, medical care, and estate planning. With Social Security, for example, you consider the implications of divorce and/or remarriage. Your estranged spouse may have a valid claim to part of your Social Security benefits (and it will not affect yours). If you marry, how will that impact your Social Security income and your new spouse's Social Security income? Contact Social Security to obtain *Understanding the Benefits* (Publication No. 05-10024). Call 1-800-772-1213 or download it from www. ssa.gov. The rules are not that difficult (far easier then understanding an IRS 1040 form).

Medical

Retirees may experience increasing legal and financial problems created by their more frequent contact with the medical system. Look, for example, at a couple of practices that are now illegal. A nursing home tries to require a "responsible" party to sign the admissions contract or to require an agreement stipulating you will pay private rates before converting to Medicaid. A hospital suddenly claims that Medicare will no longer pay your hospital costs. (The hospital must give you written notification, including the date from which you are expected to pay. You can then request through your doctor or hospital a review by the Peer Review Organization [PRO] — the local PRO phone number is available in Appendix B, State Resources, from the hospital, or from the local Social Security office.) The trend of convoluted, confusing practices such as these, unfortunately, appears to be on the rise. You must be vigilant about what you sign or agree to when you deal with these medical entities. The AARP offers free legal counseling for the elderly. You can contact your state's Department of Aging, the Medicare regional office, and your local Social Security office when you think you need assistance.

Much of the rest of special legal needs for retirees revolve around maintaining personal control of your affairs in the face of the medical and legal establishments. As one Indiana couple puts it:

> Early on, the first priority must be writing a living will for the edification of your partner, kith, kin, and medical man. There-after, do not falter. Compose your durable power of attorney for health or appointment of a health care representative.
>
> Finally, push to establish a general power of attorney to cover the overseeing of matters financial. Any steam left? Arm yourself with a lot of sourcebooks, and put together a made-for-you living trust. The thought of avoiding probate keeps you happy the whole long while this project can take.

Advanced Directives

No matter your age, one of the first legal concerns for you to consider is an advanced directive, a declaration of how you want to be treated medically when you are unable to communicate.

Living Wills

The most common directive is known as a living will. You use a preprinted form, or simply write out what you want done and what you do not want done medically if you cannot communicate (for example, if you're in a coma). All institutions that participate in Medicare are required to recognize an advance directive. Each state, however, has its own laws concerning how a directive is worded and implemented. Your best living will (fill in the blank or custom written) is tailored to your state and/or hospital. If you travel, you might carry more than one, since states differ. A few states have recently begun to require that another living will is executed if the person discovers he or she has a terminal illness.

Durable Power of Attorney

The second type of advance directive is called a durable power of attorney for health care (or, alternatively, appointment of a health-care representative or health-care proxy). In this document, you appoint someone to make medical decisions for you if you are incapacitated. You may specify conditions as you did in a living will. The paper is signed, witnessed, and notarized as is any legal document. Depending on the state, in which you live you may want to execute both of these documents. Make copies and give them to those close to you so they know about the directive(s). Ask your doctor to make them part of your permanent record.

Call 1-800-989-WILL or (410) 962-5454 to request an advance directive kit tailored to your state from Choice in Dying ($5.00 per kit), 1035 30th St. NW, Washington, DC 20007. Or, download free forms from www.choices.org. Also, check your bookstore or library for such guides as: *How to Write Your Own Living Will: With Forms (Self-Help Law Kit with Forms)* by Edward A. Haman.

Estate Planning

The term *estate planning* has become a hot topic in financial planning circles. Whenever you see a "hot" topic, you can be relatively sure a few folk have figured out how to make a lot of money off it. Simply, if you die today, you leave an estate (all of your assets and liabilities). Since some of these items have your name attached to them (house, vehicle registration, credit cards, owed taxes), some procedure is needed to take care of them—pay what is owed and dispense the rest. Each state has laws that provide for that process. In effect, you do

I have a will that's very specific about the distribution of my assets, a power of attorney (appointing my daughter to act on my behalf), and a living will so that I'm not plugged into any machines that would keep me alive unnecessarily.

RETIREE
North Carolina

not have to do anything to "plan your estate"; it's already done by your state. Of course, before you die you can put in place a few documents that will tailor to your wishes this process of paying and dispensing.

Dispensing Your Assets

The simpler your family situation and your wishes as to the dispensing of your assets, the simpler the documents needed to ensure it happens. For example, if you are married, property listed as owned by the two of you as "joint tenancy with the right of survivorship" automatically transfers to the surviving person. If you want to pre-dispense part of your estate, you can give up to $10,000 per year tax-free to each of your beneficiaries while you are alive. (This practice avoids estate taxes later and this way you experience their reaction.) Also, ensure that any life insurance policies and retirement-benefit plans have current beneficiaries listed.

Wills

The basic document everyone can (and should) put into place is a will, a written record of how you want your estate handled, who is supposed to assure it happens (the executor), and who receives what (the beneficiaries). You sign this paper, which is witnessed and notarized. After you are dead, the will stands on its own as a record of your wishes. Note that you can have only one will in effect. (The most recent one rules. After all, you might change your mind occasionally.)

Preparing a Simple Will Wills are not difficult to write and a few states still recognize the hand-written version. The easiest way to prepare simple will is to purchase some fill-in-the-blank forms or use a personal computer's family legal program. Choose the version that makes the most sense to you and your situation.

If You Need a Lawyer Most situations rarely call for a lawyer. Still, you might have complications due to your family (such as ex–stepbrothers-in-law or disgruntled former stepchildren) and/or asset holdings (such as holding companies within limited partnerships). Another reason to involve a lawyer is if you lack a capable person to serve as executor. Examine such books as *The Complete Idiot's Guide to Wills and Estates* by Stephen M. Maple and Steve Maple.

Appointing an Executor You must appoint an executor in your will (as you may be appointed an executor in someone else's will). What are the duties of an executor? Is a lawyer necessary? Since each will and each state presents special concerns, these are not simple questions. Generally, the role of an executor is almost totally administrative (picking up forms, filling them out, turning them in)—not legal or requiring legal fees. If a lawyer becomes necessary to help with a specific task, the executor can always hire one at an hourly rate (not a percentage of the estate).

Probate The steps of probate are fairly straightforward. First, the executor opens the estate for probate by going to the local probate office (usually called the registrar of wills) and procuring the correct forms to file with the court. The executor then inventories the estate, just as you did your own asset inventory in this chapter—complete with estimates of each asset's current value. This step generally has a two-month time limit. Subsequently, the executor must pay taxes: federal inheritance tax (if any), state inheritance tax (if any), and income tax from the deceased's last tax return until the time of death. The estate can then be closed (through the court) after time is allowed for the filing of any claims that might be made against the estate. Finally, according to the provisions of the will, the executor is allowed to distribute the assets to the beneficiaries.

After death, the state uses a probate court to ensure the will is executed properly. The state wants all the title name changes done correctly, debtors paid off, taxes collected, and probate fees and assessments paid. It is this last part—probate fees and assessments—that prompted one independent financial planner/lawyer to lead a revolt some thirty-five years ago against the probate system itself. Norman F. Dacey's *How to Avoid Probate* created great shockwaves throughout the probate legal establishment on its way to becoming a number-one best-seller. Dacey wrote of the good-old-boy network often found in local probate systems, detailing how the system frequently prolonged the settlement of even simple estates for years, while it garnered large fees and assessments. Dacey explicitly demonstrated how anyone can put an end to that for his or her estate.

The Dacey Trust Thus, the second major document that can ensure your wishes are carried out is the living *inter vivos* trust or, as it is now known, the Dacey trust. A living trust puts your wishes into effect now—while you are alive. You create a trust in which you, the grantor, appoint yourself as the trustee for your assets. If you are married, you can create a living bypass or family trust (so your spouse will receive the unlimited marital deduction). In the trust, you appoint a successor trustee (similar to an executor), and identify beneficiaries as in a will. Next, you transfer your assets into your trust. Assets such as bank and brokerage accounts simply require that you provide a photocopy of your trust to the institution and, perhaps, signing one of its internal trust forms. Thereafter, the John Doe account is known as the John Doe Trust account. That's it. For tangible property, such as real estate whose deed might be recorded in a county or state office, you provide a copy of the trust with a quick claim deed showing the transfer from John Doe to John Doe Trust. (There may be a small charge to register the paperwork.)

Once your assets are in a living trust, all continues as before—you still pay taxes as if the assets were in your name without the "trust" afterward. Once you die or are incapacitated, the successor trustee can step in and administer the trust. There are no probate fees or probate delays. In addition, note that the successor trustee can take charge upon your incapacitation, which makes the living trust function as if there were a durable power of attorney in effect. Other advantages of a living trust over regular probate are its privacy (not public court record) and its ability to transfer titles across state lines (good for those with assets in more than one state).

Do-It-Yourself Living Trusts If you ever decide to change your trust, simply amend it and provide copies to the institutions involved. If you decide to revoke it, follow the establishment steps in reverse. You will see advertisements and solicitations for "free" seminars on how to establish a living trust. Before you fall for these marketing gimmicks, check out a do-it-yourself book from the library or local bookstore. If you have a computer, investigate one of the personal-lawyer software programs. (Check for a simple trust form on-line in the Everyday Law Series, at www.halt.org.) For most people's situations, the standard trust forms are adequate. Many resources are available, including *Make Your Own Living Trust* by Denis Clifford; *Understanding Living Trusts: How You Can Avoid Probate, Save Taxes and Enjoy Peace of Mind* by Vickie and Jim Schumacher; *How to Properly Plan Your "Total" Estate With a Living Trust, Without the Lawyer's Fees: The National Living Trust Kit* by Benji O. Anosike; and *The Living Trust: The Failproof Way to Pass Along Your Estate to Your Heirs Without Lawyers, Courts, or the Probate System* by Henry W. Abts, III.

Do You Need an Estate-planning Expert?

Beyond the simple living trust, many variations have erupted, as legal professionals seek to offset the loss in probate income with a gain in the trust business. Several of these variations take advantage of the tax system's peculiarities. These variations may help dodge some estate taxes (especially for estates greater than $1,000,000), while they generate preparation fees for the law firm. There are a variety of irrevocable, testamentary trusts that can be used for special situations. If you think you fall into one of these categories, and tax avoidance for your heirs is high on your priority list, check with an estate-planning expert. Be sure that the expert is truly versed in estate plans. Most lawyers have had a one-semester course in trusts (all types of trusts) and are not necessarily up-to-date on the latest in the field.

Decide on Legacies

As you put your estate in order, this is the perfect time to analyze legacies you would like to establish. As one couple points out, "How much do we want to give the children? How much do we leave our community? Can we establish a quality scholarship?" In other words, where will the money you have accumulated over the years do the most good? And you can start the giving while you are alive.

Legal Summary

For other legal matters, arm yourself with as much information as possible. Try to create a paper trail (copies of everything both going and coming). Investigate whether a governmental body can help (often slow, but they're free). Check on seminars, legal clinics, self-help books, Internet resources, and so on. Some of the most comprehensive offerings to assist you (both books and software) are produced by Nolo Press, 950 Parker St., Berkeley, CA 94710; 1-800-992-6656; www.nolo.com. The more knowledge you possess, the better your chances are of obtaining what you want, with or without a lawyer.

If you need an attorney, compile a list of those in your area who handle cases similar to your needs. Seek referrals from friends or businesses. Interview those who are recommended. This interview should be be free, and the lawyer must be willing to come up with a written fee agreement. If not, keep looking.

Questions for your interview might include the following.

- What is your experience with cases similar to mine? What were the outcomes?
- What are your fees? If there is a percentage, what does it include? Are there other costs?
- How long will the work take? Who will perform the work (the lawyer, an associate, or a paralegal)? Is the billing rate the same for each?
- How will we (you and the lawyer) work together? What if something goes wrong?
- Can we put all this into a lawyer-client written agreement?

The complexity of your case dictates the type of answers and type of lawyer you want. There are wide differences in lawyers' abilities and experiences. Simple items may leave you with lots of options; complex cases may call for a more expensive, skilled specialist.

In summary, to maintain personal control of your body, complete an advance directive. To ensure control over your asset distribution, prepare your will, establish a living trust, and transfer your assets to the trust. Take out your calendar and schedule time to complete these items. Each interviewed retiree who had completed these "tasks" felt satisfied about their situation and freed from bothersome burdens. Those who had not, typically said, "For years, I've been meaning to get to it" or "I've been thinking about researching that." It often takes more energy to procrastinate than it does to accomplish a chore. Legal paperwork is no exception.

Common sense and a level head remain important. In spite of the jargon and complexity of our society, you can maintain control over your affairs.

CHAPTER SIX

Here or There Decisions: Where to Live or Travel

Deciding where to live is one of the hottest topics concerning retirement. Several books are devoted to this question, while countless newspaper and magazine articles continue to rate the best locales. People are more mobile today than a century ago, but most do not pick up and move during retirement. (Interestingly, about half of the baby boomers think they'll move when it's their turn to retire—compared with about 25 percent today.) For all the touted migration to the sunshine states, there is also a significant (though smaller) reverse migration occurring a few years later. What is important to know is your definition of home. So, ask yourself, "What makes a place my home?" Then, you can ask, "Where is best?"

Start your decision-making process with an inventory of your needs and wishes. Areas of concern and interest might include: housing, proximity of family and friends, money matters (cost of living and taxes), part-time job opportunities, availability of necessary services, transportation options, climate, travel desires, recreational opportunities, safety concerns, your comfort with the familiar, and your desire for the new and exotic. If you have a partner, compare notes. Rank your collective needs (what's necessary) and wishes (what's nice) in order of importance.

Early on, start flirting with possible retirement areas. Florida is not the only choice.

RETIRED MINISTER
South Carolina

Think and talk about the qualities that make a home. Consider your present situation. If you decide to move, how long it will take to build a support group of friends and acquaintances? It takes less time for full-time travelers or for those who choose a retirement community, since everyone's "new" to the situation.

Be pragmatic and realize that doing nothing is not always the best solution, either. Small problems (such as house and yard maintenance) may become burdens. Other people move or die. Your status changes without a "job" and its title. Most important is to predict where your retirement goals can best be fulfilled. Decide over time, jotting down ideas and saving them. One day, pull them out and evaluate. With this knowledge in hand, read through the possible choices detailed in the rest of this chapter.

There is no Utopia, but there are lots of possibilities—and you can try more than one.

Types of Housing

Before detailing the choices of where you might want to live during retirement, let's cover the type of "home" you might want to establish—for the short- or long-term. Each option has strengths and weaknesses. Know yourself, understand what you like—and what bothers you.

The Single-family House

We'll start our list with the most traditional—the single-family house. Home ownership includes such positive benefits as control, privacy, tax benefits, and possible financial gain if the property appreciates. Home ownership also includes the disadvantages of a lot of maintenance (which ties you down), property taxes, insurance, mortgage interest (if you have a loan), and difficulty in leaving (selling) when ready. During retirement, maintenance becomes increasingly problematic, as the house is aging (requiring more repairs) and your physical ability is declining (necessitating hiring others to make repairs).

Condominums

A second ownership possibility is a condominium. In most condo developments, you own the interior of your unit, while you and the rest of the owners (as an association) own the exteriors and common grounds. Compared with a stand-alone house, condos are generally cheaper. There is less maintenance to think about, lower taxes, and the possibility of financial gain if property values escalate. On the other hand, there are issues over which you have less control than in a house: privacy, management, maintenance, regime fees, and special levies. Some of these fees may escalate beyond your comfort level, and you may have difficulty selling when you are ready.

Buy all the things you need. Make all the necessary repairs to your home. You're not going to do these things later when the money isn't flowing as it once did.
ARTIST
South Carolina

Mobile Homes

You can purchase a mobile home (manufactured housing), whose main appeal is its comparatively low cost. It is the one ownership, however, that will depreciate in value rather than appreciate. The quality of the units is uneven; financing options can be few. Bad weather (such as tornadoes and hurricanes) can cause havoc with the mobile home and, consequently, your safety. If you live within a park, you could run into other problems, such as utilities, congestion, noise, and rising lot rents. If you choose this alternative, obtain *How to Buy a Manufactured Home,* Manufactured Housing Institute, 2101 Wilson Blvd., Suite 610, Arlington, VA 22201; (703) 558-0400; www.mfghome.org.

The RV or Boat Option

Another option growing in popularity is to hit the open road or seas. You own your shelter (an RV, tent, or boat), you stop in a private or public park, create your own camp on public land, moor at a marina, or anchor in a protected cove. You have high flexibility about where and when you want to "settle for a spell." However, your shelter will depreciate in value, and if you choose an RV or boat, you are likely to have significant maintenance costs. If you are a couple, you will quickly discover if you can live together twenty-four hours a day. Those who desire a more social setting can opt for travel clubs, caravans, and groups.

Living in a High-Rise

For city-lovers, a possible decision is to inhabit a high-rise. You could either buy (a condo) or rent (an apartment). High-rises offer security and low maintenance, with a feeling of community. Well-adapted inhabitants compare it to a small village that still offers personal privacy. Some tout the feature of locking up and taking off for extended trips. If this style sounds appealing, investigate how many residents leave for summer or winter. Of critical importance is how well you mesh with your neighbors and staff. You will also need to examine the building's financial records and maintenance history, because a new boiler, roof, wiring, etc., can demand hefty fees from the tenants.

Shared Housing

Rare though growing in popularity is shared housing. The idea is to have separate quarters for each individual (or couple), with shared common rooms. It is cost effective and provides social and emotional support (with the right mix of people). Think of it as a variation of a simple commune or Israeli kibbutz. Sometimes as simple as the "Housemate Wanted" classified ad to group-sponsored larger facilities, the best source for information about this alternative is from Shared Housing Resource Center, Inc., 6344 Greene St., Philadelphia, PA 19144; (215) 848-1220. For a directory of programs, write National Shared Housing Resource Center, 321 E 25th St., Baltimore, MD 21218.

Rentals

Another option is to rent an apartment, condo, or house, which has the advantages of little or no maintenance costs, property taxes, interest, etc. You can leave an apartment soon after you make the decision to do so. On the other hand, your money for rent is straight expense. You earn no equity, and privacy or noise may be a problem in some units. Retirees often use rentals as a temporary, cost-effective way to check out a possible location for their new residence. If you're looking at a particular complex, see if the owner or manager lives on the premises.

Senior Apartments

A variation of the standard rental is the senior apartment. In some locales, these are frequently government run and subsidized. In others, they are run by private or not-for-profit groups. Generally, they have design features to assist older residents, security, and, occasionally, transportation service, plus one or more meals per day.

Retirement Communities

You can also buy into or rent residences within a larger retirement community. (Many types of communities will be covered in greater depth later in the chapter.) Retirement communities are generally examined because you feel less capable and want extra services available, and you are looking for other retirees interested in similar social and recreational activities.

Status Quo

One of the first options to consider is maintaining your status quo. For those who own their own home, this decision generally means little or no mortgage payments, known strengths and flaws in your house, and not having to put up with the complications of moving. You probably have an established circle of friends and acquaintances, and you are familiar with local shops and services. If you desire part-time work or volunteer opportunities, you already know what your community has to offer. And, there is the intangible importance of maintaining one's roots. Do not discount the sentimental attachments you have accumulated over the years.

Your present situation probably involves people of different ages and interests, which can be stimulating as you age. If your neighborhood has new residents from other generations and cultures, that can be positive, too. Depending on how long you have lived in your home, you may have adapted to your climate. (It is all too common for people who move not to like their new climate any better, though for a different reason.)

Opportunities in Your Current Location

Look critically at your present situation. Try to imagine it next year, in five years, or in ten. Are you making new friends each year, or do you socialize with the same old crew? Have you recently become involved in a new activity? To stay alive and independent during retirement, you want to remain or become active. Are these opportunities available in your current location? Or are you in a deep rut?

Reverse Mortgages

A few retirees find themselves wanting to stay in their home but are unable to figure out how to do it financially. Even if you are in good financial shape now, an unforeseen medical event, nursing-home stay, or any unscheduled monetary setback can put you in the category of "house-rich, cash poor." Several financial companies have instituted reverse mortgages targeted toward people older than sixty-two whose homes are paid off and where the real estate values have greatly escalated. Basically, a loan is made to you in one of three ways: as a lump sum; a series of monthly payments; or a line of credit. (The line of credit option has proven to be the most popular.) As long as you live in the house you do not have to make a payment on the loan. Each month the amount you owe grows greater, drawing down how much of the house (equity) you own—but it can never rise higher than the value of the house. Whenever you sell, or if your estate sells, the loan must be repaid in full. You must continue to pay all taxes, insurance, as well as guarantee all repairs are done. There has been abuse within this system—be cautious. Call the Housing Community Clearinghouse, at 1-888-466-3487 to find a nearby local agency with free or low-cost counseling. You can also contact the nonprofit National Center for Home Equity Conversion, 7373 147th St. W, #115, Apple Valley, MN 55124. For $1 and a self-addressed, stamped envelope (SASE), the center will send a list of preferred counselors and lenders. In addition, you can download a conversion calculator from HUD, at http://huduser.org:73/1/2/ finance/worksheet.

Another Home in the Same Community

You might consider moving to another location within your community. This possibility allows you to build on the strength of the familiar, while providing a fresh start. If you happen to buy smaller, you may have a pocket of cash to invest.

Travel or Relocate for Part of the Year

An additional variation is to stay put most of the year, but travel or relocate for a few months. With a bit of creativity and research this option can be done inexpensively. Travelers can camp, keeping accommodations and food expenses to a minimum. One Minnesota couple posts us regularly on their exploits since retirement. Now in their seventies, they have tent-camped on all their travels. She keeps meticulous records in her journal. She recently shared that during a nine-year span, they visited places throughout North America, traveling more than 46,000 miles in their journeys. Their total expenses, including all fees for places such as Disneyworld and Opryland, were only $5,716! They count their experiences as priceless and far more fulfilling than any standard tour or traditional travel option. If you have never camped, try a few small trips first. You can often borrow or rent the equipment. If you want to try RV travel, again, borrow or rent for some trial excursions. Of course, you can rent an apartment or house for a short time in an area you find appealing. This, too, gets you out of the house and into new environs. To find the best deals, look for non-boomtowns or "forgotten" villages close to "hot" spots.

Changes You May Need to Your Current House

If you opt to stay in your house, be aware of changes you'll need. Try to organize maintenance so you can obtain help when you need it. For example, paint the interior when the house-painters need work—in the winter. Also, take steps to accident-proof your property. Less agile bodies (both yours and your friends) appreciate handrails and non-slip treads on stairs, throw rugs with nonskid pads, easy-to-use doorknobs, good lighting, grab bars, and nonslip surfaces in bathrooms. At some point, you may desire services not now required. Find out what is available for seniors while you are still active.

Volunteer a bit of your time at a service organization that helps the elderly. Your efforts will be appreciated; you will also see what is available for you in your later years.

Converting Part of Your House to a Rental Unit

Your home may have more room than you need. Some retirees have been successful at converting part of their dwelling into a separate apartment. They can enjoy additional income from rent and the reassuring presence of someone else on the premises. Local conditions dictate whether this is a good move. Look around at other rentals. Determine demand and the people you are likely to attract as renters.

Sharing space and human resources is an old, yet viable, option for various situations. On the surface, it has appealing features: cutting costs and combining personal strengths. These are the advantages similar to sharing your home by creating separate sleeping/work areas or an apartment. With family and friends, there is greater possibility of familiar emotional support in times of crisis. There is also increased peace of mind and a sense of security.

As we look more closely, however, certain problems arise.

First, consider the physical space involved. Is it adequate for your needs? Is there enough separation so all have a feeling of privacy? Next, do you enjoy being around all the people involved for any length of time. Consider how easy or difficult it might be to move on if things do not work out. (A short trial run would give everyone a good idea of how well the arrangement would function long term.) When sharing a space with family or friends, it is critical that the financial and chore arrangements be discussed at the outset.

People who try this arrangement report a higher degree of stress until everyone's role is established. If it is your children, the old parent-child relationship (on both sides) may be hard to resolve. It is difficult not to offer advice or make judgments (surefire destroyers of a pleasant relationship).Often, lifestyles do not mesh. Aspects such as food, neatness, and daily habits can become issues. You also must address the legal issues, such as a living will, durable power of attorney, who (if anyone) is a dependent, and so on.

Creating a Separate Apartment

Typical physical arrangements are accessory apartments created by making a separate apartment in a home, with one or more rooms and a separate kitchen. This conversion allows independence yet sharing as necessary.

Elder Cottage Housing

A more recent alternative in a growing number of communities is ECHO (Elder Cottage Housing Opportunity), allowing small, portable units that can be placed near a single-family house. They are equipped with plumbing and electrical wiring so that you can live independently yet be close to your family or friend's support system. Since placing a cottage on the property involves a zoning decision, you must check locally to see if one is permitted. One entrepreneur has designed a "tiny house" that is a handsome, all-wood, stick-built unit that can be constructed inexpensively by two people. Contact Tiny House, at 1-800-499-3201 or goodearth@rockbridge.ne.

New Locale

You want to investigate the possibility of relocating. People dream of a better climate with easier living and new beginnings. These dreams are most potent during a spell of lousy weather at home or when daily life has become unrewarding. Before you take off to find your Shangri-la, re-examine your self-evaluation and emotional planning for retirement. Have firmly in mind (or minds, if you are part of a couple) the kind of relationships and opportunities you want to experience in the next twenty years. These desires are far more important than the weather.

Why Aren't You Happy Where You Are?

Probably, the most critical question to ask is: What keeps you from being really happy where you are? Identify the concerns you have about your area (booming too quickly, escalating cost of living, or deteriorating neighborhood). Perhaps you have health concerns that suggest a move. Whatever your reason, the location of your home should provide the activities you want to enjoy during retirement. Consider your past record of making new friends. One well-adapted couple shares, "Because we had moved five times in the ten years or so of working, it was easy for us to readily make new friends at our chosen retirement location."

To find locales that will offer you the most promising possibilities, begin with the size of community you like. Choose a city with all its excitement, shops, events, and activities, and you also get the city's noise, pollution, traffic, and crime. Or, you could move to suburbia with access to shopping and city lights, and rapid changes, increasing congestion, and, often, sterile neighborhoods. Small towns offer basic services, a few accessible clubs and volunteer groups, the likelihood of stronger neighborhoods, and little traffic.

On the other hand, small towns can be stifling, suspicious of newcomers, and deficient in a wide range of opportunities. Villages can provide a feeling of community and togetherness (if open to strangers) yet bore many. Rural life provides a sense of independence and privacy but little social stimulation. Too often, no land-use planning or zoning can destroy your "perfect" retreat.

No place is ideal. You cannot use a guide to the best 100 and expect miracles. Know what you are looking for and why.

Retirement-Site Criteria

Natural Setting Let's examine possible criteria to use when searching. We would put the natural setting at the top of our list. That factor includes climate and scenic beauty. Do you relish woods, desert, ocean, mountains, or canyons? When you think of climate and comfort, go beyond mere temperature extremes. How do you feel about high versus low humidity? In one case, you may experience mold and mildew, in the other, dust and pollen. Try a few days in the "worst" season to see how you will adapt. Consider the probabilities of storms (hurricanes, tornados, thunder, blizzards), earthquakes, and floods. For accurate data on all of these conditions, contact the National Climatic Data Center, Federal Building, 151 Patton Ave., Asheville, NC 28801-5001; (828) 271-4800; www.ncdc.noaa.gov. You are narrowing down your list to what you prefer.

The small town we chose is intellectually stimulating—no more do we have to listen to other seniors' "organ" recitals. Too, the town is this Peyton Place. It's a microcosm of life, with all these strata of power struggles, for example, between natives and newcomers. I'm getting to know and relate to some of the locals.

RETIRED

TRANSPORTATION

CONSULTANT

Pennsylvania

Housing The next criteria might be the type of available housing (depending on your preferences). Look at the choices, availability, and prices. Cost of housing includes the land, structure, property taxes, energy costs, and maintenance requirements. If you are considering a condo, apartment, or other "managed" unit, examine the construction quality, noise factors, parking, pets, quality of management, and upkeep. At this point, you are not trying to buy. You are simply scrutinizing several geographic locales.

Community Aliveness A third criteria, and one that should raise a warning flag, is the presence (or lack) of warmth and aliveness within a community. This is hard to gauge, but there is a world of difference between quality of life in a warm, friendly setting and in a cold, uncaring one. Does your potential new home welcome retirees? Are services available? Are seniors who have moved here over the past few years actively involved in local events? Ask them. Were they accepted? Look for an abundance of cultural, recreational, and entertainment openings that match your interests. Do not overlook continuing education courses, lectures, workshops, and volunteer programs. Are the prevailing political and philosophical leanings comfortable? Are there intellectual challenges? Does this community have a good age mix? (For those who prefer to separate themselves from younger folk, read the retirement community section below.) In short, discern whether you live and flourish rather than merely survive here.

A Region's Economic Conditions Another criteria for limiting your search might be the region's economic conditions—an especially important consideration for those on a fixed income. Money will last longer in a "poor" area, but if you need part-time work, will it be available? Take the expense report you completed in Chapter 5, "Financial and Legal Issues," and examine how your expenses might be affected in this new community. The big-ticket items, such as insurance and taxes, may be higher or lower than in your current location. Check the costs on variables such as groceries, entertainment, and recreation. If you are concerned about taxes, look at comparative analyses on-line at www.taxadmin.org (or write Federation of Tax Administrators, 444 N. Capitol St. NW, Washington, DC 20001). While one category may be higher, several others might offset it. For example, a location near a fine-arts school may offer quality concerts, recitals, and art shows for free (or at a fraction of big-city prices), or a resort locale may have expensive food prices (especially in season).

How to Create Your Own List of Viable Choices

You can develop your own list of viable choices. One commercial Internet site, www.homefair.com, allows you to choose criteria with its "Lifestyle Optimizer." You can subscribe to the magazine *Where to Retire*, 1502 Augusta, Suite 415, Houston, TX 77057; (713) 974-6903. Or, you can take the initiative, as did computer user Gene Ledbetter, who looked at *Money* magazine's Web site, www.pathfinder. com/money/bestplaces, and found a list of 300 U.S. cities, with sixty-three quality-of-life factors for each. He picked three expenses most important to him: price of homes, property taxes, and cost of living. After some manipulation (tossing out the half with high-price housing), he came up with a ranked listing of eighty-six inexpensive cities. For him, the 1998 top ten were: (1) Sharon, Pennsylvania; (2) Decatur, Illinois; (3) Youngstown, Ohio; (4) Steubenville, Ohio; (5) Scranton/Wilkes-Barre, Pennsylvania; (6) Killeen/Temple, Texas; (7) Duluth, Minnesota; (8) Rochester, Minnesota; (9) Texarkana, Texas; and (10) Lawton, Oklahoma. Ledbetter didn't consider such factors as utility costs or entertainment options. That's why it is important for you to develop a list of factors important to the way you want to live.

Personal Safety As we age, we naturally become more concerned about personal safety. No one wants to live in a crime-riddled neighborhood. Media sensationalism aside, older people are less likely than any other group to be victims of violent crime. The single most effective weapon is to live in a close-knit, neighborhood community with a low transient

I've loved traveling and living abroad. My experiences have given me the expatriate's advantage of a broader outlook and a greater appreciation for living in this older home, this small but cosmopolitan town that's rather distinctive for America. These same experiences give me the courage to live my life the way I want.

WORLD TRAVELER

rate. If you use crime statistics to aid your search, focus on the burglary and mugging rates. (Those crimes most often affect the elderly.) In addition, check out the quality of both the police and fire departments.

Another safety issue is the presence of appropriate health-care facilities. Ideally, you would find well-rounded care and reasonable costs. You will probably have to settle for less, so it is doubly important to predict what you might require in the coming years. Look at your family and personal health history. Are you looking for good preventive programs, a solid choice in an HMO, long-term care possibilities, or alternative medicine? Each community will have strong and weak points in the medical-services arena, so you must prioritize your wishes.

How Do You Want to Live? Finally, look at how you want to live. If you enjoy travel, will you be close to highways and airports? Will day-to-day shopping be easy or a chore? Don't overlook the presence (or absence) of public transportation. Can you use a motorcycle or bicycle? Can you walk to nearby places? Can you share rides with others? Do local stores or food services deliver to the home? Aging can create problems with getting around. So it's nice to know you have options if you need them.

Entertainment How about entertainment? What are your desires for cultural opportunities? Be open, however, for as one self-proclaimed "cultural snob" reveals, "I didn't think I could live without the city. But in a small town, we all have parts in the community tapestry—doing, supporting. . . ."

Helpful Community Services If you would like to live independently as long as possible, then start creating a list of community services that may aid you. Look for personal and home health care, meals (such as meals-on-wheels), companionship, caregiver support, adult day care, chore assistance, and home repair. When you have a car that you can no longer use, consider donating it to the Kidney Cars Program, at 1-800-488-CARS. If you are part of a couple, several seniors suggest you consider what the locale will be like for a single person (the one left behind) in the event of one of your deaths.

Subscribe to Local Papers Once you have narrowed down your list of possible locations, subscribe to the local paper(s) for several months. These periodicals will show you opportunities and "introduce" you to other people in your new area. After several issues, you will sense how you might (or might not) fit in. If there is no local paper, how are notices communicated? Live a few months in your selected areas to evaluate firsthand your potential new home.

Check Out the New Location Before Moving Don't move before you've adequately checked out the new location. Employ the advantages of renting for a while. While there, reexamine all your day-to-day habits for the situations you forgot to consider. How is the local library? What is the restaurant situation (for quality and affordability)? Examine the nitty-gritty, too. For example, you have a couple of dogs that love to run free, but the town you've chosen has a strictly enforced leash law. Or, can you burn trash (a real concern of one Dallas, Texas, retiree)? Then, when ready to purchase, be careful not to spend more on housing than you can afford. (In other words, live below your means.)

As you build excitement for relocating, maintain your perspective. You may be moving away from family and friends, and will have to create a new support network. At this point, you might benefit from creating a systematic checklist for the house hunt. Develop your own list based on your personal preferences. The following categories might be useful:

- *General*: price, square footage, price per foot, financing, age, utility costs
- *Floor plan*: site orientation, size of each room with color scheme, and window treatments
- *Interior*: insulation, fireplaces, appliances, wall and floor treatments, wiring, and plumbing

- *Exterior*: deck, porches, fences, landscaping, trees, foundation, siding, and roof
- *Neighborhood*: overall appearance, zoning, traffic, power lines, privacy, restrictions, susceptibility to acts of nature, inclement weather provisions, drive time to services, and neighbors

For other checklists and tips, use your federal government by writing for a free catalog (with several home-buying booklets) from Consumer Information Center, Pueblo, CO 81009; (719) 948-3334; www.pueblo.gsa.gov (download free booklets), or try www.hud.gov.

The Final Test

Beauty is important in
a home.
RETIRED COUPLE
North Carolina

The last tip we'll pass along is to spend time on the lot where you think you'll build, in the house you think you'll buy, or the apartment you'll rent. Ask yourself, "Does this place feel right?" The process may sound magical. Of all the retirees we interviewed, those who seemed most satisfied say they had made their final choice only after using this "test."

Full-time Travel

A viable option for many is not to stay in one place, but to travel—domestically or abroad. We have traveled almost full-time during a ten-year period and are happy to report the experience exceeded our best estimates. Our travel has been restricted to North America; you might want to experience the world.

The crucial key to happy traveling is psychological. If you are with another person, how well do you get along (twenty-four hours a day, seven days a week)? Your attitude makes a world of difference. There will be frustrating times (as there are anywhere), but they can be magnified because you're in unfamiliar territory. With a sense of humor and wonder, however, the endless possibilities eclipse those moments of uncertainty.

You Can Choose Any State As Your Place of Residence

The mundane tasks are easy to handle. If you have no home base (primary residence or job), then you can choose any state as your place of residence. Consider one without a state income tax, such as Alaska, Florida, Nevada, South Dakota, Texas, Washington, or Wyoming. With permission to use the address of a friend or relative in one of those states, you can register to vote, obtain vehicle tags, etc. There are commercial services that will perform these services for you (for a small fee), including forwarding your mail. Look for ads in the back of *Trailer Life* magazine.

Forwarding Mail, Paying Bills, and Banking

With mail forwarding, we have never experienced a serious problem. Out of thousands of pieces, only a few political flyers and one roll of film were lost. When traveling, our mail is forwarded to us in care of general delivery at a small-town post office (where it is less likely to be misfiled). As for bills, we avoid those that must be paid traditionally. We charge everything to a credit card and then have the card's monthly total debited from our checking account. If a company cannot debit our credit card, we find a competitor that can. For banking service, try to choose interest-bearing checking, no-fee credit cards, and quality phone assistance. Our bank and its credit-card division have toll-free numbers so we can always check on our accounts. Our brokerage house is set up for travelers. We can monitor our account, as well as buy and sell stocks from any Touch-Tone phone.

Shopping

Shopping on this continent is easy, with little need for cash. If a grocery store does not take a charge card it will probably take your out-of-state check for the amount of purchase. (This is true in non-tourist areas only.) Also, traveler's checks are often available without service fees from auto clubs.

No Home Base

If you opt for full-time travel without maintaining a home base, you may be surprised at how inexpensively you can enjoy life. (When we travel we spend about one-third to one-half of what we spend when we're "settled down.") You will be freed of wondering how the place is holding up and of ensuring that all bills and taxes are paid on time. If the time to settle down arrives, you'll know. And you will have many more possibilities in mind thanks to your traveling experiences.

It Can Be an Adventure

If you like adventure, there are many avenues to explore. For example, one couple retired in their fifties (one was a college professor; the other, an elementary school teacher) and decided to try things that were new to both of them. Since neither had hiked, they elected to head east from Nevada and hike the Appalachian Trail! To become fit, they spent the winter on Gulf beaches, walking with empty packs on their backs. Each week they added a brick for weight, slowly preparing for the trek. They joined the other hikers in Georgia during the early spring and trekked half the trail to Harper's Ferry, Virginia. Then, to avoid harsh winter weather, they took the bus to Maine and hiked down the trail toward Virginia. They were soon passing the young hikers they had accompanied on the first half of the trail and enjoying a reunion party every night. After the hike, they taught themselves sailing, bought a small sailboat, and spent a year along the Intracoastal Waterway.

One winter, they rented a small house in a remote Labrador village. During a summer, they focused on visiting national wildlife refuges. There was a year vanning around Australia. Their retirement has been anything but boring.

Living Abroad

Traveling and Staying in other Countries

Foreign travel can take various forms. For many retirees, the extra benefit of time allows a leisurely sojourn—perhaps staying for years. When you have to travel fast (days and weeks), you are forced to spend more money, as convenience becomes a priority. A more leisurely pace allows you to rent and buy as the locals do, cutting costs and giving you a truer feel for the country. You can stay in hostels, boardinghouses, rented rooms, even American-style retreats or enclaves. (Do choose countries that welcome Americans.) Eat like the natives and try your hand at fixing the country's recipes. For ideas, start with *The Lonely Planet* guides, either in book form (at most libraries and bookstores) or on the Internet, at www.lonelyplanet.com.

Social Security and Medical Care

Special concerns about lengthy foreign travel or relocation revolve around Social Security and medical care. Several of the Medigap insurance policies do cover foreign care. Obviously, Medicare is not in effect. The quality of medical service varies widely around the world. It is wise to investigate any known needs before you set out.

Currency, Language, and Citizenship

Other concerns involve money, language, and citizenship. Currency fluctuations make budget predictions more difficult. Trying to speak the native language becomes a huge asset and you improve as you practice. In some countries, visas may require you to return "home" once or twice a year. Consider becoming a permanent resident and holding dual citizenship. The hardest adjustment for most, however, is the reality of being an alien. Information for Americans considering living abroad is available at www. escapeartist.com.

Retirement Community

The last ten years have seen rapid growth in retirement community options. Currently, less than 6 percent of the retired population choose these options, but that may change. The communities today may be merely a prelude of things to come to accommodate the aging boomers. Classifying the offerings by their foci and services creates a great overlap. The one factor common to all the community choices is age segregation. At some point, alternatives that do not impose such a barrier will likely arise. The first caveat for any of these alternatives: You will talk to the marketing people, who will show you the best possible side of their community. That's their job. Once you're "sold," you will have little contact with them. Therefore, you want to meet and evaluate the manager, the recreational or social director, and the dining hall personnel. These are the people you will deal with every day.

The Resort Community

The first classification we'll call a *resort community*. This is an outgrowth of country clubs and vacation resorts. Often built around a golf course, a pool, a beach, a horse riding area, etc., its emphasis is on leisure and recreation, focusing on the services it offers. The marketing is intense for the initial buyers, which makes resale (if you so decide) tricky, at best. While the community is being developed, many promises are made. Your concern must be the developer's solvency and the ongoing project's management. The board and the management company are the keys to success or failure. There are generally lots of recreational fees and no guarantee they won't change. For example, the facilities (such as the golf course or tennis courts) could be sold later to a separate organization, requiring you to join in order to use them. Investigate the clubhouse (or other center of activities) and look for your favorite interests. One of the most pressing concerns for many is: Will you find any mental stimulation? If you've decided on one of these resorts, the last caution is not to overbuy.

A Leisure Retirement Village

The next classification is a variation of the first, the leisure retirement village. The best-known examples of this group are the Sun Cities, developed by the Del Webb Corporation. Independent research studies reveal that retirees who adapt to these villages are indeed happy. The same studies indicate that these villages are less than a perfect choice for everyone. There are many appealing features. The ambience is one of country-club living. Often, the landscaping and lawns are taken care of for you. There are low property taxes because there are no children. (This is an adults-only community.) You can develop a network of people who are like you. There is a plethora of activities. And, for the fearful, there are security gates. For each of these benefits, there is a drawback: The assessments can rise (sometimes, dramatically); shopping may not be convenient; your grandchildren (or other children) can visit but not for extended times; individualism (even of your own place) can be frowned upon. (An architectural committee may want all units to look alike.) These villages are aware of current trends and are preparing additional features (such as work-at-home offices) for what they feel the baby-boomer generation will desire.

Smaller versions of retirement villages are also springing up. Many are offering more focused interests to enhance their market niche. One type is tied (or situated close) to a university or college setting. There, you can attend special or regular classes, take advantage of the cultural opportunities, and still be around younger people while maintaining a senior setting. Investigate these with the same caution you would use in any of the other options.

Active Adult Retirement Communities

Another group of living choices offers more than recreational activities; they include daily services, from food to medical. For example, all utilities, one or more daily meals, and all exterior maintenance may be included. Thus, on the surface they tend to be far more expensive compared with similar housing elsewhere. To accurately compare the financial aspects, you need to list all the services provided by any community you're considering. Next to each service write down what you spend each month for that category. Total your entries, compare, and obtain a truer picture of the costs. All of the above options have been lumped together by a few writers into a category called Active Adult Retirement Communities (AARC) to distinguish them from the choices below.

Continuing Care Retirement Communities

Geared toward the health consequences of aging, the next choice is generally known as Continuing Care Retirement Communities (CCRC). They offer long-term contracts to provide for many needs in one location. These communities attempt to maintain the full range of possible support services as you need them. Typically, you start in an independent-living section. As your health dictates, you can change to assisted-living or even skilled medical care. You have shelter and dining privileges (room and board), social assistance, health care, and support services all under your contractual arrangement. Most communities maintain public spaces, with additional services, such as a bank, library, hair dresser, café, and ice-cream parlor. Recreational and special programs are part of the features. There are generally no restrictions on your lifestyle. You may continue to travel, volunteer, and enjoy life outside the community.

Rentals or Equity-Based CCRCs can be divided into two groups: rental, and equity-based (those you purchase). The rental fees are based on yearly leases and often include meals. The rates do go up periodically, or, in CCRC lingo, "are adjusted." Find out the procedure of the community that interests you. In an equity community, you buy a condo that you or your heirs might be able to sell. (There may be a 90 percent buyback in place.) Many require a stiff entrance fee that may be partially refundable depending on the length of time you stay there. (This fee may be partially tax-deductible as medical expense—ask the CCRC.) You may still have a monthly fee. The ownership and management of these communities are often by for-profit corporations, whose responsiveness to the residents may vary greatly.

Accreditation for CCRCs The Continuing Care Accreditation Commission (CCAC) is the nation's only accreditation program for CCRCs. It is a big plus if the communities you're examining are accredited. Obtain a free Accredited Communities List from CCAC Publications, 901 E St. NW, Suite 500, Washington, DC 20004-2037; (202) 783-7286; www.ccacon line.org. Also of interest is www.retirement living.com, an Internet site hosted by the publisher of guides in the mid-Atlantic region, *The Guide to Retirement Living*, P.O. Box 7512, McLean, VA 22106-7512; 1-800-394-9990.

The Financial Aspects As you investigate these alternatives, attend closely to the financial aspect (can you afford it?), the small units (compared with your present dwelling), and whether you would be happy with the current residents. There are restrictive rules in this type of facility. If the community is sponsored by a nonprofit group, does it have any legal or financial responsibility (or does it simply have its name on the letterhead)? Look at the board of directors and management company. Is there an active residents' association? Look for a long-term vision and plan. (After all, this is a long-term promise.) What does the monthly fee cover? Any medical benefits? Can you choose your own doctor? Additional or extended services are often available for an extra fee. Thoroughly investigate the meal plan and setting, which typically becomes the heart of all social interaction. Talk to the residents. If at all possible, spend a couple of days at the center going through the day-to-day activities as if you were already a permanent resident.

Know All Aspects Before Signing a Resident Agreement
Finally, before you sign a resident agreement, read it carefully. Ensure that the community is properly licensed and certified, and, hopefully, accredited. Examine its disclosure documents, paying particular attention to its financial health. Can the CCRC require you to leave (for what causes and, if so, what happens to your entry fee)? You may sign a health-care coverage agreement. These can be categorized as extensive (all-inclusive, with little or no increase in monthly payments); modified (specified amounts of care per year before increasing charges); and fee-for-service (lower fees initially, but higher if you need more care later).

Ideally, as one pamphlet claims, "a CCRC is a network of caring and support—friends and family, neighbors, staff, and volunteers work together to provide a rich, challenging, comfortable, interesting, and secure future for retired people." In reality, this type of living requires flexibility, tolerance, and good humor.

Congregate Housing

Similar to a CCRC, though less comprehensive, is a retirement development called congregate housing, a complex with added services, such as meals, linens, housekeeping, security, even medical. It's pricey, making it an option for upper middle-class and above. It tries to appear like traditional rental-type living (with a few support services), which alleviates the stigma of the elderly living in isolation.

Assisted-Living Facilities

Looking much like congregate housing are assisted-living facilities, rental complexes that generally provide an apartment, utilities, three meals a day, housekeeping, laundry and linen services, emergency call, and, often, help as required. Van transportation and medical services may also be available. They may have other personal services, such as a beauty shop or bank, with limited hours. They do not have facilities for those who need extended skilled-nursing care (nor are they licensed as nursing homes). As with any of these service-oriented options, it is a good idea to visit more than one so that you recognize the range in quality. Pay attention to which of these services you're most likely to use (since you're paying for all of them). Which conditions may force you to move (for example, Alzheimer's disease)? Two groups that represent assisted-living facilities can provide more detailed information. Contact the Assisted Living Federation of America, 10300 Eaton Pl., Suite 400, Fairfax, VA 22030; (703) 691-8100; www.alfa.org; or the American Health Care Association, 1201 L St. NW, Washington, DC 20005; (202) 842-4444; www.ahca.org.

Nursing Homes

Finally, there are nursing homes. It is useful to think of two levels of homes—immediate care (custodial), and skilled-nursing care—though some provide both. You may find this type of care available in the previously mentioned choices of residential care, continuing care, and assisted living. Because of the high staff demands, with twenty-four-hour, seven-day-per-week coverage, the nursing home has become expensive. Most residents pay out-of-pocket, though a substantial number are on Medicaid (which some homes do not accept). Medicare pays only for skilled-nursing care—full for twenty days, and partial for the next eighty days.

Look first to methods that allow you to remain independent where you are. Certain conditions may interfere with that option: physical or mental disabilities, special care, or special devices unavailable in a typical home setting. For more information, contact the National Association for Home Care, 228 Seventh St. SE, Washington, DC 20003; (202) 547-7424; www.nahc.org.

Survey the Choices Beforehand Since the nursing home becomes the option of last resort (meaning you can no longer live independently, at least for a while), the decision-making process often involves another (spouse, child, medical spokesperson, etc.). It's a good idea to have surveyed the choices before you need them. Make a checklist of your concerns. If possible, talk to other residents to acquire a firsthand impression of the quality of care. When going over the details, watch for hidden costs. (Obtain a list of all fees.) Insist on looking at the nursing home's required bill of rights (mandated by the Nursing Home Reform Law of 1987). These include citizenship, residence, personal property, dignity, privacy, information, freedom, choice, expression, and care. Arm yourself with a copy of Robert Bua's *The Inside Guide to America's Nursing Homes.*

Certifications and Physical Attributes To check out a home, you need common sense, a few visits, and the knowledge of which categories to cover. First are the certifications. The home needs a current operating license from the state, and the administrator must have an up-to-date license. If you anticipate Medicare or Medicaid help, the home must be certified to receive it. Does the home comply with the standards of your state's Peer Review Committee? Next, observe the physical attributes. A location that makes regular visits by family and friends easy is a real bonus. The grounds should be appealing. Inside, the home must have handrails in hallways, grab bars in bathrooms, and other features aimed at accident prevention, clearly marked exits and unobstructed paths to these exits (and compliance with all fire codes), bedrooms that open onto a corridor and windows for emergency exit, hallways wide enough to permit two wheelchairs to pass with ease, toilet facilities designed to accommodate wheelchair residents, and wheelchair ramps for easy access in and out of the home. The overall decor should be light and airy; individual rooms should feature a comfortable, homelike appearance. (Does each room have an individual thermostat?)

Check Out the Medical Facilities You should also explore the medical facilities. A physician must be available for emergencies. The home should have arrangements for the full range of medical needs (dental, optometry, physical therapy, pharmacy, etc.). Nurses should be licensed. In skilled-nursing care, nurses must be registered.

Check Out Daily Operations and Resident Care Walk around and notice the day-to-day operation. For example, you should detect no heavy odors, whether offensive stenches or pleasant sprays that mask smells. The kitchen should separate its food preparation, garbage, and dishwashing areas, and perishable foods must be refrigerated. Is the resident dining room attractive, with tables convenient for wheelchairs? Is the food appetizing? Do the residents look clean, alert, and dressed for a full day of activity and social interaction? Do they talk with each other and with you? Are they encouraged to go outside? Notice, too, whether residents who need help receive it. Finally, determine if there appears to be a commitment to a philosophy of care in which physical and chemical restraints are minimally used—or not at all. What happens if a resident does not like his room (too noisy, incompatible roommate, etc.)? Is there an activity room or designated space for residents who can enjoy reading, crafts, and social activities? Look for a friendly and available staff that appears pleasant, caring, and accommodating to residents and visitors. Also, determine if there is an active resident council or a resident participation program that enables residents to recommend changes within the home.

In summary, a quality nursing home offers a full array of necessary services, including medical, nursing, therapeutic, dining, laundry, social, and recreational. A full staff includes nurses, activities coordinator, dietician, social worker, and counselors. Extra icing on the cake is the presence of many volunteers, who help residents with daily activities.

Help from Agencies and Groups

Various agencies and groups will point you in the right direction. The U.S. Administration on Aging (AOA) is a federal agency that helps people locate long-term care services. Contact AOA at 330 Independence Ave. SW, Washington, DC 20201; (202) 619-0724); www.aoa.dhhs.gov. AOA maintains *The Directory of State and Area Agencies on Aging* (often available in your library or on-line at www.aoa.dhhs.gov/aoa/pages/ltcomb.html). Each state agency on aging (see Appendix B, State Resources) can refer you to help with your specific needs. *The National Directory for Eldercare Information and Referral* has additional information about various home health and other services. This is the printed version of the information given over the telephone when you call the Eldercare Locator, at 1-800-677-1116. A national nonprofit organization representing nearly 5,000 not-for-profit assisted-living facilities for the aging is The American Association of Homes and Services for the Aging (AAHSA), 901 E St. NW, Suite 500, Washington, DC 20004-2037; 1-800-508-9442; www.aahsa.org. One commercial service is attempting to offer an on-line listing of all senior assisted-living residences at www.seniorservicesguide.com.

Over the next few years, retirement communities, from resorts to nursing homes, are expected to multiply rapidly. As the competition mounts, you will witness exaggerated claims and a lot of hard-sale tactics. If you think one of these places is right for you, you have a broad range of options

Summary

Those preparing to retire today have the widest range of living options available in human history. There is no better way to determine what is best for you than a complete, honest self-analysis. If you can picture how you would like to live day-by-day and month-by-month for the next twenty years, focus on the regular activities you want to enjoy. You'll have a much easier time of sorting through your choices. If all you know is, "I want a warmer climate," then you're setting yourself up for disappointment. Think critically. Then, go for your best dream—whether you stay where you are, or set out for an idyllic village. Maybe you crave city lights, a senior mecca, or desire full-time travel to foreign shores. The choices are yours.

CHAPTER SEVEN

Safety and Security Concerns

Fear—a paralyzing emotion that can render one incapable of rational thought or action—erupts from perceived danger. As we progress in life, especially as we feel our bodies change, fear can escalate. We need to discern the essential steps we can take to minimize potential dangers in order to continue to enjoy a full life. That way, we can put fear to rest. "To conquer fear is the beginning of wisdom," writes Bertrand Russell in his *Unpopular Essays*.

In this chapter, we'll examine the possibilities of physical dangers, property risks, and financial scams. Many of the more publicized perils, such as assaults, are rare for older adults, while the con games and marketing ploys are on the increase. There are ways to avoid all this unpleasantness so you can feel safe and secure during your retirement years.

We are, perhaps uniquely among the earth's creatures, the worrying animal. We worry away our lives, fearing the future, discontent with the present, unable to take in the idea of dying, unable to sit still.

LEWIS THOMAS, M.D.
Author

Accident Prevention

By far, the most common physical dangers are situations we create—accidents. Naturally, there are accidents out of our control, such as a falling tree limb, a lightning bolt, or a drunk driver. Even with this type of danger, you are not helpless. Regularly check the health of your trees; head for low ground during a thunderstorm; drive defensively. Focus your attention and energy on prevention within your typical day-to-day habits and routines. The following tips listed may appear to be common sense, and more appropriate for someone less capable than yourself. Consider them a warm-up for things to come.

Reduce Home Accidents

You can reduce the chance of accidents in your home. Explore your living space as if you were trying to find every hazard a small grandchild might encounter. A great place to start is with handguns. How are they secured? Do you have trigger locks? There are far more "accidental" deaths by firearms than there are "successful" defenses of one's personal safety. In fact, FBI statistics show that handguns at home kill loved ones far more often than they protect them.

The Bath Inventory several basic items around your home. (If you help care for others who are older than you, execute this effective exercise in their homes, too.) Start with the most dangerous room—the bath. It is dangerous because of the hard, slippery surfaces that are unforgiving when you fall. Simple changes can lower risks. Install a railing in the bathtub or shower. Add a nonskid surface in the tub and, if necessary, a seat. Mark hot and cold water taps clearly. Ensure that the water heater is set for 120 degrees Fahrenheit to prevent accidental scalds and to save on your utility bill. Move to a thorough inspection of the medicine cabinet. Clean it out, discarding all out-of-date medicines. Every container needs to be clearly labeled.

The Kitchen Analyze your kitchen. If you are beginning to feel a bit unsteady handling sharp knives, check out heavy-duty scissors—they work almost as well with a lot less hazard. Put heavy items where you can reach them without straining. Use a small, sturdy step-stool to reach the higher cabinets. Each year 3,000 people older than sixty-five are treated for falls from standing on a chair. When cooking, use longer-handled tools, such as barbecue tongs, to keep from burning yourself. Clearly mark all stove controls. Seventy percent of all people who die of clothing fires are older than sixty-five years of age. Never cook while wearing loose-fitting long-sleeve garments; they can dangle onto a hot burner or into a gas flame.

Check Out Smoke Alarms Every year, check out all smoke alarms on a given date, such as your birthday. The majority of retirees who die in fires either do not own a smoke alarm or have a malfunctioning one. Never smoke in bed and know all possible escape routes, in case of fire. Hold a home fire drill. Similarly, rehearse storm or earthquake emergency procedures. If you wait until you need them, it is too late.

Other Things to Do for Safety Look for other needs throughout your house. Ensure that all your rugs are skid-proof. Check stairs for nonslip treads. Remove or reroute any electrical wires or telephone cords that might trip anyone. Keep a list of up-to-date emergency and other important phone numbers next to every telephone. (This list is of even greater importance if you live alone.) As you become less agile, you can also make your house—and your life—more convenient. For an idea-prompting journey, examine Doreen Brenner Greenstein's *Easy Things to Make to Make Things Easy.*

Safe Driving

When it comes to your automobile, do not let false pride keep you from critically analyzing your driving skills. There is no guarantee you can drive forever in a safe manner. Retirees have more accidents per miles driven than almost any other age group. Young males have a slightly worse rate due to their tendency to speed. Retirees, on the other hand, have a high number of accidents when attempting to make left turns across traffic. Eyes become weaker; depth perception is flatter; reactions have slowed. Be alert to other sloppy driving practices, such as not stopping for stop signs, driving consistently below the speed limit, weaving or temporarily losing control, not sig-naling lane changes or turns, and misreading traffic signs. Take the advice of many retirees and enroll in AARP's 55 ALIVE/ Mature Driving Course. (Depending on your state, course completion may lower your auto insurance bill.) When you or someone you know is becoming more and more unsafe while driving, curb the car. Bring it to a halt before a serious accident occurs. Driving is a privilege—not a right.

Crime

When discussing crime, it is important to maintain a rational outlook. Minimize the likelihood of your becoming a victim without overreacting to hypothetical possibilities. Retirees have the lowest incidence rates of being victims of crimes except for purse-snatching and pickpocketing. You must be alert, however, and take precautions when in a high-risk situa-tion. For example, in crowds, carry your wallet in a front pocket or wear a waist purse. Carry a whistle or sound alarm to alert others, if necessary. If you're concerned about pickpock-eting, especially if you intend to travel to a high-risk country, order the $3.95 booklet *Foiling Pickpockets & Bag Snatchers and Other Travel-Related Crimes or Scams* from Jens Jurgen, P.O. Box 833, Amityville, NY 11701; (516) 454-0880.

Most retirees fear burglaries, muggings, and carjackings far more than the common pickpocketing incident. Though the odds of one of these scary scenarios happening to you are low, it is certainly possible. Where you live has a great deal to do with your odds—the larger the metropolitan area you live in, the higher the chance of an incident.

Lower Your Risks at Home

There are many actions you can take to lower your risk of being burglarized. The first priority is to protect yourself—not your property. Assume that all burglars are armed and don't want to be caught. Do not play the hero. (Your life is worth more than the value of your stereo.)

Burglar Alarms Examine your house the way a burglar does. Most intruders look for the easiest possible mark. The welcome target is an unlocked, unwatched, and no-one-at-home dwelling that contains firearms, cash, credit cards, and jewelry. Make your dwelling a less appealing prize. Use deadbolt locks on all exterior doors. (Window locks are generally worthless, since a determined burglar finds it easy to jimmy the lock or break the glass.) If possible, enroll your neighborhood in a watch program. No one can be home all the time, but neighbors can be alert to a strange vehicle or suspicious activity. If you live in a high-crime area, install a burglar alarm. This is an expensive option and cannot guarantee you will not be burgled. Too, while an alarm system may reduce your homeowner's insurance premium, a false alarm may provoke a fine from the police. The common belief among policemen, however, is that an alarm system does deter burglaries. If you are considering an alarm system, contact the nonprofit National Burglar and Fire Alarm Association, 7101 Wisconsin Ave. #901, Bethesda, MD 20814; (301) 907-3202; www.alarm.org.

Don't Make It Easy for a Burglar If you plan to be away from your dwelling for more than twenty-four hours, make it look as if someone is there. Set light timers; turn on a radio; stop papers and mail delivery; keep valuables well hidden. Most burglars want to be in and out quickly, so make their treasure hunt difficult. If you are home or come home while a burglary is in process, make a lot of noise, give the burglar an exit route, and call the police.

Auto Theft

Another type of burglary that may infringe on your life is auto theft. Once again, where you live or drive determines the likelihood of theft. If car theft were a legitimate business in large cities, it would rank as one of the largest in terms of economic impact. If a thief wants your car, he can get it—often in less than thirty seconds. Your best course of action is to make his job as difficult as possible. Lock your car and take your keys. If possible, leave nothing in view that looks tempting. Try to leave your car in well-lit areas. Turn your wheels against a curb and always set your emergency brake, which makes quick towing far more difficult. Etch your vehicle number on all glass windows.

Carjacking Once again, in auto theft as in home burglary, your main concern remains protecting yourself from bodily harm. One of the more disturbing variations of auto theft is carjacking—it often involves physical assault. This somewhat recent phenomenon is fairly infrequent and is generally restricted to larger cities. The thief takes the car by force, using a gun in more than 90 percent of reported cases. It may involve the setup of a minor accident, such as bumping your vehicle from the rear or stopping suddenly in front of you. When you step out to inspect the damage, one of the group hops into your automobile and takes off. Other carjackings are as straightforward as someone approaching you when you stop at a traffic light or when you park. Your best bet in any carjacking is to readily give up the car and do not attempt to follow it. Contact the police.

One woman acquaintance, who has traveled alone for many years, always tries to take a higher position—the sidewalk instead of the street, a higher step on the stairs, the highest side or point of a path—when encountering a stranger. The superior position makes her appear taller and in greater control of the situation.

Muggings

Muggings are almost nonexistent in many areas of the country, but, unfortunately, they are not so rare in and around larger cities. As you age, your physical appearance can make you look like less of a threat to a would-be assailant. Learn to carry yourself tall and strong. Be alert when in a high-risk area. Look for safe havens (crowded stores, offices, or uniformed people) to use if someone (or a group) threatens you. Have your keys ready when you approach your car. Carry a whistle or sound alarm. Walk with a dog. Take a self-defense course—

it may help build your confidence, as well as provide valuable tips. Try not to live in fear because of the nightly news' latest sensational report. Instead, reexamine your location and the actual threats—if any—that you are likely to encounter.

High-pressure Tactics

It is much more likely that you'll become a victim in a financial transaction rather than a physical assault. Throughout your life, you have encountered questionable individuals whose goal is to separate you from your money. In your retirement, you will notice these people's tactics will shift increasingly to the use of intimidation, confusion, and/or fear. Most of the people who employ such offensive tactics work for legitimate companies but sell products or services you probably do not need; a few of these people represent disreputable organizations.

Rid Yourself of Junk Mail

Retirement is the perfect time to simplify your life. Rid yourself of unwanted junk mail, and don't take telephone calls designed to make others richer and you poorer. Write a letter to the Direct Marketing Association (DMA) requesting that your name be permanently removed from all mailing lists. Send your name and address to DMA Mail Preference Service, P.O. Box 9008, Farmingdale, NY 11735-9008. To delete your phone number from telemarketing lists, send your name, address, and phone number to DMA Telephone Preference Service, P.O. Box 9014, Farmingdale, NY 11735-9014. These requests must be written and signed. For additional information, explore the DMA Web site at www. the-dma.org.

Stop Recurring Phone Calls

To stop recurring telephone calls, write down the date, time, and company name, as well as the name of the person who made the call. Tell the person you demand that your name be put on a "do-not-call" list. The Telephone Consumer Protection Act of 1991 provides that if you receive another call from that same company, the violator is liable for up to $500 per call or up to $1,500 for willful violations—so, be sure to keep a record of the date, time, company name, and caller's name.

Improve Your Consumer Skills

Next, hone your consumer analytic skills. As baby boomers approach retirement age, the marketing blitz that has followed them through their lives will offer many new and revitalized products now targeted for seniors. As the competition increases and companies scramble for their niches, the touted claims will grow wilder. Be cautious about purchasing services and products that may not be a wise choice. Certain insurance policies, such as specific-disease health insurance, many types of life insurance, and some of the medical "geriatric" insurance offerings, tend to strongly favor the company far more than the policyholder. When any product is heavily advertised or if individual salesmen are used to pitch it, large commissions and profit margins are in place. Someone, namely you—the potential purchaser—must pay for these expenses. Look at your options. Use third-party publications such as *Consumer Reports*. If you have the slightest question, check with your state's department of aging, departments of insurance, or the Better Business Bureau.

Beware of Unnecessary Medical Procedures

The current trend indicates that this high-pressure selling of dubious offerings will also grow in the medical field. Notice the implications in this paragraph from *Your Medicare Handbook* by the Health Care Financing Administration:

> Additionally, any doctor who does not participate in
> Medicare and who provides you a service that he or she

knows or has reason to believe Medicare will determine to be medically unnecessary, and thus will not pay for, must tell you that in writing before performing the service. If written notice is not given, and you did not know that Medicare would not pay, you cannot be held liable to pay for that service. However, if you did receive written notice and signed an agreement to pay for the service, you will be held liable to pay.

In other words, a confused patient could sign a "release" for treatment. Afterward, he would receive a huge bill because Medicare will not pay for it—which the doctor knew all along.

Do Business with People Who Don't Pressure You

Hopefully, you will not transact business with professionals and/or salespeople who engage in these tactics. The odds are increasing, however, that you will encounter one or more who will. Even though such practices are legal (or use a legal loophole), it does not mean it is in your best interest. Do not sign away your rights. You must decide when a deal is a good deal. After all, it is your life and your money.

One retiree tells us that she does business only with people she has known for several years in her town. She may pay a bit more for a product or a service, but she has never been "taken"—after all, they have to face her the next day.

Telemarketing

Retirees have become targets for unscrupulous telemarketers. There are many legitimate telemarketing campaigns; the scams are in the minority. This potent group of professional crooks, however, is "stealing" an estimated $40 billion per year! And most of that amount comes from the purses and pockets of retirees. (Up to 80 percent of the illegitimate operations specifically target seniors.) Focusing on their "mark," these unscrupulous operations call upon well-educated, socially active retirees with above-average incomes. Do not allow yourself or someone you care about to become a victim. If you suspect a telemarketing scam, immediately notify the National Fraud Information Center, at P.O. Box 65868, Washington, DC 20035; 1-800-876-7060; www.fraud.org.

A couple of things in life I'd change are all this telephone marketing and all those phone menus. They can be very frustrating.

RETIRED TEACHER
North Carolina

Fraudulent Telemarketers

Fraudulent telemarketers are successful because they understand human tendencies, particularly those of seniors. As the National Fraud Information Center points out, most people find it hard to tell if a caller is legitimate. Once you are on the line, you find it hard to hang up. Your politeness can be manipulated by someone pretending to be friendly or using high-pressure, bullying tactics. Seniors tend to be more trusting than others, and crooks use that trust in their pitch. They know the other side of human nature. Most of us want to believe we have won something or have earned the "chance of a lifetime." If we succumb to a scam, we become like an alcoholic—we refuse to listen to family or friends because we want to believe we were right.

If you think you could never become a "mooch" (telemarketer slang for victim), realize that the telemarketer almost always knows more about you than you do about him. They try to garner information about your preferences so they can hit one of your emotional triggers. They are skilled liars with excellent verbal comebacks; they sound legitimate. If you give them any money, there is little hope you will ever see it again.

Some possible warning signs are shown in Exhibit 7.1, page 220–21. These warning signs are guides. There are more creative scams evolving every day. You must learn to diligently reject these schemes. It is not easy. Some seniors have lost all or a large part of their life's savings. When in doubt, remember to call the National Fraud Information Center Hot Line, at 1-800-876-7060 or E-mail it through www.fraud.org. You can also write the information center at the previously referenced address—or its parent organization, The National Consumers League, 1701 K St. NW, Suite 1200, Washington, DC 20006;

(202) 835-3323. Chances are that the scam artist will not wait around for an answer.

Fraudulent Charities

Unfortunately, fraudulent operations masquerade as legitimate charities. Avoid giving them your money. You can request free reports on up to three charities from the Philanthropic Advisory Service, Council of Better Business Bureaus, 4200 Wilson Blvd., Arlington, VA 22203, or download the information from www.bbb.org/reports/charity.html. You can order a report on-line from the National Charities Information Bureau at www.give.org.

Another frequent problem is that once a charity or action group receives a donation from you, it immediately sends another request for more money. An interviewee (who helps others with financial concerns) shares, "One woman client was on so many charity mailing lists that together we created a list. We investigated each charity, then we created a chart of the ones she wanted to support. Now when the client sends a check, she notes it on her chart. Then she does not send any additional dollars until a year has gone by."

For those connected to the Internet, all of the above scams plus more will crowd your E-mail box. (They are called *spam.*) After all, sending an E-mail message is much cheaper than a bulk-mail letter or a long-distance telephone call.

Other Cons, Swindles, and Frauds

Con Games

Anyone who has seen the movie *The Sting* knows that con games can be great entertainment—unless you happen to be the pigeon. At the heart of a con game is personal greed—the belief that one can get something for nothing. The best games are designed so that you never see the trap until it is too late.

Exhibit 7.1: Fraudulent Telemarketing Ploys

Action	Reaction
High-pressure sales tactics.	Legitimate offers allow you to rationally decide; fraudulent ones push you into an emotional decision.
Insistence on an immediate decision.	All decisions must be given deliberate consideration. The need for an immediate decision is an excellent indicator of a fly-by-night operation.
Unwillingness to send written information.	Legitimate companies readily furnish printed material. A con artist, however, may not have printed materials. The unwillingness to send printed information indicates you are talking to a con artist.
Sounds too good to be true.	It is!
Request a credit-card number for any purpose other than to make a purchase you have initiated.	Chances are, if you did not originate this call, you are being robbed over the phone lines. The same is true if the caller asks for your Social Security number, your bank account number, or any other financial data.
Offer to send someone to your home or office to pick up the money—or employ some other method such as a private courier or wiring of funds.	By avoiding the postal system, con artists dodge federal laws and are harder to trace. Fraudulent operators love cash because it is easily laundered.

For example, the Ponzi scheme (and its variants) promises a nice return (such as 20 percent within a month) and actually pays off. Then, you reinvest everything or add more money —and your money disappears.

Con artists generally work in pairs, though they sometimes use more people for an elaborate game. They use fake identities (bank examiner, repairman, or inspector). They promise actual work, such as a home-improvement project. ("We happen to be in your neighborhood with leftover materials," or "We'd like to use your house for a model.") What a con operation cannot stand is slow, methodical examination by the would-be pigeon. Call to check on these "businesses," verify their references, and obtain written specifications. Do not accept any verbal promises—get them in writing. Never sign

Exhibit 7.1: Fraudulent Telemarketing Ploys, *continued*

Action	Reaction
State that something is "free" or that you have won a prize, followed by a requirement that you pay for something else.	This technique is illegal.
Offer of investment that is "without risk."	All investments have risks. Anyone who says otherwise is lying. A variation is a franchise or home business with guaranteed profits for little or no effort. All businesses require effort and none can guarantee profits.
Unwillingness to provide references such as a bank or names of satisfied customers in your area you can contact.	Legitimate companies provide these sources without hassle.
Suggest that you "should" make a purchase or investment on the basis of "trust."	This is a shameful technique to play on your nobler instincts. Hang up!
Request a donation for an unknown charity.	Demand information to verify the charity and how much of the money goes to services rather than overhead. All legitimate charities are happy to oblige.
Variations of a chain letter.	These are illegal and guaranteed to take your money.
Offer to obtain a loan, credit card, or to "repair" your bad credit if you pay an up-front fee.	Legitimate operations do not demand payment in advance. Besides, no one can remove bad credit information, if that information is accurate. A variation is the offer to help you recover money lost to another fraudulent scheme. Advance payment for this "service" is illegal. Most likely, you are talking to the same company that took your money the first time.

a document with blank entries. Face the facts. When someone approaches you (a cold call) rather than your having sought a necessary product or service, be skeptical.

Standard tip-offs that you are being hustled are: getting rich quick; finding something for nothing; letting you in on secret plans; telling you this is your last chance; insisting you must act now; and guaranteeing big money without risk. Again, if it sounds too good to be true, it is.

Swindles or Scams

Swindles or scams are orchestrated attempts to sell you a worthless (or nearly worthless) product or service. For example, an old but a popular version is the land scam. You want to buy property long-distance? First, did you receive and analyze the property report (required for all advertised out-of-state offerings by the Office of Interstate Land Sales Registration)? Have you investigated how close the lot is to other facilities, ensured that the actual measurements are on the legal description, checked on the soil and subsoil analysis, and calculated the possibilities of flooding or erosion? Do you understand the water and mineral rights? Have you received, analyzed, and verified the developer's detailed financial statement? Always check with local officials about the reputation of this operation. In other words, do your homework. Scams do not stand up to scrutiny.

Quackery

Quackery is another standard scam on the increase. You will find magic cures for arthritis and cancer, surefire weight-loss programs, and pills to reverse impotency. These are generally sold by mail-order and use "testimonials" to convince you of the efficacy of their product. Beware. Secret formulas, breakthroughs, and miracles belong in the fiction category, not legitimate medicine.

Door-to-Door Sales

Door-to-door sales still exist. Be cautious, since legitimate door-to-door offers are rare. You do have three days to cancel a door-to-door sale, but that does not help if you have paid cash, taken an item on approval, or signed a document waiving your right to change your mind.

Business opportunity frauds advertised through the mail are also popular. Most work-at-home schemes, self-employment offers, chain-referral techniques, and pyramid marketing gimmicks (that involve all your family and friends) are simply devices to separate you from your money. These personalized offers can come in "official"-looking packages. Most are sent by bulk mail—an easy tip-off.

Legitimate Solicitations

There are legitimate solicitations, including high-yield investment offerings, home improvement services, business franchise openings, or retirement sites and opportunities. Yet each of these four areas is highly infiltrated with fraudulent operators. If you do not understand the investment or product, do not buy it. Demand the name, address, and phone of any company that contacts you. Ask for references. Find out the name of the state and federal agencies responsible for the company's regulation or registration. If they claim none, become highly suspicious. If they provide a name, check it out via a phone call or letter. For a major purchase or investment, request that duplicate information be sent to someone you trust (a family member, friend, accountant, lawyer, etc.). We saw one slick set of papers selling an oil partnership; it was laced with carefully hidden traps. Since then, the company has changed names many times, and the individual's $20,000 investment has become worthless. Investigate! Fraudulent operations hate scrutiny.

One couple has implemented a simple procedure. Whenever either one is tempted to buy anything beyond groceries, they write it on a list and date the entry. Thirty days later they discuss whether they really want to purchase the item or service. Often, they cannot remember what it was or why they had considered buying it in the first place. This cooling-off period seems to be a great way to find perspective on necessities and niceties.

Security is mostly a superstition. It does not exist in nature, nor do the children of men as a whole experience it. Avoiding danger is no safer in the long run than outright exposure. Life is either a daring adventure or nothing.

HELEN KELLER
Author and lecturer

Summary

We have no guarantees that our lives will be without danger. Fortunately, our rational minds can come to our aid. As you deal with this quickly changing, complex society, understand that few humans provide "essential" goods and services— what you need to survive. Most people work in jobs that market goods and services that could be categorized as niceties, luxuries, or worthless. And, a few people deal in the illegal. Use your intelligence and common sense to keep your retirement simple and enjoyable. Whether it is avoiding a crime-ridden area at night or saying no to the next telemarketer, you can maximize your safety and security and minimize unnecessary unhappiness.

Epilogue

Retirement can be the most exciting period of your life. You are more independent than ever. You have abundant possibilities for how to structure the years ahead. Approach this special time with wonder. This attitude will encourage you to place a priority on learning and trying new roles. Your increased enthusiasm will show and attract others.

As you examine how to use your time, allot ample hours to keep your body and mind performing at their highest levels. There is abundant knowledge available about how to stay healthy. By incorporating these ideas into your daily life, you diminish the possibilities of pain and suffering. When you do need medical assistance, become an active patient. Do your own research and seek second opinions as needed. Medicine is an inexact science, so do not be afraid to ask questions.

Consider scheduling more time devoted to caring for friends, family, and community. This emphasis will help strengthen your own positive emotional state. Continue to enlarge your circle of friends. This practice will pay off in the years ahead.

Find ways to stay involved and engaged with the world around you. Develop hobbies, a wide range of interests, new careers (if you desire), and leisure activities. Explore your spiritual side. Retirement is a period when there is little reason to become bored.

Money does not have to be a problem for most retirees. When you seek rewarding experiences, you will discover they are available for little or no cost. You will find a higher quality of life by following your passions, not by accumulating more "stuff." To keep concerns to a minimum, organize your financial and legal affairs.

You may want to consider relocating or engaging in extensive travel. The options are numerous, and you can increase the chance of satisfaction by doing your homework. Flirt with all the possibilities but understand what you (and your partner) most enjoy. When you know what makes you happy, it is much harder to be swept into a poor decision by slick marketing tactics.

Retirement is all about choices. You can make your "golden years" shine.

Organizational Contacts

Government Agencies

Administration on Aging
330 Independence Ave. SW
Washington, DC 20201
(202) 619-0724
www.aoa.dhhs.gov

Consumer Information Catalog
P.O. Box 100
Pueblo, CO 81002
(719) 948-3334
www.pueblo.gsa.gov

Consumer Product Safety Commission
4330 East-West Hwy.
Bethesda, MD 20207
1-800-638-2772
www.cpsc.gov

Cooperative Extension Office
(check local phone book under
federal, state, or county listings)

*Corporation for National Service
(AmeriCorps & Senior Corps)*
1201 New York Ave. NW
Washington, DC 20525
1-888-507-5962
www.cns.gov

Federal Trade Commission
CRC-240
Washington, DC 20580
(202) FTC-HELP
www.ftc.gov

Health Care Financing Administration (HCFA)
7500 Security Blvd.
Baltimore, MD 21244-1850
1-800-638-6833
www.hcfa.gov

National Aging Information Center,
330 Independence Ave. SW, Room 4656
Washington, DC 20201
(202) 619-7501
www.aoa.dhhs.gov/naic

National Climatic Data Center
Federal Building
151 Patton Ave.
Asheville, NC 28801-5001
(828) 271-4800
www.ncdc.noaa.gov

National Institute on Aging
P.O. Box 8057
Gaithersburg, MD 20898-8057
1-800-222-2225
www.nih.gov/nia

Pension Benefit Guaranty Corp. (PBGC)
1200 K St. NW
Washington, DC 20005-4026
(202) 326-4000
www.pbgc.gov

Pension Welfare and Benefits Administration
U.S. Department of Labor
200 Constitution Ave. NW, Room N-5619
Washington, DC 20210
1-800-998-7542
www.dol.gov/dol/pwba

Social Security Administration
6401 Security Blvd.
Baltimore, MD 21235
1-800-234-5772
www.ssa.gov

Veterans Administration
810 Vermont Ave. NW
Washington, DC 20420
1-800-827-1000
www.va.gov

Associations

American Association of Retired Persons (AARP)
601 E St. NW
Washington, DC 20049
1-800-424-3410
www.aarp.org

American Bar Association
Legal Problems of the Elderly
740 Fifteenth St. NW
Washington, DC 20005-1022
(202) 662-8690
www.abanet.org/elderly

American Health Care Association
1201 L St. NW
Washington, DC 20005
(202) 842-4444
www.ahca.org

Assisted Living Federation of America
10300 Eaton Pl., Suite 400
Fairfax, VA 22030
(703) 691-8100
www.alfa.org

Center for Creative Retirement
1 University Heights
Asheville, NC 28804
(704) 251-6140

Center for the Study of Services
733 15th St. NW, Suite 820
Washington, DC 20005
1-800-475-7283
www.checkbook.org

Choice in Dying
1035 30th St. NW
Washington, DC 20007
(212) 366-5540
www.choices.org

Common Cause
1250 Connecticut Ave. NW, #600
Washington, DC 20036
(202) 833-1200
www.commoncause.org

Consumers Union of the United States
101 Truman Ave.
Yonkers, NY 10703-1057
(914) 378-2000
www.consunion.org

Continuing Care Accreditation Commission
901 E St. NW, Suite 500
Washington, DC 20004-2037
(202) 783-7286
www.ccaconline.org

Direct Marketing Association
1120 Ave. of the Americas
New York, NY 10036-6700
(212) 768-7277
www.the-dma.org

Eldercare Locator
1112 16th St. NW
Washington, DC 20036
1-800-677-1116
www.ageinfo.org/elderloc

Federation of Tax Administrators
444 N. Capitol St. NW
Washington, DC 20001
www.taxadmin.org

Friends Life Care at Home
1777 Sentry Pkwy. W
Dublin Hall, Suite 210
Blue Bell, PA 19422-2246
(215) 628-8964
www.friendslifecareathome.com

Gray Panthers
2025 Pennsylvania Ave. NW, Suite 821
Washington, DC 20006
1-800-280-5362
http://combi.agri.ch/graue-panther/pae_addr.htm

National Association for Home Care
228 Seventh St. SE
Washington, DC 20003
(202) 547-7424
www.nahc.org

National Association of Securities Dealers
1735 K St. NW
Washington, DC 20006-1500
1-800-289-9999
www.nasd.com

National Burglar and Fire Alarm Association
7101 Wisconsin Ave., #901
Bethesda, MD 20814
(301) 907-3202
www.alarm.org

National Center for Home Equity Conversion
7373 147th St. W, #115
Apple Valley, MN 55124
(612) 953-4474

National Council of Senior Citizens
8403 Colesville Rd., Suite 1200
Silver Spring, MD 20910-3314
1-888-3-SENIOR
www.ncscinc.org

National Council on the Aging
409 Third St. SW, Suite 200
Washington, DC 20024
(202) 479-1200
www.shs.net/ncoa/ncoa.htm

National Fraud Information Center
P.O. Box 65868
Washington, DC 20035
1-800-876-7060
www.fraud.org

National Shared Housing Resource Center
321 E 25th St.
Baltimore, MD 21218

Older Women's League
666 Eleventh St. NW, Suite 700
Washington, DC 20001
(202) 783-6686

SeniorNet
121 Second St., 7th Floor
San Francisco, CA 94105
(415) 495-4990
www.seniornet.org

Shared Housing Resource Center, Inc.
6344 Greene St.
Philadelphia, PA 19144
(215) 848-1220

*The American Association of Homes and
Services for the Aging (AAHSA)*
901 E St. NW, Suite 500
Washington, DC 20004-2037
1-800-508-9442
www.aahsa.org

The American Association of Individual Investors (AAII)
625 N. Michigan Ave.
Chicago, IL 60611
1-800-428-2244
www.aaii.com

Business and Financial Resources
Better Business Bureau
4200 Wilson Blvd., Suite 800
Arlington, VA 22203-1804
www.bbb.org

Institute of Certified Financial Planners
3801 E. Florida Ave., Suite 708
Denver, CO 80210-2544
1-800-282-7526
www.icfp.org

Investment Company Institute
1401 H St. NW
Washington, DC 20005
www.ici.org

Mutual Fund Education Alliance
P.O. Box 419263
Kansas City, MO 64193-0148
(816) 454-9422
www.mfea.com

*National Association of Personal
Financial Advisors (NAPFA)*
355 W. Dundee Rd., Suite 200
Buffalo Grove, IL 60089
1-888-FEE-ONLY
www.napfa.org

Operation ABLE
16250 Northland Dr., Suite 102
Southfield, MI 48075-5226
1-800-922-4473

Service Corps of Retired Executives (SCORE)
409 3rd St. SW, 6th Floor
Washington, DC 20024
1-800-634-0245
www.score.org

U.S. Small Business Administration
1441 L St. NW
Washington, DC 20549
1-800-827-5722
www.sbaonline.sba.gov

Health-Related Groups

Albert Ellis Institute
45 E. 65th St.
New York, NY 10021
1-800-323-4738
www.REBT.org

American Academy of Family Physicians,
8880 Ward Pkwy.
Kansas City, MO 64114
(816) 333-9700
www.aafp.org

American Academy of Ophthalmology (AAO)
P.O. Box 7424
San Francisco, CA 94120-7424
1-800-222-EYES
www.eyenet.org

American Association of Geriatric Psychiatry
7910 Woodmont Ave., Suite 1350
Bethesda, MD 20814
1-800-573-4433
www.aagpgpa.org

American Cancer Society
1-800-227-2345
www.cancer.org

American College of Surgeons
633 N. Saint Clair St.
Chicago, IL 60611
(312) 202-5000
www.facs.org

American Diabetes Association
1660 Duke St.
Alexandria, VA 22314
1-800-232-3472
www.diabetes.org

American Dietetic Association
216 W. Jackson Blvd., Suite 800
Chicago, IL 60606-6995
1-800-366-1655
www.eatright.org

American Heart Association
National Center
7272 Greenville Ave.
Dallas, TX 75231
1-800-AHA-USA1
www.americanheart.org

American Hospital Association
1 N. Franklin
Chicago, IL 60606
(312) 422-3000
www.aha.org

American Institute for Cancer Research
1759 R St. NW
Washington, DC 20009
1-800-843-8114
www.aicr.org

American Optometric Association
243 N. Lindbergh Blvd.
St. Louis, MO 63141
(314) 991-4100
www.aoanet.org

American Osteopathic Association
142 E. Ontario St.
Chicago, IL 60611
1-800-621-1773
www.am-osteo-assn.org

Arthritis Foundation
1330 W. Peachtree St.
Atlanta, GA 30309
1-800-283-7800
www.arthritis.org

Better Hearing Institute
5021-B Backlick Rd.
Annandale, VA 22003
1-800-EAR-WELL
www.betterhearing.org

Center for Science in the Public Interest
1875 Connecticut Ave. NW, Suite 300
Washington, DC 20009-5728
(202) 332-9110
www.cspinet.org

DEPRESSION Awareness, Recognition, and Treatment (D/ART)
National Institutes of Mental Health
5600 Fishers Ln., Room 14C-02
Rockville, MD 20857
www.nimh.nih.gov

Fifty-Plus Runners Association
P.O. Box D
Stanford, CA 94309-9790
(415) 723-9790

Food and Nutrition Information Center
10301 Baltimore Ave.
Beltsville, MD 20705-2351
1-800-535-4555
www.nal.usda.gov/fnic

Foundation for Hospice & Home Care
519 C St. NE
Washington, DC 20002
(202) 547-6586

Joint Commission on Accreditation of Hospitals
875 N. Michigan Ave.
Chicago, IL 60611

National Association for Home Care
228 Seventh St. SE
Washington, DC 20003
(202) 547-7424
www.nahc.org

National Association of Mall Walkers
P.O. Box 191
Hermann, MO 65041
(313) 486-3945

National Cancer Institute
Building 31, Room 10A0731
Center Dr., MSC 2580
Bethesda, MD 20892-2580
1-800-4-CANCER
www.nci.nih.gov

National Committee for Quality Assurance (NCQA)
2000 L St. NW, Suite 500
Washington, DC 20036
1-888-275-7585
www.ncqa.org

National Eye Institute
2020 Vision Pl.
Bethesda, MD 20892-3655
(301) 496-5248
www.nei.nih.gov

National Health Information Center
P.O. Box 1133
Washington, DC 20013-1133
1-800-336-4797
www.healthfinder.gov

National Hospice Organization
1901 N. Moore St., Suite 901
Arlington, VA 22209-1714
1-800-658-8898
www.nho.org

National Institute of Allergy & Infectious Diseases
Building 31, Room 7A-50
31 Center Dr., MSC 2520
Bethesda, MD 20892-2520
(301) 496-5717
www.niaid.nih.gov

National Mental Health Association
1021 Prince St.
Alexandria, VA 22314-2971
1-800-969-NMHA
www.nmha.org

National Osteoporosis Foundation
1150 17th St. NW, Suite 500
Washington, DC 20036-4603
(202) 223-2226
www.nof.org

People's Medical Society
462 Walnut St.
Allentown, PA 18102
(610) 770-1670
www.peoplesmed.org

Shape Up America!
6707 Democracy Blvd., Suite 306
Bethesda, MD 20817
(301) 493-5368
www.shapeup.org

Society of Gynecologic Oncologists
401 N. Michigan Ave.
Chicago, IL 60611
1-800-444-4441
www.sgo.org

The Alzheimer's Association
919 N. Michigan Ave., Suite 1000
Chicago, IL 60611-1676
1-800-272-3900
www.alz.org

The Lighthouse, Inc.
111 E. 59th St.
New York, NY 10022
1-800-829-0500
www.lighthouse.org

Weight Watchers
175 Crossways Park W
Woodbury, NY 11797
1-800-726-6108
www.weightwatchers.com

Travel Sources

Consumer Reports Travel Letter
P.O. Box 53629
Boulder, CO 80322-3629
1-800-365-0396
www.consumerreports.org

Earthwatch Expeditions, Inc.
P.O. Box 9104
680 Mt. Auburn St.
Watertown, MA 02272
1-800-776-0188
www.earthwatch.org

Elderhostel
75 Federal St.
Boston, MA 02110-1941
(617) 426-7788
www.elderhostel.org

International Association for Medical Assistance to Travelers,
736 Center St.
Lewiston, NY 14092
(716) 754-4883
www.sentex.net/~iamat

Lifestyle Explorations
101 Federal St., Suite 1900
Boston, MA 02110
(508) 371-4814

The Mature Traveler
P.O. Box 50820
Reno, NV 89513
(702) 786-7419

The Over-Fifty Thrifty Traveler
P.O. Box 8168
Clearwater, FL 33758
1-800-532-5731
www.thriftytraveler.com

Travel Companion Exchange
P.O. Box 833
Amityville, NY 11701-0833
(516) 457-0880
www.whytravelalone.com

Volunteer Possibilities

AARP Volunteer Talent Bank
601 E St. NW
Washington, DC 20049
1-800-727-7788
www.aarp.org

American Red Cross
8111 Gatehouse Rd., 6th Floor
Falls Church, VA 22042
1-800-HELP-NOW
www.red.cross.org

Amnesty International, USA
322 8th Ave.
New York, NY 10001
1-800-AMNESTY
www.amnesty-usa.org

Friendship Force
57 Forsyth St. NW, #900
Atlanta, GA 30303-2213
(404) 522-9490
www.friendship-force.org

Global Art Project
P.O. Box 40445
Tucson, AZ 85717
(520) 628-8353
www.global-art.org

Greenpeace
1436 U St. NW
Washington, DC 20009
(202) 462-1177
www.greenpeaceusa.org

Habitat for Humanity
121 Habitat St.
Americus, GA 31709
(912) 924-6935
www.habitat.org

International Executive Service Corps
P.O. Box 10005
Stamford, CT 06904-2005
1-800-243-4372
www.iesc.org

National Association of Partners in Education
901 N. Pitt St., Suite 320
Alexandria, VA 22314
(703) 836-4880
www.NAPEhq.org

*National Association for the Advancement
of Colored People (NAACP)*
4805 Mt. Hope Dr.
Baltimore, MD 21215
(410) 521-4939
www.naacp.org

National Audubon Society
700 Broadway
New York, NY 10003
(212) 979-3000
www.audubon.org

National Coalition Against Domestic Violence
P.O. Box 18749
Denver, CO 80218
(303) 839-1852
www.ncadv.org

National Executive Service Corps
257 Park Ave. S
New York, NY 10010-7304
(212) 529-6660

The Nature Conservancy
1815 N. Lynn St.
Arlington, VA 22209
(703) 841-5300
www.tnc.org

Parents Anonymous
675 W. Foothill Blvd., Suite 220
Claremont, CA 91711-3475
(909) 621-6184
www.parentsanonymous-natl.org

Partners of the Americas
1424 K St. NW, #700
Washington, DC 20005
1-800-322-7844
www.partners.net

Peace Corps
1990 K St. NW
Washington, DC 20526
1-800-424-8580
www.peacecorps.gov

Prison Fellowship Ministries
P.O. Box 17500
Washington, DC 20041-0500
(703) 478-0100
www.pfm.org

Service Corps of Retired Executives (SCORE)
409 3rd St. SW, 6th Floor
Washington, DC 20024
1-800-634-0245
www.score.org

Sierra Club
85 Second St., Second Floor
San Francisco, CA 94105-3441
(415) 977-5500
www.sierraclub.org

Special Olympics
1325 G St. NW, Suite 500
Washington, DC 20005
(202) 628-3630
www.specialolympics.org

United States Committee for UNICEF
333 E. 38th St.
New York, NY 10016
(212) 922-2613
www.unicefusa.org

United Way of America
701 N. Fairfax St.
Alexandria, VA 22314-2045
(703) 836-7100
www.unitedway.org

This list of volunteer possibilities is partial. Many other deserving
medical organizations, religious ministries, museums, libraries, and
interest groups welcome volunteer efforts.

State Resources

Alabama

State Department of Aging
Commission on Aging
770 Washington Ave., Suite 470
P.O. Box 301851
Montgomery, AL 36130
1-800-243-5463
(334) 242-5594

Insurance Counseling
1-800-243-5463

State Insurance Office
Insurance Department, Consumer Service Division
P.O. Box 303351
135 S. Union St.
Montgomery, AL 36130-3351
(334) 269-3550

State Ombudsman
(501) 682-2441

Peer Review Organization
Alabama Quality Assurance Foundation
1-800-760-3540

Medicare Regional Office
(404) 331-2044

Medicare Part B Claims
Blue Cross/Blue Shield of Alabama
1-800-292-8855
(205) 988-2244

Durable Medical Equipment Regional Carrier
Palmetto Government Benefits Administrators
1-800-213-5452
1-800-213-5446 (Spanish)

Alaska

State Department of Aging
Division of Senior Services
3601 C St., Suite 310
Anchorage, AK 99503
(907) 563-5654

Insurance Counseling
1-800-478-6065
(907) 562-7249

State Insurance Office
Division of Insurance
3601 C St., Suite 1324
Anchorage, AK 99503
(907) 269-7900

State Ombudsman
(907) 563-6393

Peer Review Organization
PRO-WEST
1-800-445-6941
(503) 562-2252 (Anchorage)

Medicare Regional Office
(206) 615-2354

Medicare Part B Claims
Medicare Part B
1-800-444-4606

Durable Medical Equipment Regional Carrier
CIGNA Medicare
1-800-899-7095

American Samoa

State Department of Aging
Territorial Administration on Aging
Government of American Samoa
Pago Pago, AS 96799
011 (684) 633-1252

State Insurance Office
Insurance Department
Office of the Governor
Pago Pago, AS 96799
011 (684) 633-4116

Peer Review Organization
Mountain Pacific Quality Health Foundation
1-800-524-6550
(808) 545-2550

Medicare Part B Claims
Medicare Part B
1-800-444-4606

Durable Medical Equipment Regional Carrier
CIGNA Medicare
1-800-899-7095

Arizona

State Department of Aging
Department of Economic Security
Aging & Adult Administration
1789 W. Jefferson St.
Phoenix, AZ 85007
(602) 542-4446

Insurance Counseling
1-800-432-4040
(501) 371-2640

State Insurance Office
Insurance Department
Consumer Affairs Division
2910 N. 44th St.
Phoenix, AZ 85018
(602) 912-8444

State Ombudsman
(602) 542-4446

Peer Review Organization
Health Services Advisory Group, Inc.
1-800-626-1577

Medicare Regional Office
(415) 744-3602

Medicare Part B Claims
Medicare Part B
1-800-444-4606

Durable Medical Equipment Regional Carrier
CIGNA Medicare
1-800-899-7095

Arkansas

State Department of Aging
Division of Aging and Adult Services
1417 Donaghey Plaza S
P.O. Box 1437, Slot 1412
Little Rock, AR 72203-1437
(501) 682-2441

Insurance Counseling
1-800-852-5494
(501) 371-2640

State Insurance Office
Insurance Department
Seniors Insurance Network
1123 S. University Ave., Suite 400
Little Rock, AR 72204
1-800-852-5494

State Ombudsman
(501) 682-2441

Peer Review Organization
Arkansas Foundation for Medical Care, Inc.
1-800-272-5528

Medicare Regional Office
(214) 767-6401

Medicare Part B Claims
Blue Cross/Blue Shield
1-800-482-5525
(501) 378-2320

Durable Medical Equipment Regional Carrier
Palmetto Government Benefits Administrators
1-800-213-5452

California

State Department of Aging
Department of Aging
Health Insurance Counseling and Advocacy Branch
1600 K St.
Sacramento, CA 95814
(916) 322-3887

Insurance Counseling
1-800-434-0222
(916) 323-7315

State Insurance Office
Insurance Department, Consumer Services Division
300 Capitol Mall
Sacramento, CA 95814
(916) 445-5544

State Ombudsman
(916) 323-6681

Peer Review Organization
California Medical Review, Inc.
1-800-841-1602
(415) 882-5800

Medicare Regional Office
(415) 744-3602

Medicare Part B Claims
Counties of Los Angeles, Orange, San Diego, Ventura, Imperial,
San Luis Obispo, and Santa Barbara:
Transamerica Occidental Life Insurance Company
1-800-675-2266
(213) 748-2311
Rest of State:
National Heritage Insurance Company
1-800-952-8627
(916) 743-1583

Durable Medical Equipment Regional Carrier
CIGNA Medicare
1-800-899-7095

Colorado

State Department of Aging
Aging and Adult Services
Department of Social Services
110 16th St., Suite 200
Denver, CO 80203-1714
(303) 620-4147

Insurance Counseling
1-800-544-9181
(303) 894-7499, ext. 356

State Insurance Office
Insurance Division
1560 Broadway, Suite 850
Denver, CO 80202
(303) 894-7499, ext. 356

State Ombudsman
(303) 722-0300

Peer Review Organization
Colorado Foundation for Medical Care
1-800-727-7086
(303) 695-3333

Medicare Regional Office
(303) 844-4024

Medicare Part B Claims
Blue Shield
1-800-322-6681
(303) 831-2661

Durable Medical Equipment Regional Carrier
Palmetto Government Benefits Administrators
1-800-213-5452

Connecticut

State Department of Aging
Commission on Aging
25 Sigourney St.
Hartford, CT 06106-5033
(806) 424-5360

Insurance Counseling
1-800-994-9422

State Insurance Office
Insurance Department
P.O. Box 816
Hartford, CT 06142-0816
(203) 297-3800

State Ombudsman
(860) 424-5200

Peer Review Organization
Programs for Health Insurance Assistance
Outreach, Information and Referral (CHOICES)
Connecticut Peer Review Organization, Inc.
1-800-553-7590
(860) 632-2008

Medicare Regional Office
(617) 565-1232

Medicare Part B Claims
MetraHealth Insurance Company
1-800-982-6819
(203) 237-8592 (Meriden)

Durable Medical Equipment Regional Carrier
United Health Care Insurance Company
1-800-842-2052

Delaware

State Department of Aging
Services for Aging & Adults with Physical Disabilities
Department of Health & Social Services
1901 N. DuPont Highway
2nd Floor Annex Administration Building
New Castle, DE 19720
1-800-223-9074
(302) 577-4791

Insurance Counseling
1-800-336-9500

State Insurance Office
Insurance Department
Rodney Building
841 Silver Lake Blvd.
Dover, DE 19904
1-800-282-8611
(302) 739-4251

State Ombudsman
(302) 453-3820

Peer Review Organization
West Virginia Medical Institute, Inc.
1-800-642-8686 ext. 266
(302) 655-3077 (Wilmington)

Medicare Regional Office
(215) 596-1335

Medicare Part B Claims
Xact Medicare Services
1-800-851-3535

Durable Medical Equipment Regional Carrier
United Health Care Insurance Company
1-800-842-2052

District of Columbia

State Department of Aging
Office on Aging
441 4th St. NW, 9th Floor
Washington, DC 20001
(202) 724-5626
(202) 724-5622

Insurance Counseling
(202) 676-3900

State Insurance Office
Insurance Department
Consumer & Professional Services Bureau
441 4th St. NW, Suite 850-N
Washington, DC 20001
(202) 727-8000

State Ombudsman
(202) 662-4933

Peer Review Organization
Delmarva Foundation for Medical Care, Inc.
1-800-999-3362 (DC)
1-800-492-5811 (MD)

Medicare Regional Office
(215) 596-1335

Medicare Part B Claims
Xact Medicare Services
1-800-233-1124

Durable Medical Equipment Regional Carrier
AdminaStar Federal, Inc.
1-800-270-2313

Florida

State Department of Aging
Department of Elder Affairs
4040 Esplanade Way, Suite 260
Tallahassee, FL 32399-7000
(904) 414-2060

Insurance Counseling
1-800-963-5337
(904) 414-2060

State Insurance Office
Department of Insurance
200 E. Gaines St.
Tallahassee, FL 32399-0300
(904) 922-3100

State Ombudsman
(904) 488-6190

Peer Review Organization
Florida Medical Quality Assurance, Inc.
1-800-844-0795
(813) 354-9111

Medicare Regional Office
(404) 331-2044

Medicare Part B Claims
Blue Cross/Blue Shield of Florida
1-800-333-7586
(904) 355-3680

Durable Medical Equipment Regional Carrier
Palmetto Government Benefits Administrators
1-800-213-5452

Georgia

State Department of Aging
Division of Aging Services
Department of Human Resources
2 Peachtree St. NW, Room 18.403
Atlanta, GA 30303
(404) 657-5258

Insurance Counseling
1-800-669-8387
(404) 657-5334

State Insurance Office
Insurance Department
2 Martin Luther King, Jr., Dr.
716 W. Tower
Atlanta, GA 30334
(404) 656-2056

State Ombudsman
(404) 657-5319

Peer Review Organization
Georgia Medical Care Foundation
1-800-982-0411
(404) 982-0411

Medicare Regional Office
(404) 331-2044

Medicare Part B Claims
Cahaba Government Benefits Administrators
1-800-727-0827
(912) 920-2412

Durable Medical Equipment Regional Carrier
Palmetto Government Benefits Administrators
1-800-213-5452

Guam

State Department of Aging
Division of Senior Citizens
Department of Public Health and Social Services
P.O. Box 2816
Agana, GU 96910
011 (671) 475-0262/3

Insurance Counseling
011 (671) 475-0262/3

State Insurance Office
Insurance Division
Department of Revenue & Taxation
P.O. Box 23607
GMF Barrigada, GU 96921
011 (671) 475-5000

Peer Review Organization
Mountain Pacific Quality Health Foundation
1-800-524-6550
(808) 545-2550

Medicare Regional Office
(415) 744-3602

Medicare Part B Claims
Medicare Part B
1-800-444-4606

Durable Medical Equipment Regional Carrier
CIGNA Medicare
1-800-899-7095

Hawaii

State Department of Aging
Executive Office on Aging
250 S. Hotel St., Suite 107
Honolulu, HI 96813
(808) 586-0100

Insurance Counseling
(808) 586-0100

State Insurance Office

Department of Commerce and Consumer Affairs
Insurance Division
P.O. Box 3614
Honolulu, HI 96811
(808) 586-2790

State Ombudsman
(808) 586-0100

Peer Review Organization
Mountain Pacific Quality Health Foundation
1-800-524-6550
(808) 545-2550 (Oahu)

Medicare Regional Office
(415) 744-3602

Medicare Part B Claims
SAGE PLUS
(808) 586-0100

Durable Medical Equipment Regional Carrier
CIGNA Medicare
1-800-899-7095

Idaho

State Department of Aging
Office on Aging
Statehouse, Room 108
Boise, ID 83720
(208) 334-3833

Insurance Counseling
1-800-247-442 (SW)
1-800-488-5725 (N)
1-800-488-5764 (SE)
1-800-488-5731 (C)

State Insurance Office
Insurance Department
SHIBA Program
700 W. State St., 3rd Floor
Boise, ID 83720-0043
(208) 334-4350

State Ombudsman
(208) 334-3822

Peer Review Organization
PRO-WEST
1-800-445-6941
(208) 343-4617

Medicare Regional Office
(206) 615-2354

Medicare Part B Claims
Medicare Part B
1-800-627-2782
(615) 244-5650

Durable Medical Equipment Regional Carrier
CIGNA Medicare
1-800-899-7095

Illinois

State Department of Aging
Department on Aging
421 E. Capitol Ave., #100
Springfield, IL 62701-1789
1-800-252-8966

Insurance Counseling
1-800-548-9034
(217) 785-9021

State Insurance Office
Insurance Department
320 W. Washington St., 4th Floor
Springfield, IL 62767
(217) 782-4515

State Ombudsman
(217) 785-3143

Peer Review Organization
Illinois Foundation for Medical Care
1-800-647-8089

Medicare Regional Office
(312) 353-7180

Medicare Part B Claims
Claims/Health Care Service Corp.
1-800-642-6930
1-800-535-6152 (TTY/TDD)
(312) 938-8000

Durable Medical Equipment Regional Carrier
AdminaStar Federal Inc.
1-800-270-2313

Indiana

State Department of Aging
Division of Aging & Rehabilitative Services
402 W. Washington St.
P.O. Box 7083
Indianapolis, IN 46207-7083
1-800-545-7763
(317) 232-7020

Insurance Counseling
1-800-452-4800
(317) 233-3475
(317) 232-5299

State Insurance Office
Insurance Department
311 W. Washington St., Suite 300
Indianapolis, IN 46204
1-800-622-4461
(317) 232-2395

State Ombudsman
(317) 232-7134

Peer Review Organization
Health Care Excel, Inc.
1-800-288-1499

Medicare Regional Office
(312) 353-7180

Medicare Part B Claims
AdminaStar Federal
1-800-622-4792
(317) 842-4151

Durable Medical Equipment Regional Carrier
AdminaStar Federal
1-800-270-2313

Iowa

State Department of Aging
Department of Elder Affairs
200 10th St., Third Floor
Des Moines, IA 50309-3709
(515) 281-5187

Insurance Counseling
1-800-351-4664

State Insurance Office
Insurance Division
Lucas State Office Building, 6th Floor
E 12th & Grand Streets
Des Moines, IA 50319
(515) 281-5705

State Ombudsman
(515) 281-4656

Peer Review Organization
Iowa Foundation for Medical Care
1-800-752-7014
(515) 223-2900

Medicare Regional Office
(816) 426-2866

Medicare Part B Claims
IASD Health Services Corporation
Blue Cross/Blue Shield of Iowa
1-800-532-1285
(515) 245-4785

Durable Medical Equipment Regional Carrier
CIGNA Medicare
1-800-899-7095

Kansas

State Department of Aging
Department on Aging
150-S Docking State Office Building
915 S.W. Harrison
Topeka, KS 66612-1500
(913) 296-4986

Insurance Counseling
1-800-860-5260

State Insurance Office
Insurance Department
420 S.W. 9th St.
Topeka, KS 66612
1-800-432-2484
(913) 296-3071

State Ombudsman
(913) 296-6539

Peer Review Organization
The Kansas Foundation for Medical Care
1-800-432-0407
(913) 273-2552

Medicare Regional Office
(816) 426-2866

Medicare Part B Claims
Medicare/Blue Cross/Blue Shield of Kansas
1-800-432-3531
(913) 232-3773

Durable Medical Equipment Regional Carrier
CIGNA Medicare
1-800-899-7095

Kentucky

State Department of Aging
Division of Aging Services
Cabinet of Family & Children
275 E. Main St.
Frankfort, KY 40621
(502) 564-7372

Insurance Counseling
1-800-372-2973
(502) 564-7372

State Insurance Office
Insurance Department
215 W. Main St.
P.O. Box 517
Frankfort, KY 40602
1-800-595-6053
(502) 564-3630

State Ombudsman
(502) 564-6930

Peer Review Organization
Health Care Excel, Inc.
1-800-288-1499

Medicare Regional Office
(404) 331-2044

Medicare Part B Claims
AdminaStar of Kentucky
1-800-999-7608
(502) 425-6759

Durable Medical Equipment Regional Carrier
Palmetto Government Benefits Administrators
1-800-213-5452

Louisiana

State Department of Aging
Governor's Office of Elderly Affairs
4550 N. Blvd.
P.O. Box 80374
Baton Rouge, LA 70806-0374
(504) 925-1700

Insurance Counseling
1-800-259-5301
(504) 342-5301

State Insurance Office
Department of Insurance
P.O. Box 94214
Baton Rouge, LA 70804-9214
1-800-259-5301
(504) 342-5301

State Ombudsman
(504) 342-7100

Peer Review Organization
Louisiana Health Care Review, Inc.
1-800-433-4958
(504) 926-6353

Medicare Regional Office
(214) 767-6401

Medicare Part B Claims
Louisiana Medicare Part B
1-800-462-9666
(504) 927-3490 (Baton Rouge)

Durable Medical Equipment Regional Carrier
Palmetto Government Benefits Administrators
1-800-213-5452

Maine

State Department of Aging
Bureau of Elder and Adult Services
State House, Station 11
Augusta, ME 04333
(207) 624-5335

Insurance Counseling
1-800-750-5353
(207) 623-1797

State Insurance Office
Bureau of Insurance
34 State House Station
Augusta, ME 04333
(207) 624-8475

State Ombudsman
1-800-499-0229

Peer Review Organization
Northeast Health Care Quality Foundation
1-800-722-0151

Medicare Regional Office
(617) 565-1232

Medicare Part B Claims
National Heritage Insurance Company
1-800-492-0919

Durable Medical Equipment Regional Carrier
United Health Care Insurance Co.
1-800-842-2052

Maryland

State Department of Aging
Office on Aging
301 W. Preston St., Room 1007
Baltimore, MD 21201
(410) 767-1074

Insurance Counseling
1-800-243-3425
(410) 767-1074

State Insurance Office
Insurance Administration, Complaints and Investigation
Unit-Life & Health
501 St. Paul Pl.
Baltimore, MD 21202-2272
(410) 333-2793
(410) 333-2770

State Ombudsman
(410) 225-1074

Peer Review Organization
Delmarva Foundation for Medical Care
1-800-492-5811
1-800-645-0011 (outside Maryland)

Medicare Regional Office
(215) 596-1335

Medicare Part B Claims
Counties of Montgomery & Prince Georges:
Exact Medicare Services
1-800-444-4606,
Rest of state:
Trail Blazer Enterprises
1-800-444-4606

Durable Medical Equipment Regional Carrier
AdminaStar Federal Inc.
1-800-270-2313

Massachusetts

State Department of Aging
Executive Office of Elder Affairs
1 Ashburton Place, 5th Floor
Boston, MA 02108
1-800-882-2003
(617) 727-7750

Insurance Counseling
1-800-882-2003
(617) 727-7750

State Insurance Office
Insurance Division, Consumer Services Section
470 Atlantic Ave.
Boston, MA 02210-2223
(617) 521-7777

State Ombudsman
(617) 727-7750

Peer Review Organization
Massachusetts Peer Review Organization
1-800-252-5533
(617) 890-0011

Medicare Regional Office
(617) 565-1232

Medicare Part B Claims
National Heritage Insurance Company
1-800-882-1228

Durable Medical Equipment Regional Carrier
United Health Care Insurance Co.
1-800-842-2052

Michigan

State Department of Aging
Office of Services to the Aging
611 W. Ottawa St.
P.O. Box 30026
Lansing, MI 48909
(517) 373-8230

Insurance Counseling
1-800-803-7174

State Insurance Office
Insurance Bureau
P.O. Box 30220
Lansing, MI 48909
(517) 373-0240 (general assistance)
(517) 335-1702 (senior issues)

State Ombudsman
AdminaStar Federal Inc.
1-800-270-2313

Peer Review Organization
Medicare/Medicaid Assistance Program
1-800-803-7174

Medicare Regional Office
(312) 353-7180

Medicare Part B Claims
Michigan Medicare Claims
1-800-562-7802 (906 area code)
1-800-482-4045 (rest of state)
(313) 225-8200

Durable Medical Equipment Regional Carrier
Michigan Peer Review Organization
1-800-365-5899

Minnesota

State Department of Aging
Board on Aging
Human Services Building, 4th Floor
444 Lafayette Rd.
St. Paul, MN 55155-3843
(612) 296-2770

Insurance Counseling
1-800-882-6262
(612) 296-2770

State Insurance Office
Insurance Department
Department of Commerce
133 E. 7th St.
St. Paul, MN 55101-2362
(612) 296-4026

State Ombudsman
(612) 296-0382

Peer Review Organization
Stratis Health
1-800-444-3423
(612) 854-3306

Medicare Regional Office
(312) 353-7180

Medicare Part B Claims
MetraHealth Medicare
1-800-352-2762
(612) 884-7171

Durable Medical Equipment Regional Carrier
AdminaStar Federal Inc.
1-800-270-2313

Mississippi

State Department of Aging
Division of Aging & Adult Services
750 N. State St.
Jackson, MS 39202
1-800-948-3090
(601) 359-4929

Insurance Counseling
1-800-948-3090

State Insurance Office
Insurance Department
Consumer Assistance Division
P.O. Box 79
Jackson, MS 39205
(601) 359-3569

State Ombudsman
(601) 359-4929

Peer Review Organization
Foundation for Medical Care
1-800-844-0600
(601) 354-0304

Medicare Regional Office
(404) 331-2044

Medicare Part B Claims
United Health Care Insurance Company
1-800-682-5417
(601) 956-0372

Durable Medical Equipment Regional Carrier
Palmetto Government Benefits Administrators
1-800-213-5452

Missouri

State Department of Aging
Division of Aging, Department of Social Services
615 Howerton Ct.
Jefferson City, MO 65109-1337
1-800-285-5503
(573) 751-3082

Insurance Counseling
1-800-390-3330
(573) 893-7900

State Insurance Office
Department of Insurance, Consumer Services Section
P.O. Box 690
Jefferson City, MO 65102-0690
1-800-726-7390
(314) 751-2640

State Ombudsman
(573) 526-0727

Peer Review Organization
Missouri Patient Care Review Foundation
1-800-347-1016

Medicare Regional Office
(816) 426-2866

Medicare Part B Claims
Counties of Andrew, Atchison, Bates, Benton, Buchanan,
Caldwell, Carroll, Cass, Clay, Clinton, Daviess, DeKalb, Gentry,
Grundy, Harrison, Henry, Holt, Jackson, Johnson, Lafayette,
Livingston, Mercer, Nodaway, Pettis, Platte, Ray, St. Claire, Saline,
Vernon, and Worth:
Blue Cross/Blue Shield of Kansas
1-800-892-5900
(816) 561-0900

Rest of State:
Medicare General American Life Insurance Company
1-800-392-3070
(314) 843-8880

Durable Medical Equipment Regional Carrier
CIGNA Medicare
1-800-899-7095

Montana

State Department of Aging
Division of Senior & Long-Term Care/DPHHS
48 N. Last Chance Gulch
P.O. Box 4210
Helena, MT 59604-8005
1-800-332-2272
(406) 444-7781

Insurance Counseling
1-800-332-2272

State Insurance Office
Insurance Department
126 N. Sanders
Mitchell Building, Room 270
P.O. Box 4009
Helena, MT 59601
(406) 444-2040

State Ombudsman
(406) 444-5900

Peer Review Organization
Mountain Pacific Quality Health Foundation
1-800-497-8232
(406) 443-4020

Medicare Regional Office
(303) 844-4024

Medicare Part B Claims
Blue Cross/Blue Shield of Montana
1-800-332-6146
(406) 444-8350

Durable Medical Equipment Regional Carrier
CIGNA Medicare
1-800-899-7095

State Department of Aging
Department on Aging
State Office Building
301 Centennial Mall S
Lincoln, NE 68509-5044
1-800-942-7830
(402) 471-2306

Insurance Counseling
(402) 471-2201

State Insurance Office
Insurance Department
Terminal Building
941 O St., Suite 400
Lincoln, NE 68508
(402) 471-2201

State Ombudsman
(402) 471-2306

Peer Review Organization
The Sunderbruch Corp. of Nebraska
1-800-247-3004
(402) 474-7471

Medicare Regional Office
(816) 426-2866

267
Appendix B
State Resources

Medicare Part B Claims
Medicare Part B
Blue Cross/Blue Shield of Kansas
1-800-633-1113

Durable Medical Equipment Regional Carrier
CIGNA Medicare
1-800-899-7095

Nevada

State Department of Aging
Department of Human Resources
Division for Aging Services
340 N. 11th St., Suite 114
Las Vegas, NV 89101
1-800-243-3638
(702) 486-3545

Insurance Counseling
1-800-307-4444
(702) 486-4602

State Insurance Office
Department of Business & Industry
Division of Insurance
1665 Hot Springs Rd., Suite 152
Carson City, NV 89710
1-800-992-0900
(702) 687-4270

State Ombudsman
(702) 486-3545

Peer Review Organization
HealthInsight
1-800-748-6773
(702) 385-9933

Medicare Regional Office
(415) 744-3602

Medicare Part B Claims
Medicare Part B
1-800-444-4606

Durable Medical Equipment Regional Carrier
CIGNA Medicare
1-800-899-7095

New Hampshire

State Department of Aging
Department of Health & Human Services
Division of Elderly & Adult Services
State Office Park South, Annex Building Number 1
115 Pleasant St.
Concord, NH 03301
(603) 271-4680

Insurance Counseling
1-800-852-3388
(603) 225-9000

State Insurance Office
Insurance Department
Life and Health Division
169 Manchester St.
Concord, NH 03301
1-800-852-3416
(603) 271-2261

State Ombudsman
1-800-443-5640 (in-state only)
(603) 271-4375

Peer Review Organization
Northeast Health Care Quality Foundation
1-800-772-0151
(603) 749-1641

Medicare Regional Office
(617) 565-1232

Medicare Part B Claims
National Heritage Insurance Company
1-800-447-1142

Durable Medical Equipment Regional Carrier
United Health Care Insurance Company
1-800-842-2052
(603) 749-1641

New Jersey

State Department of Aging
Health & Human Services Division
Department of Senior Affairs
101 S. Broad St., CN 807
Trenton, NJ 08625-0807
1-800-792-8820
(609) 984-3951

Insurance Counseling
1-800-792-8820

State Insurance Office
Insurance Department
Roebling Building, CN 325
20 W. State St.
Trenton, NJ 08625
(609) 292-5363

State Ombudsman
(609) 984-7831

Peer Review Organization
The PRO of New Jersey Inc.
1-800-624-4557
(908) 238-5570

Medicare Regional Office
(212) 264-3657

Medicare Part B Claims
Xact Medicare Services
1-800-462-9306

Durable Medical Equipment Regional Carrier
United Health Care Insurance Company
1-800-842-2052

New Mexico

State Department of Aging
State Agency on Aging
La Villa Rivera Building
224 E. Palace Ave.
Santa Fe, NM 87501
1-800-432-2080
(505) 827-7640

Insurance Counseling
1-800-432-2080
(505) 827-7640

State Insurance Office Insurance Department
P.O. Drawer 1269
Santa Fe, NM 87504-1269
(505) 827-4601

State Ombudsman
(505) 827-7663

Peer Review Organization
New Mexico Medical Review Association
1-800-279-6824
(505) 842-6236

Medicare Regional Office
(214) 767-6401

Medicare Part B Claims
Medicare Services New Mexico
1-800-423-2925
(505) 821-3350

Durable Medical Equipment Regional Carrier
Palmetto Government Benefits Administrators
1-800-213-5452

New York

State Department of Aging
State Office for the Aging
2 Empire State Plaza
Albany, NY 12223-0001
1-800-342-9871
(518) 474-9871

Insurance Counseling
1-800-333-4114
(212) 869-3850 (New York City area)

State Insurance Office
Insurance Department
160 W. Broadway
New York, NY 10013
(212) 602-0203
1-800-342-3736 (outside of New York City)

State Ombudsman
(518) 474-0108

Peer Review Organization
Island Peer Review Organization, Inc.
1-800-331-7767
(516) 326-7767

Medicare Regional Office
(212) 264-3657

Medicare Part B Claims
Counties of Bronx, Columbia, Delaware, Dutchess, Greene,
Kings, Nassau, New York, Orange, Putnam, Richmond, Rockland,
Suffolk, Sullivan, Ulster, and Westchester:
Empire Medicare Services
1-800-442-8430
(516) 244-5100
Queens City Group Health
(212) 721-1770
Rest of State:
BC/BS of Western NY
1-800-252-6550
(607) 766-6223

Durable Medical Equipment Regional Carrier
United Health Insurance Company
1-800-842-2052

North Carolina

State Department of Aging
Division of Aging
Caller Box 29531
693 Palmer Dr.
Raleigh, NC 27626-0531
(919) 733-3983

Insurance Counseling
1-800-443-9354

State Insurance Office
Insurance Department
Seniors' Health Insurance Information Program (SHIIP)
P.O. Box 26387
Raleigh, NC 27611
1-800-662-7777 (consumer services)
(919) 733-0111 (SHIIP)

State Ombudsman
(919) 733-3983

Peer Review Organization
Medical Review of North Carolina
1-800-722-0468
(919) 851-2955

Medicare Regional Office
(404) 331-2044

Medicare Part B Claims
CIGNA
1-800-672-3071
(910) 665-0348

Durable Medical Equipment Regional Carrier
Palmetto Government Benefits Administrators
1-800-213-5452

North Dakota

State Department of Aging
Department of Human Services
Aging Services Division
P.O. Box 7070
Bismarck, ND 58507-7070
1-800-755-8521
(701) 328-8910

Insurance Counseling
1-800-247-0560

State Insurance Office
Insurance Department
Senior Health Insurance Counseling
600 East Blvd.
Bismarck, ND 58505-0320
1-800-247-0560
(701) 328-2440

State Ombudsman
(701) 328-2577

Peer Review Organization
North Dakota Health Care Review, Inc.
1-800-472-2902
(701) 852-4231

Medicare Regional Office
(303) 844-4024

Medicare Part B Claims
Blue Shield of North Dakota
1-800-247-2267
(701) 277-2363

Durable Medical Equipment Regional Carrier
CIGNA Medicare
1-800-899-7095

Ohio

State Department of Aging
Department of Aging
50 W. Broad St., 9th Floor
Columbus, OH 43215-5928
1-800-282-1206
(614) 466-1221

Insurance Counseling
1-800-686-1578
(614) 644-3458

State Insurance Office
Insurance Department
Consumer Services Division
2100 Stella Ct.
Columbus, OH 43215-1067
1-800-686-1526
(614) 644-2673

State Ombudsman
(614) 466-7922

Peer Review Organization
Peer Review Systems, Inc.
1-800-837-0664
1-800-589-7337

Medicare Regional Office
(312) 353-7180

Medicare Part B Claims
Medicare/Nationwide Mutual Insurance Company
1-800-282-0530
(614) 249-7157

Durable Medical Equipment Regional Carrier
AdminaStar Federal Inc.
1-800-270-2313

Oklahoma

State Department of Aging
Department of Human Services
Aging Services Division
312 NE 28th St.
Oklahoma City, OK 73125
(405) 521-2327

Insurance Counseling
1-800-763-2828
(405) 521-6628

State Insurance Office
Insurance Department
P.O. Box 53408
Oklahoma City, OK 73152
1-800-522-0071
(405) 521-2828

State Ombudsman
(405) 521-6734

Peer Review Organization
Oklahoma Foundation for Medical Quality
1-800-522-3414
(405) 840-2891

Medicare Regional Office
(214) 767-6401

Medicare Part B Claims
Medicare Services Oklahoma
1-800-522-9079
(405) 848-7711

Durable Medical Equipment Regional Carrier
Palmetto Government Benefits Administrators
1-800-213-5452

Oregon

State Department of Aging
Department of Human Resources
Senior & Disabled Services Division
500 Summer St. NE, 2nd Floor
Salem, OR 97310-1015
1-800-232-3020
(503) 945-5811

Insurance Counseling
1-800-722-4134
(503) 378-4636 ext.600

State Insurance Office
Department of Consumer & Business Services,
Senior Health Insurance, Benefits Assistance
350 Winter St. NE, Room 440
Salem, OR 97310
1-800-722-4134
(503) 378-4484

State Ombudsman
(503) 378-6533

Peer Review Organization
Oregon Medical Professional Review Org.
1-800-344-4354
(503) 279-0100

Medicare Regional Office
(206) 615-2354

Medicare Part B Claims
Medicare Part B
1-800-444-4606

Durable Medical Equipment Regional Carrier
CIGNA Medicare
1-800-899-7095

Pennsylvania

State Department of Aging
Department of Aging
"Apprise" Health Insurance, Counseling and Assistance
Rachel Carson State Office Building
400 Market St.
Harrisburg, PA 17101
1-800-783-7067

Insurance Counseling
1-800-783-7067

State Insurance Office
Insurance Department
Consumer Services Bureau
1321 Strawberry Sq.
Harrisburg, PA 17120
(717) 787-2317

State Ombudsman
(717) 783-7247

Peer Review Organization
Keystone Peer Review Organization, Inc.
1-800-222-0711
(717) 564-8288

Medicare Regional Office
(215) 596-1335

Medicare Part B Claims
Xact Medicare Services
1-800-382-1274

Durable Medical Equipment Regional Carrier
United Health Care Insurance Company
1-800-842-2052

Puerto Rico

State Department of Aging
Governor's Office of Elderly Affairs
Gericulture Commission
Box 11398
Santurce, PR 00910
(809) 722-2429

Insurance Counseling
(809) 721-5710
(809) 721-8590

State Insurance Office
Office of the Commissioner of Insurance
P.O. Box 8330
San Juan, PR 00910-8330
(809) 722-8686

State Ombudsman
(809) 721-8225

Peer Review Organization
Quality Improvement Professional Research Organization
(787) 753-6705
(787) 753-6708

Medicare Regional Office
(212) 264-3657

Medicare Part B Claims
Triple-S, Inc.
San Juan Metro area:
(787) 749-4900
Rest of Puerto Rico:
1-800-981-7015

Durable Medical Equipment Regional Carrier
Palmetto Government Benefits Administrators
1-800-213-5452

Rhode Island

State Department of Aging
Department of Elderly Affairs
160 Pine St.
Providence, RI 02903
(401) 277-2880

Insurance Counseling
1-800-322-2880

State Insurance Office
Insurance Division
233 Richmond St., Suite 233
Providence, RI 02903-4233
(401) 277-2223

State Ombudsman
(401) 277-2858

Peer Review Organization
Rhode Island Quality Partners, Inc.
1-800-553-7590

Medicare Regional Office
(617) 565-1232

Medicare Part B Claims
Blue Cross/Blue Shield of Rhode Island
1-800-662-5170
(401) 861-2273

Durable Medical Equipment Regional Carrier
United Health Care Insurance Company
1-800-842-2052

South Carolina

State Department of Aging
Division on Aging
202 Arbor Lake Dr., Suite 301
Columbia, SC 29223-4554
(803) 737-7500

Insurance Counseling
1-800-868-9095
(803) 737-7500

State Insurance Office
Department of Insurance
Consumer Services Section
P.O. Box 100105
Columbia, SC 29202-3105
1-800-768-3467
(803) 737-6180

State Ombudsman
(803) 737-7500

Peer Review Organization
Carolina Medical Review
1-800-685-1512
(803) 731-8225

Medicare Regional Office
(404) 331-2044

Medicare Part B Claims
Palmetto Government Benefits Administrators
1-800-868-2522
(803) 788-3882

Durable Medical Equipment Regional Carrier
Palmetto Government Benefits Administrators
1-800-213-5452

South Dakota

State Department of Aging
Office of Adult Services and Aging
700 Governors Dr.
Pierre, SD 57501-2291
(605) 773-3656

Insurance Counseling
1-800-822-8804
(605) 773-3656

State Insurance Office
Insurance Department
500 E. Capitol Ave.
Pierre, SD 57501-5070
(605) 773-3563

State Ombudsman
(605) 773-3656

Peer Review Organization
South Dakota Foundation for Medical Care
1-800-658-2285
(605) 336-3505

Medicare Regional Office
(303) 844-4024

Medicare Part B Claims
Blue Shield
1-800-437-4762
(701) 277-2363

Durable Medical Equipment Regional Carrier
CIGNA Medicare
1-800-899-7095

Tennessee

State Department of Aging
Commission on Aging
Andrew Jackson Building
500 Deaderick St., 9th Floor
Nashville, TN 37243
(615) 741-2056

Insurance Counseling
1-800-525-2816

State Insurance Office
Department of Commerce & Insurance
Insurance Assistance Office
500 James Robertson Pkwy., 4th Floor
Nashville, TN 37243
1-800-525-2816
(615) 741-4955

State Ombudsman
(615) 741-2056

Peer Review Organization
Mid-South Foundation for Medical Care
1-800-489-4633

Medicare Regional Office
(404) 331-2044

Medicare Part B Claims
CIGNA Medicare
1-800-342-8900
(615) 244-5650

Durable Medical Equipment Regional Carrier
Palmetto Government Benefits Administrators
1-800-213-5452

Texas

State Department of Aging
Department on Aging
P.O. Box 12786 (78711)
1949 I-35 S
Austin, TX 78741
1-800-252-9240
(512) 424-6840

Insurance Counseling
1-800-252-3439
1-800-252-9240

State Insurance Office
Department of Insurance
Complaints Resolution (MC 111-1A)
P.O. Box 149091
333 Guadalupe St. (78701)
Austin, TX 78714-9091
1-800-252-3439
(512) 463-6515

State Ombudsman
(512) 444-2727

Peer Review Organization
Texas Medical Foundation
1-800-725-8315
(512) 329-6610

Medicare Regional Office
(214) 767-6401

Medicare Part B Claims
Blue Cross & Blue Shield of Texas
1-800-442-2620
(214) 235-3433

Durable Medical Equipment Regional Carrier
Palmetto Government Benefits Administrators
1-800-213-5452

Utah

State Department of Aging
Division of Aging and Adult Services
120 N. 200 W
Salt Lake City, UT 84103
(801) 538-3910

Insurance Counseling
1-800-439-3805
(801) 538-3910

State Insurance Office
Insurance Department
Consumer Services
3110 State Office Building
Salt Lake City, UT 84114-6901
1-800-439-3805
(801) 538-3805

State Ombudsman
(801) 538-3910

Peer Review Organization
HealthInsight
1-800-274-2290

Medicare Regional Office
(303) 844-4024

Medicare Part B Claims
Blue Shield of Utah
1-800-426-3477
(801) 481-6196

Durable Medical Equipment Regional Carrier
CIGNA Medicare
1-800-899-7095

Vermont

State Department of Aging
Department of Aging & Disabilities
Waterbury Complex
103 S. Main St.
Waterbury, VT 05671-2301
(802) 241-2400

Insurance Counseling
1-800-642-5119
(802) 861-1577

State Insurance Office
Department of Banking & Insurance
Consumer Complaint Division
Drawer 20
89 Main St.
Montpelier, VT 05620-3101
(802) 828-3302

State Ombudsman
(802) 863-5620

Peer Review Organization
Northeast Health Care Quality Foundation
1-800-772-0151
(603) 749-1641

Medicare Regional Office
(617) 565-1232

Medicare Part B Claims
National Heritage Insurance Company
1-800-447-1142

Durable Medical Equipment Regional Carrier
United Health Care Insurance Company
1-800-842-2052

Virginia

State Department of Aging
Department for the Aging
700 Centre, 10th Floor
700 E. Franklin St.
Richmond, VA 23219-2327
1-800-552-3402
(804) 225-2271

Insurance Counseling
1-800-552-3402

State Insurance Office Bureau of Insurance
1300 E. Main St.
Richmond, VA 23219
1-800-552-7945
(804) 371-9691

State Ombudsman
AdminaStar Federal Inc.
1-800-270-2313

Peer Review Organization
Virginia Health Quality Center
1-800-545-3814
(804) 289-5320,
(804) 289-5397 (Richmond)

Medicare Regional Office
(215) 596-1335

Medicare Part B Claims
Counties of Arlington, Fairfax:
Xact Medicare Services
1-800-233-1124
Rest of state:
MetraHealth
1-800-552-3423
(804) 330-4786

Durable Medical Equipment Regional Carrier
Virginia Health Quality Center
1-800-545-3814 (District of Columbia, Maryland, Virginia)
(804) 289-5320
(804) 289-5397 (Richmond)

Virgin Islands

State Department of Aging
Senior Citizen Affairs Division
Department of Human Services
19 Estate Diamond
Fredericksted, St. Croix, VI 00840
(809) 772-0930

Insurance Counseling
(809) 774-2991

State Insurance Office
Insurance Department
Kongens Gade, #18
St. Thomas, VI 00802
(809) 773-6449, ext. 248

Peer Review Organization
Virgin Islands Medical Institute, Inc.
(809) 778-6470

Medicare Regional Office
(212) 264-3657

Medicare Part B Claims
Triple-S, Inc.
1-800-474-7448

Durable Medical Equipment Regional Carrier
Palmetto Government Benefits Administrators
1-800-213-5452

Washington

State Department of Aging
Aging & Adult Services Administration
Department of Social & Health Services
P.O. Box 45600
Olympia, WN 98504-5600
(360) 493-2500

Insurance Counseling
1-800-605-6299
1-800-397-4422

State Insurance Office
Insurance Department
4224 6th Ave. SE, Bldg 4
P.O. Box 40256
Lacey, WN 98504-0256
1-800-397-4422
(360) 407-0383

State Ombudsman
(206) 838-6810

Peer Review Organization
PRO-WEST
1-800-445-6941
(206) 368-8272

Medicare Regional Office
(206) 615-2354

Medicare Part B Claims
Medicare Part B
1-800-444-4606

Durable Medical Equipment Regional Carrier
CIGNA Medicare
1-800-899-7095

West Virginia

State Department of Aging
Commission on Aging
State Capitol Complex, Holly Grove
1900 E. Kanawha Blvd.
Charleston, WV 25305-0160
(304) 558-3317

Insurance Counseling
1-800-642-9004
(304) 558-3317

State Insurance Office
Insurance Department
Consumer Service
P.O. Box 50540
2019 E. Washington St.
Charleston, WV 25305-0540
1-800-642-9004
1-800-435-7381 (hearing impaired)
(304) 558-3386

State Ombudsman
(304) 558-3317

Peer Review Organization
West Virginia Medical Institute, Inc.
1-800-642-8686, ext. 266
(304) 346-9864 (Charleston)

Medicare Regional Office
(215) 596-1335

Medicare Part B Claims
Nationwide Mutual Insurance Co.
1-800-848-0106
(614) 249-7157

Durable Medical Equipment Regional Carrier
AdminaStar Federal Inc.
1-800-270-2313

Wisconsin

State Department of Aging
Board on Aging and Long-Term Care
214 N. Hamilton St.
Madison, WI 53703
1-800-242-1060
(608) 266-8944

Insurance Counseling
1-800-242-1060

State Insurance Office
Insurance Department, Complaints Department
P.O. Box 7873
Madison, WI 53707
1-800-236-8517
(608) 266-0103

State Ombudsman
(608) 266-8944

Peer Review Organization
Wisconsin Peer Review Organization
1-800-362-2320
(608) 274-1940

Medicare Regional Office
(312) 353-7180

Medicare Part B Claims
Medicare/WPS
1-800-944-0051
(608) 221-3330
1-800-828-2837 (TTY/TDD)

Durable Medical Equipment Regional Carrier
AdminaStar Federal Inc.
1-800-270-2313

Wyoming

State Department of Aging
Division on Aging
Hathaway Building
2300 Capitol Ave., Room 139
Cheyenne, WY 82002
1-800-442-2766
(307) 777-7986

Insurance Counseling
1-800-856-4398
(307) 856-6880

State Insurance Office
Insurance Department
Herschler Building
122 W. 25th St.
Cheyenne, WY 82002
1-800-438-5768
(307) 777-7401

State Ombudsman
(307) 322-5553

Peer Review Organization
Mountain Pacific Quality Health Foundation
1-800-497-8232
(406) 443-4020

Medicare Regional Office
(303) 844-4024

Medicare Part B Claims
Blue Cross & Blue Shield of North Dakota
1-800-442-2371
(307) 632-9381

Durable Medical Equipment Regional Carrier
CIGNA Medicare
1-800-899-7095

Bibliography

ABTS, III, HENRY W. *The Living Trust: The Failproof Way to Pass Along Your Estate to Your Heirs Without Lawyers, Courts, or the Probate System.* Chicago: NTC/Contemporary Publishing, 1997.

AMERICAN ASSOCIATION OF HOMES AND SERVICES FOR THE AGING. *The Consumers' Directory of Continuing Care Communities.* Washington, D.C.: AAHSA, 1997.

ANDERSON, BARBARA GALLATIN. *The Aging Game.* New York: McGraw-Hill, 1979.

ANDERSON, BOB and JEAN ANDERSON. *Stretching.* Bolinas, Calif: Shelter Publications, 1987.

ANDERSON, BOB, ET AL. *Getting In Shape: Workout Programs for Men and Women.* Bolinas, Calif.: Shelter Publications, 1994.

ANOSIKE, BENJI O. *How to Properly Plan Your "Total" Estate with a Living Trust, Without the Lawyer's Fees: The National Living Trust Kit.* Newark, N.J.: Do It Yourself Legal Publications, 1995.

ANRIG, JR., GREG. "How to Retire Early." *Money*, November 1988.

BADGWELL, NANCY. "To Rekindle the Marital Fire," *Women in Their Dynamic Years.* Washington, D.C.: AARP, 1989.

BERMAN, PHILLIP L. BERMAN and CONNIE GOLDMAN. *The Ageless Spirit.* New York: Ballantine Books, 1992.

BIRACREE, TOM and NANCY BIRACREE. *Over Fifty: The Resource Book for the Better Half of Your Life.* New York: Harper Collins, 1991.

BIRKENDAHL, NONIE. *Older & Wiser.* Oakland, Calif.: New Harbinger Publications, 1991.

BLAND, JOHN H. *Live Long, Die Fast.* Minneapolis: Fairview Press, 1997.

BOLLES, RICHARD N. *The Three Boxes of Life*. Berkeley, Calif.: Ten Speed Press, 1978.

BOYER, RICHARD and DAVID SAVAGEAU. *Places Rated Retirement Guide*. Chicago: Rand McNally & Company, 1983.

BUA, ROBERT. *The Inside Guide to America's Nursing Homes*. New York: Warner Books, 1997.

CARLIN, VIRGINIA AND RUTH MANSBERG. *If I Live to be 100*. Princeton, N.J.: Princeton Book Company, 1989.

CARPER, JEAN. *Stop Aging Now!* New York: HarperCollins, 1995.

CARTER, JIMMY and ROSALYNN. *Everything to Gain*. New York: Random House, 1987.

CHASE, MARILYN. "Feed Your Brain, and It May Thrive in Old Age," *The Wall Street Journal*, 21 November, 1994.

CHOPRA, DEEPAK, M.D. *Ageless Body, Timeless Mind: The Quantum Alternative to Growing Old*. New York: Harmony Books, 1993.

CIRINO, LINDA D. *On Your Own: The Seniors' Guide to An Independent Life*. New York: Hearst Books, 1995.

CLEVELAND, JOAN. *Everything You Need to Know About Retirement Housing*. New York: Penguin Books, 1996.

CLIFFORD, DENIS. *Make Your Own Living Trust*. San Francisco: Nolo Press, 1998.

COLLIER, JAMES LINCOLN. "Most of Worry Doesn't Do Any Good." *Reader's Digest*, April 1988.

COMFORT, ALEX. *A Good Age*. New York: Crown Publishers, 1976.

Consumer Reports, "How Will You Pay for Your Old Age?" October 1997.

COOPER, LESLIE and ROBERT COOPER. *Low-Fat Living Cookbook*. Emmaus, Pa.: Rodale Press, 1998.

CORT-VAN ARSDALE, DIANA NEWMAN, AND PHYLLIS NEWMAN. *Transitions: A Woman's Guide to Successful Retirement*. New York: HarperCollins, 1991.

COSBY, BILL. *Time Flies*. New York: Doubleday, 1987.

COUDERT, JO. "Risky Business." *Woman's Day*, 24 March 1987.

COWLEY, GEOFFREY. "Melatonin," *Newsweek*. 7 August, 1975.

DACEY, NORMAN. *How to Avoid Probate*. New York: Macmillan Publishing, 1990.

DACYCZYN, AMY. *The Tightwad Gazette*. New York: Villard Books, 1993.

DANGOTT, LILLIAN. *A Time to Enjoy: The Pleasures of Aging*. Los Angeles: Spectrum Books, 1978.

DICKINSON, PETER. *The Complete Retirement Planning Book*. New York: E. P. Dutton and Company, 1976.

DICKMAN, BARRY, TRUDY LIEBERMAN, and *Consumer Reports* Editors. *How to Plan for a Secure Retirement*. Yonkers, N.Y.: Consumers Union, 1992.

DILLER, PHYLLIS. *The Joys of Aging & How to Avoid Them*. Garden City, N.J.: Doubleday & Company, Inc., 1981.

DOMINGUEZ, JOE and VICKI ROBINS. *Your Money or Your Life*. New York: Penguin Books, 1992.

DOWNS, HUGH. *Fifty to Forever*. Nashville, Tenn.: Thomas Nelson Publishers, 1994.

DOWNS, HUGH with RICHARD J. ROLL. *The Best Years Book*. New York: Delacorte Press, 1981.

DYCHTWALD, KEN and JOE FOWLER. *Age Wave: The Challenges and Opportunities of an Aging America*. Los Angeles: Jeremy P. Tarcher, Inc. 1989.

EDITORS OF CONSUMERS GUIDE. *Your Retirement: A Complete Planning Guide*. New York: A&W Publishers, 1981.

ELLIS, ALBERT and RONALD HARPER. *A New Guide to Rational Living*. North Hollywood, Calif.: Wilshire Books, 1976.

ETTINGER, JR., WALTER H., BRENDA MITCHELL, and STEVEN BLAIR. *Fitness After 50*. St. Louis, Mo.: Beverly Cracom Publications, 1996.

Financial Freedom Report, "The Courage to Keep a Dream Alive," April 1989.

Fortune, "The Future of Retirement: It's Not What You Think," 19 August, 1996.

FRENKEL-BRUNSWIK, ELSE. "Adjustments and Reorientations in the Course of the Life Span," *Middle Age and Aging*, Bernice Neugarten, ed. Chicago: University of Chicago Press, 1968.

FRIEDMAN, ROSLYN and ANNETTE NUSSBAUM. *Coping With Your Husband's Retirement*. New York: Simon & Schuster, Inc. 1986.

GREENSTEIN, DOREEN BRENNER. *Easy Things to Make to Make Things Easy*. Cambridge, Mass.: Brookline Books, 1997.

GROSS, ANDREA. *Shifting Gears*. New York: Crown Publishers, 1991.

HANSEN, LEONARD J. *Life Begins At 50: A Handbook for Creative Retirement Planning*. New York: Barron's, 1989.

HAUSER, LEO and VINCENT MILLER. *Retirement: New Beginnings, New Challenges, New Successes*. Wayzata, Minn.: DCI Publishing, Inc., 1989.

HAZEN-HAMMOND, SUSAN. "Twice in a Lifetime." *Mature Outlook*, July/August 1988.

HEILMAN, JOAN RATTNER. *Unbelievably Good Deals and Great Adventures That You Absolutely Can't Get Unless You're Over 50* (10th ed). Chicago: NTC/Contemporary Publishing, 1998.

HOBBS, FRANK and BONNIE L. DAMON. *65+ in the United States*. Washington, D.C.: U.S. Government Printing Office, 1996.

HOBMAN, DAVID. *The Social Challenge of Aging*. New York: Saint Martin's Press, 1987.

JONES, LAURIE. "Imagery May Help You Cope with Stress." *Minneapolis Star Tribune*, 28 March, 1989.

KAUFMAN, LOIS L. *Old Age Is Not for Sissies*. White Plains, N.Y.: Peter Pauper Press, Inc. 1989.

KENZEL, ROBERT. *Retirement: Creating Promise Out of Threat*. New York: American Management Association, 1979.

KNOWLES, ANN. "Think Your Way out of Depression." *Dynamic Years*, January /February 1983.

KÜBLER-ROSS, ELISABETH. *The Wheel of Life: A Memoir of Living and Dying*. New York: Touchstone Books, 1998.

LEDERER, WILLIAM J. and DON D. JACKSON, M.D. *Mirages of Marriage*. Washington, D.C.: Action for Independent Maturity, 1977.

LEE, ALICE and FRED LEE. *A Field Guide to Retirement*. New York: Doubleday Dell Publishing Group, Inc., 1991.

LINDEMAN, BRAD. "Keeping Love Alive," *50-Plus*, September 1986.

LUNSFORD, CHARLOTTE J. "Volunteering in 2001," *Vital Speeches of the Day* 54, no. 23, 15 September, 1988.

MCGINNIS, ALAN LOY. *The Friendship Factor*. Minneapolis: Augsburg Publishing House, 1979.

MAPLE, STEPHEN M. and STEVE MAPLE. *The Complete Idiot's Guide to Wills and Estates*. New York: Macmillan General Reference, 1997.

MARTINDALE, JUDITH and MARY MOSES. *Creating Your Own Future: A Woman's Guide to Retirement Planning*.Naperville, Ill.: Sourcebooks Trade, 1991.

MARZYNSKI, MARIAN. *A Look at the Land of Our Second Chance*. Boston: WGBH Frontline, 1998.

Money, "Taking a Hard Look at AARP's Deals," July 1995.

MOUSTAKAS, CLARK. *Loneliness and Love*. Englewood Cliffs, N.J.: Prentice-Hall, 1972.

MYERS, ALBERT. *Success Over Sixty.* New York: Summit Books, 1984.

MYERS, ALBERT and CHRISTOPHER ANDERSON. *Success Over Sixty: How to Plant It, How to Harvest It, How to Live by It.* New York: Summit Books, 1984.

NEILL, ROLFE. "Viewpoint." *The Charlotte Observer,* 10 December, 1995.

NEWCOMBE, GEORGE RUSSELL. *On Second Thought.* Landrum, S.C.: John Lawrence Press, 1991.

OLMSTEAD, ALAN H. *Threshold: The First Days of Retirement.* New York: Harper and Row, 1975.

PAGE, CYNTHIA L., ed. *Your Retirement.* New York: Arco Publishing, Inc., 1984.

POGREBIN, LETTY COTTIN. *Getting Over Getting Older.* Boston: Little, Brown and Company, 1996.

PRAGER, DENNIS. "The Secret of True Happiness." *Redbook,* February 1989.

ROGERS, CARL. *On Becoming A Person: A Therapist's View of Psychotherapy.* Boston: Houghton Mifflin, 1961.

ROWE, JOHN W. and ROBERT L. KAHN. *Successful Aging.* New York: Pantheon Books, 1998.

RUSSELL, BERTRAND. *Unpopular Essays.* New York: Routledge, 1997.

RUSSELL, CHERYL. "The Ungraying of America." *American Demographics,* July 1997.

SAMPSON, ANTHONY and SALLY SAMPSON. *The Oxford Book of Ages.* Oxford, England: Oxford University Press, 1985.

SARTON, MAY. *At Eighty-Two: A Journal.* New York: W. W. Norton & Company, Inc., 1997.

SCHUMACHER, VICKIE and JIM SCHUMACHER. *Understanding Living Trusts: How You Can Avoid Probate, Save Taxes and Enjoy Peace of Mind.* Santa Monica, Calif.: Schumacher & Company, 1998.

SELTZER, MILDRED, SHERRY CORBETT, and ROBERT ATCHLEY. *Social Problems of the Aging: Readings.* Belmont, Calif.: Wadsworth Publishing, 1978.

Sex Over Forty, "You Want More Sex, Your Partner Doesn't: What to Do When Desire Differs," 8, no. 2, April 1990.

SHANK, HOWARD. *Managing Retirement.* Chicago: Contemporary Books, Inc., 1985.

SHEEHY, GAIL. *Passages: Predictable Crises of Adult Life.* New York: E. P. Dutton & Co., Inc., 1976

SHI, DAVID E. *The Simple Life*. New York: Oxford University Press, 1985.

SILVERSTONE, BARBARA and HELEN KANDEL HYMAN. *Growing Older Together*. New York: Pantheon Books, 1992.

SIMON, SIDNEY B. *Meeting Yourself Halfway*. Niles, Ill.: Argus Communications, 1974.

SKINNER, B.F. and M.E. VAUGHAN. *Enjoy Old Age: A Program of Self-Management*. New York: W.W. Norton & Company, Inc., 1983.

SMITH, KATHY and ROD STRYKER. *New Yoga Video*. New York: BodyVision, 1994.

SMITH, WESLEY J. *The Senior Citizens' Handbook: A Nuts and Bolts Approach to More Comfortable Living*. Los Angeles: Price Stern Sloan, 1989.

SODDY, KENNETH AND MARY KIDSON. *Men in Middle Life*. Philadelphia: J.B. Lippincott, 1967.

SPARROW, MALCOLM. *License to Steal*. Boulder, Colo.: Westview Press, 1996.

SPRAGINS, ELLYN. *Choosing and Using an HMO*. Princeton, N.J.: Bloomberg Press, 1998.

STANLEY, THOMAS and WILLIAM DANKO. *The Millionaire Next Door*. Marietta, Ga.: Longstreet Press, 1996.

STATON, BILL. *The America's Finest Companies Investment Plan*. New York: Hyperion, 1998.

STERN, KEN. *Lee and Saralee Rosenberg's 50 Fabulous Places to Retire in America*. Franklin Lakes, N.J.: Career Press, 1996.

STOKELL, MARJORIE and BONNIE KENNEDY. *The Senior Citizen Handbook: A Self-Help and Resource Guide*. Englewood Cliffs, N.J.: Prentice-Hall, Inc., 1985.

STREIB, GORDON F. and CLEMENT J. SCHNEIDER. *Retirement in American Society: Impact and Process*. Ithaca, N.Y.: Cornell University Press, 1971.

SUNSET BOOKS. *Complete Book of Low-fat Cooking*. Menlo Park, Calif.: Sunset Publishing, 1996.

TAVES, ISABELLA. *The Widow's Guide*. New York: Schocken Books, 1981.

THEODOSAKIS, M.D., JASON. *The Arthritis Cure*. New York: St. Martins Press, 1997.

TOBIAS, ANDREW. *The Only Investment Guide You'll Ever Need (Revised and Updated Edition)*. New York: Harcourt Brace, 1996.

TOPOLNICKI, DENISE M. "The Pre-Retiree: A Supersaver, a Positive Thinker, a Terrible Planner." *Money*, April 1989.

UNITED NATIONS. *Earth Summit Press Release.* New York: United Nations, June, 1997.

UPDEGRAVE, WALTER L. "Six Smart Ways to Plan for Retirement Income." *Family Wealth*, Spring 1989.

VENINGA, ROBERT L. *Your Renaissance Years: Making Retirement the Best Years of Your Life.* Boston: Little Brown & Company, 1991.

VICKERY, M.D., DONALD M. *LifePlan: Your Own Master Plan for Maintaining Health and Preventing Illness.* Golden, Colo.: Health Decisions, Inc., 1990.

VIORST, JUDITH. "What Is This Thing Called Love?" *Redbook*, February 1975.

WALFORD, ROY L. *The 120-Year Diet: How to Double Your Vital Years.* New York: Pocket Books, 1986.

WARNER, DIANE. *How to Have a Great Retirement on a Limited Budget.* Cincinnati, Ohio: Writer's Digest Books, 1992.

WARNER, RALPH. *Get a Life.* Berkeley, Calif.: Nolo Press, 1996.

WEIHOFEN, DONNA and CHRISTINA MARINO. *The Cancer Survival Cookbook.* Minneapolis: Chronimed Publishing, 1998.

WEINSTEIN, GRACE W. *Life Plans: Looking Forward to Retirement.* New York: Holt, Rinehart and Winston, 1979.

WHALEY, EMILY. *Mrs. Whaley and Her Charleston Garden.* New York: Simon & Schuster, 1997.

WILDER, LELAND EFFIE. *Older but Wilder (More Notes from the Pasture).* Atlanta, Ga.: Peachtree Publishers, Ltd., 1995.

———. *Out to Pasture (but Not over the Hill).* Atlanta, Ga.: Peachtree Publishers, Ltd., 1995.

———. *Over What Hill?: Notes from the Pasture.* Atlanta, Ga.: Peachtree Publishers, Ltd., 1996.

WISCHMEYER, BOB. *Guacamole Infinity.* Chelsea, Mich.: Bookcrafters, 1994.

YANKELOVICH GROUP, DANIEL. "The Mature Americans," *Modern Maturity*, September/October, 1987.

YENCKEL, JAMES T. "Cheap Living Abroad Leaves More Money for Retirement Travel." *Minneapolis Star Tribune*, 20 March, 1988.

Index